Praise for

BROOKLYN BOUNCE

"An excellent book on [the] Nets first season in Brooklyn."

—Adrian Wojnarowski, *Yahoo! Sports*

"Appleman's account is a breezy, cautionary tale for modern sports fans in an era in which money trumps all, and owners who know nothing about the NBA meddle destructively."

—*Booklist*

"*Brooklyn Bounce* is full of insights on the small dramas. . . . I'm a lifelong Lakers nut and found myself interested in the Nets for the first time in my life."

—Man Cave Daily, CBS Local

"A very fun, interesting read, and that over time will become an important piece of NBA history. . . . Whether you're 'in the know,' a diehard fan, or even a casual NBA fan, there's a taste for everyone in this book."

—NetsDaily

"Must-read material."

—*Complex Sports*

"A fun read."

—*Good Times Magazine*

"Appleman's wit, enthusiasm for his subject, and familiarity with the players lift *Brooklyn Bounce* above most season chronicles."

—*The Boston Globe*

BROOKLYN BOUNCE

THE RISE OF THE BROOKLYN NETS

JAKE APPLEMAN

SCRIBNER

New York   London   Toronto   Sydney   New Delhi

SCRIBNER
A Division of Simon & Schuster, Inc.
1230 Avenue of the Americas
New York, NY 10020

Copyright © 2014 by Jake Appleman

First Scribner trade paperback edition February 2015

SCRIBNER and design are registered trademarks of The Gale Group, Inc.,
used under license by Simon & Schuster, Inc., the publisher of this work.

For information about special discounts for bulk purchases,
please contact Simon & Schuster Special Sales at 1-866-506-1949
or business@simonandschuster.com.

The Simon & Schuster Speakers Bureau can bring authors to your live event.
For more information or to book an event contact the Simon & Schuster Speakers Bureau
at 1-866-248-3049 or visit our website at www.simonspeakers.com.

Cover design by Julius Reyes
Cover photograph © Mark Halmas/Icon SMI/Corbis

Manufactured in the United States of America

3   5   7   9   10   8   6   4   2

Library of Congress Control Number: 2013042088

ISBN 978-1-4767-2676-2
ISBN 978-1-4767-2677-9 (ebook)

Insert photograph credits: 1 and 2 © Jesse D. Garrabrant/Getty Images; 3 © Taylor
Hill/Getty Images; 4, 5, and 13 © Jim McIsaac/Getty Images; 6, 7, 8, 9, 15, and 16 ©
Nathaniel S. Butler/Getty Images; 10 © David Becker/Getty Images; 11 © Mike Stobe/
Getty Images; 12 © Andrew D. Bernstein/Getty Images; 14 © Stan Hoda/Getty Images

For my father, who encouraged my love of sports, taught me about writing, and always gave me great books to read.

For my mother, wonderfully original, whose unique voice, collaborative spirit, and example still inspire.

For my younger brother, the most talented person I know, who consistently reminds me what it means to honor a craft.

For my grandfather, who remains quick-witted at ninety-eight, twenty years after helping construct a city kid's suburban refuge: a basketball court.

And for anyone else who has nurtured my dreams.

Contents

Author's Note

To a young adolescent, there's nothing like sleepaway camp. The drudgery of school is replaced with a few great friends and a new world. Organized days revolve around subpar food but a consistent schedule, interrupted by philosophical conversation with international counselors, candy purchases at the canteen (or a bunk), and campers giving other campers haircuts. Youngsters play amid the trees while teenage awkwardness and sugar-fueled dance parties provide more than enough energy to burnish everlasting memories if you're into that sort of thing. Friends and mentors help nurture a developing identity, be it kid with a wicked jump shot or girl with Hollywood aspirations. If the kid with the wicked jump shot is lucky enough, he gets to kiss the girl with Hollywood aspirations.

For two summers, I joined my cousin Aaron at sleepaway camp. Aaron wowed our camp friends with tales about the spontaneous ass-kickings that took place on Brooklyn playgrounds. Our second summer together, Aaron brought his lifelong friend Greg. Greg was the only black male teenage camper around for a few weeks. He lived a life of serene routine and enjoyed the change of pace.

He described the feeling as, "I'm here. I don't care what you say. I'm allowed to be here."

To many in a group of adolescents well versed in the cloistered torture of the suburbs, the volatility of Brooklyn in the nineties—

what was projected as the Brooklyn brand—came off as intoxicatingly cool. Building on the death of the Notorious B.I.G. (his funeral had erupted into a wild block party complete with a motorcade and a casket)—and a rising force named Jay-Z—Brooklyn's cultural identity became a touchstone of the decade. On his last day, one of the many foreign counselors bet Greg that he couldn't dunk a miniature basketball. Not yet fifteen, or even six feet tall, Greg, looking like an urban construction worker, crammed the ball through the hoop in a pair of Lugz boots. His parting gift was a case or two of soda.

Yet Greg didn't mind the black-kid-can-jump stereotype in the least. He was—and is—happier around the gentrification that changed Park Slope and many other Brooklyn neighborhoods.

"Absolutely," he said. "Absolutely. Less crack cocaine. Less fiends on the avenue. It's . . ."

He paused. "It's not a hood anymore. It's more of a neighborhood . . . avenue might smell bad once in a blue, but it's still a good area."

Greg took the subway to John Dewey High School, where he couldn't play basketball because there was no team. Dewey was near fabled Abraham Lincoln High School in Coney Island, and students would meet underground at Thirty-Sixth Street in Brooklyn to decide if they wanted to take the F train and witness early-morning danger (robberies, kids getting roughed up) or catch some sleep on the B train, which didn't stop near Lincoln. "It's eight in the fucking morning," Greg said, remembering. "Why are you robbing somebody?"

My cousin Aaron wasn't particularly pleased with new Brooklyn.

"There's no real concrete way to describe it," he said. "It's just silly. Silly place now. People who move here don't know anything about what it was before and they act like they have any idea what used to take place or how things looked."

At camp, Greg and Aaron brought a style that wouldn't have otherwise made its way to a sleepy little town near the New York/

Massachusetts border. "He's from Brooklyn" was a thing giggling girls said.

Born in the East Village and growing up in West Nyack, New York, I have been the outsider observing Brooklyn from Greg and Aaron's perspective. Both lived in Brooklyn during the Nets' inaugural season. One went to games and promoted a picture of three fists resting on Brooklyn Nets coffee mugs from the team store, the other seethes when thinking about Barclays Center. They are two sides of the same Brooklyn coin, a microcosm of an enormous borough with wide-ranging cultural reach where neighbors often exist as the embodiment of a friendship/disagreement hybrid lifestyle, something like the urban version of the eternal Homer Simpson/Ned Flanders archetype.

Justin Bieber was throwing a concert on the night I interviewed Greg and Aaron on a bench outside of a bar mere feet from where the movies *Clockers* and *Lotto Land* were shot. The bar promoted the Brooklyn Cyclones, the New York Mets, Boca Juniors, and a library-styled magazine rack. Earlier in the day, I passed under the Barclays Center Oculus, weaving through a sea of Beliebers, while listening to the lyrically dense rapper Ghostface Killah's "One" through my earbuds. While I was interviewing Greg a few Bieber fans walked past, a strange juxtaposition against earlier sounds of motorcycles passing down Fifth Avenue in Park Slope. "Bieber tweeters," Greg said.

Aaron couldn't really be bothered with popular culture or NBA basketball and went on an epic rant a little while later that included: "So you take these kids that are good at ball and you take them out of this bad neighborhood and all of a sudden they're like these demigods to people and you leave everybody else behind and they have shit lives and you gotta work at McDonald's and shit. Why did this person get taken out of the hood? Because they can shoot a basketball. They can dribble well. They got these talents and they worked on them. Okay. But these other people that they left behind, they gotta live in their fucking shit, you know. And this person becomes like a multimillionaire, into sellin' Pepsi, makin' kids fat, and shit. For what? You can dunk a basketball because you can drink a Five-Hour Energy or drink some Sprite. It's nonsense. It's a way to distract us."

Some of my earliest memories are of watching the NBA on an old television in a Nolita apartment before it was a Nolita apartment, James Worthy, the Lakers' goggle-wearing small forward, catching my eye. I was one of many eighties kids obsessively bouncing balls off of walls under the influence of siren sounds, raw New York conversations (with oneself or another), and pure youthful inspiration.

"I should be in the fucking NBA right now," Greg said.

After getting cut from the freshman team at my public high school, I briefly joined Aaron on a team in Park Slope. I remember how the game was different, raw and improvisational. The energy inside the gym was unique, like you were playing in front of a party. People weren't watching you as much as they *were almost out there with you*. The baggy clothes that the kids in the suburbs emulated via music videos and magazines—kids in Brooklyn oozed that as if it was a birthright.

This imbued in me, between sleepaway camp summers, a teenage revenge fantasy that played out as a recurring daydream while I walked home from school: I would bring my Brooklyn team back to the suburbs and we would wipe the floor with the freshman team that cut me. Sadly, between the facts that physically I was fourteen going on twelve and that Brooklyn was a good hour away—traffic depending—my initial foray into Brooklyn basketball didn't last. Still, it was good to get a bit more acquainted with the area.

With the league in Brooklyn off-limits, I needed to intensify my focus on a distraction. Lucky for me, the 1997–98 New Jersey Nets were perhaps the most interesting average basketball team in the history of interesting average basketball teams. I had been a diehard Knicks fan as a kid. The tears flowed every year from '93 to '97, released from faucets of frustration. April showers bring May flowers, May flowers bring *you've gotta be shitting me.*

At some point I realized that there needed to be something more than projected passion. I wanted to try to understand adults playing the game; athletes had to be more than just idols in localized tribal colors. The '98 Nets proved that, and their individual personalities shined through.

My journey as a freelance sportswriter observing Nets point guards has ebbed and flowed—from Stephon Marbury (high school sportswriting project) to Jason Kidd (*SLAM*) to Devin Harris (NBA.com) to Deron Williams (the *New York Times*)—but the Nets have remained pretty consistent in my life. The idea of rooting for them like a fan faded a long time ago, but the nostalgia for that '98 team, eliminated by the Chicago Bulls as Michael Jordan began his final championship quest, lingers: Sam Cassell bringing the ball up the court, backing into his man, talking trash; Kerry Kittles running the court like a gazelle; high-flier Kendall Gill, the greatest onetime Nickelodeon guest star of all time, asked about ice cream by an actor playing a Charlotte, North Carolina, sportswriter; Keith Van Horn, the great white hope, justifying much of the hype, averaging just a shade under 20 points per game as a rookie; and Jayson Williams, a jokester off the court, picking rebounds out of the air with a comedian's timing.

Fifteen years ago, I began to try to understand Brooklyn and I began to try to understand the Nets. This book represents another beginning, for both a franchise and an adult.

BROOKLYN
BOUNCE

Pinnacle Is Prologue

The pinnacle of the Nets' first season in Brooklyn came on April 20, 2013, a party inside their plush new pad, the billion-dollar Barclays Center, in which almost every seat is a good seat and even the macaroni and cheese is deluxe. Served with Jamaican Jerk chicken, pineapple slices, and coconut shavings mixed into it, it's delicious, but your palate has absolutely no idea what's going on.

The Nets are introducing Brooklyn to playoff basketball, and reintroducing the franchise to high-stakes postseason play after a six-year absence. They will not trail in game 1 against the Chicago Bulls, a stellar performance punctuated by a reverse dunk from a franchise player, Deron Williams, who, one month earlier, was still having trouble levitating.

The franchise is foisting a thorough rebranding on its fans even though the team was rebranded at the beginning of the season with the catchy #HelloBrooklyn slogan, an improvement over their previous tagline "Jersey Strong, Brooklyn Ready."

The night has been branded as the Blackout in Brooklyn, so the Nets wear their sleek black road uniforms after getting special permission from the NBA. Fans receive free black T-shirts. Per usual, "Public Service Announcement" off of Jay-Z's *Black Album* blares over the arena loudspeakers during warm-ups. The song features the most resonant lyric of all: "allow me to reintroduce myself." It also frequently sounds off when a player scores for the first time in a while.

From his customary courtside seat next to the Nets' bench, Jay-Z is reintroducing himself too, this time as a sports agent affiliated with Creative Artists Agency. You could probably technically say that Jay-Z was allowing himself to reintroduce himself, and that's pretty much the point. If you reintroduce yourself enough, people will remember who you are, and that's what the Nets are trying to accomplish: settling into a massive borough after a nomadic past, they want you—non-diehard NBA fan—to remember who they are.

Jay-Z has returned from a controversial vacation in Cuba, a trip that managed to get the attention of the White House, having sold his reported $350,000 stake in the Nets late in the season. That's right, a $350,000 stake, .0015 percent of the Nets, but he still controls the cool. He was to the Nets what a mole was to Cindy Crawford in her early modeling days: almost nothing, the key to everything, and the chance at an identity. He still has his microphone, but he just signed Robinson Cano, a baseball player named after Jackie Robinson. Jackie Robinson broke baseball's color barrier in Brooklyn sixty-six years earlier. There's even a movie out about Jackie Robinson (*42*), and Jay-Z is on the sound track. Ubiquity is the gospel when you're a rapper who can call himself GOD MC in front of the unblinking masses.

Inspired by old subway stations and the grittiness of a Brooklyn that feels like a historical footnote, black and white, the Nets' new colors (at the behest of Jay-Z), also appear in tandem throughout the arena. In the media room: black-and-white M&Ms, black-and-white lollipops, and #HelloPlayoffs black-and-white cookies. Yes, the Nets hash-tagged cookies.*

There are black-and-white drums during a performance on the

---

* My most fun experience playing basketball thus far came when I played on a team featuring a black backcourt and a white frontcourt. Our coach dubbed the five of us "Cookies and Cream." The roster composition flipped the traditional and somewhat racist basketball narrative of black size versus white teamwork on its head, as our coach, K-Boy, would hoot and holler when we pressed the other team into submission, yelling, "I got cookies. Woo! I got cookies!" And indeed, more often than not, K-Boy and his players had cookies.

court when play stops and a black-and-white television on the big screen during the Nets' player introduction makeover. Williams, superimposed inside the graphic of the black-and-white television on the JumboTron, taps on the fake glass and asks, "Is anybody here? Is this thing on?"

The media are even served black-and-white ravioli on black plates that say Playoffs on them (as if we might otherwise forget). Before a dispiriting game 7 against the Bulls, the Nets continued to look to the pasta, rolling out trays of black-and-white tortellini, to no avail.

The black-and-white color scheme perfectly represented the paradox that was the first rendition of the Brooklyn Nets. They were the most improved team in the NBA in 2013, but they lost game 7 at home to a battered Bulls team missing three of its best players, mainstream woofing about gutlessness, and a lack of heart echoing down the hallway as they readied for the year-two reload. The Nets had scorers who struggled with rebounding, and rebounders who rarely scored. They were branded as the cool kids, but when they threw an alley-oop, it was rare; reporters acted as if a comet had just streaked past. They were laconic big-money stars forcefully marketed to the masses, and gregarious fellas fighting for bigger roles. They had the best road record in franchise history as they adjusted to their new home.

By traditional statistical metrics (points scored and allowed), the Nets, out of thirty teams, had the seventeenth-best offense and sixth-best defense. By advanced metrics (points scored/allowed per possession), they had the eighth-best offense and eighteenth-best defense. The latter felt a little bit more accurate. The Nets played basketball at a snail's pace but were an efficient offensive team. You didn't need to refocus as often when you watched the Brooklyn Nets run their sets—offensive rebounds and an acceptance of late shot clock opportunities kept the ball in their half with great frequency. Just stare and it was sort of an optical illusion; your eyes strained at the sight of success. Especially against inferior competition, it worked. On defense, they were perpetually one stop, one great stand away from something to call Mom about.

Deron Williams, the epicenter of every move made to build the team, spent from mid-February on reintroducing himself in preparation for the playoffs. It was only nine weeks earlier when he was playing as if weighed down by invisible snowshoes. Now, after three cortisone shots, a juice cleanse, and platelet-rich plasma therapy, in which his own blood was spun around in a centrifuge and reintroduced into his ankles, he dropped fifteen to twenty pounds and was playing like an MVP candidate, the star one might logically build a franchise around. Williams is the leader of the team, the point guard of the paradox, a franchise player who stalks through the locker room with the presence of a storm cloud. He was originally acquired with the hope that he could be paired with the attention-seeking center Dwight Howard. But Howard waived the early-termination option in his contract in March 2012, essentially vetoing his ability to force the Orlando Magic to trade him to the Nets, and was dealt to the Lakers in the off-season, leaving Williams alone on Franchise Player Island. In his introductory press conference after being acquired from the Utah Jazz in February 2011, there was an extended sequence during which Williams and a Nets public relations official clarified how to pronounce his first name—*Dare-wren, not Duh-ron or Der-rin*—but that didn't exactly get the message out. Jay-Z rapped about "Duh-ron" onstage at the first concert at Barclays Center with Williams and his teammates present in the luxury box that Williams and his family received as part of his contract when he re-signed with the Nets. The hosts of the BET show *106 & Park* introduced "Duh-ron" to a live studio audience, only to come back from a commercial and apologize. When Williams was on the cusp of tying an NBA record for three-pointers in a game against the Washington Wizards, amped-up fans went absolutely apeshit at reserve swingman Keith Bogans because he didn't get the ball to "Duh-ron" for a cheeky attempt at history.

Williams loathed when people mispronounced his name, just

as he loathed many of the trappings of being an NBA superstar. He valued space, whether reveling in the open expanse of a golf course or chiding reporters waiting for him well after a game had ended, for crossing what must have been a small, invisible moat surrounding his locker. He appreciated your concern for his health, in that his appreciation of your concern for his health was a snarky stock answer he gave to queries about how he was feeling.

In business, popularity was work if you weren't already popular, as the Nets' branding efforts revealed. Both to his credit and to his detriment, Williams didn't want to do the work to be popular like so many upper-echelon NBA players. The result was a double-edged sword. He came off as a bit more real, a little bit more honest than most of his peers, but he definitely didn't dress up as a long-lost mustachioed twin during postseason commercials. *SLAM* labeled him "your favorite point guard's favorite point guard."

"With Deron Williams running the show, it's always about what opportunities present themselves," Julius "Dr. J" Erving said.

The candor and perspective from an intelligent player such as Williams were refreshing. The acid wasn't. Williams has a tattoo of a panther on his right arm and a tattoo of a coiled snake on his left. For the foreseeable future, the Nets will go only as far as Snake-Panther will lead them.

Like Williams, Gerald Wallace was looking to reintroduce himself after a disjointed, often disappointing, regular season. Wallace was nicknamed Crash because of his penchant for turning courtside patrons into bowling pins with his tenacious hustle. His streaky jump shot and inability to finish at the rim mitigated his positive contributions on defense during the regular season, his play adding a small mountain of dandruff to the head-scratching four-year $40 million contract that the Nets signed him to in the off-season. Still, if you plunked down a few grand for courtside seats, there was a small but very real chance that Wallace would make a beeline for a loose ball headed in your general vicinity.

Wallace was the most consistently accessible and emotionally available member of the team's four leading men—branded as the "Core Four"—a man who usually spoke out about needing to take responsibility, whether personal or collective. It was always reassuring to know that Crash was legitimately pissed off after losses. His nasal inflection seemed to slow time down as he spoke; there were even rare instances when he was too upset to talk. Wallace was forever a warrior midgrimace. When it wasn't his sore foot, it was his lower leg contusion, or his banged-up heel, or his bruised rib, or his bruised knee, or his sprained ankle. On the wrong side of thirty after a career that has seen a partially punctured lung and a concussion so severe an NFL team was consulted, Crash was a man at war with himself, his physical gifts deteriorating, his pride on the line every night.

Wallace often tried to recenter conversations with the press on whatever his "main thing" was at any given moment. For as much as Wallace would share his honesty, if we could circle back to his "main thing"—whether it was honor, hustle, or a belief in oneself—at some point during a group interview, it felt like an offering to the basketball gods, as if everything would end up being all right if Wallace's foremost focus was acknowledged. Wallace even admitted late in April that he had lost all confidence in his shot.

"My whole concept is just that you can't come out of the game if you're not missing shots," he said.

Brook Lopez made the All-Star team after an injury-marred 2012 campaign and was about to make his playoff debut. Lopez's work ethic was off the charts during his first Brooklyn season. Arrive super early at Barclays Center and the sight of Lopez working on his midrange jumper hours before tip-off—with arena employees still socializing on the concourse awaiting orders—was common.

Lopez generally strayed from the distractions that come with the NBA lifestyle. A cross section of nifty shots and automated behavior, he seemed to exist in a different realm. He hated talking about basketball and—it would blatantly seem—was intentionally dull during interviews, injecting the words "you know" into almost every sentence.

The press generally chalked up Lopez—a twin born on April 1, 1988—as a horrible quote and everybody moved on, even though Lopez is the future of the franchise. It was actually pretty savvy: Lopez created no new drama and succeeded at maintaining the compartmentalized life that he wanted to lead. By the time the bulging New York media gathered around Williams's locker waiting for answers, Lopez was usually well on his way home. It seems remarkable that someone can work so hard at his craft, only to have the game vanish from his mind when the buzzer sounds.

Lopez sounds like your friendly neighborhood surfer dude. He is dorky and easy to relate to when not talking about basketball, though he still comes off kind of like a seven-foot version of Tom Hanks in *Big*: an overgrown, comic-book-loving kid whose wish from the Zoltar machine was a unique combination of height and skill on the basketball court and for people to just leave him alone off of it. Asked about his opinion of the Knicks, Lopez once responded, "I'm probably the wrong guy to ask about watching basketball."

Power forward Reggie Evans and Lopez made a fascinating inside tandem, one of the NBA's most bizarre odd couples. When Evans burst on to the scene in late November, he started calling Lopez "Brookzilla." During the Nets' final practice before the playoffs, it was just "Lo." Evans has a rose gold chain honoring his nickname: "The Joker." Lopez loves Batman. Evans became more physical in his appreciation of Lopez, giving him semi bear hugs before games. Lopez is very private and organized; Evans's beard might exist in two different area codes, and he says whatever pops into his head.

Like: "I love watching NBA games, but ain't gonna get caught up in the whole business of the NBA. 'Oh, they just traded me. Oh, they did this.' Man, man, please. This is a business. This is nothing, strictly business, nothing personal. People trying to win. . . . Why are they so emotional? Some players like females, they take stuff too emotional. 'Oh, they just traded me. Oh, they just traded me to this team. Oh, I don't want to be here.' Man, there's a million more people who would love to be where you are."

It was the best season of Evans's career. Not bad for the Core Four's fifth wheel.

Of the Nets' Core Four—the starters promoted on the front of the arena, near a running ticker that proudly noted Brooklyn was home to the first ATM, in 1967—only Joe Johnson, the $123 million shooting guard, is taking his time reintroducing himself. But Johnson is a chameleon on and off the court, a scorer in perpetual but graceful slow motion. Johnson can score over anyone at any time—degree of difficulty be damned. Johnson's late-game exploits provided many of the signature moments in the Nets' inaugural season.

It's a little after five o'clock before game 1 against the Bulls and on the TV in the media room, the Knicks were taking the lead against the Celtics behind former Nets Jason Kidd and Kenyon Martin, leaders of the Nets' back-to-back NBA Finals runs a decade ago. Fifteen minutes later, Kidd's hustle yields a chant in his honor at Madison Square Garden. Kidd is the greatest player in the Nets' NBA history. Kidd is Williams's favorite player and they have the same agent. Kidd is, leadershipwise, what the consistently inconsistent Nets need. Kevin Garnett, Paul Pierce, and Jason Terry of the Celtics are on or near Kidd on the floor, and next season they will join Kidd in Brooklyn.

Back in Brooklyn, Williams chats courtside with Nets general manager Billy King. He traded for Wallace and Johnson to convince Williams to stay, but, more accurately, to preserve his job. King's nickname at Duke when he played basketball in the '80s was the Senator. He had extensive prior relationships that greased the wheels for the Williams and Johnson trades. Workers affix a playoff decal near the midcourt sideline, and the future is bright.

King is a few days away from a contract extension. The symbolism is pretty simple. After a second helping of black-and-white ravioli, it's back to the court for the pregame festivities. Nets forward Jerry Stackhouse sings the national anthem. Aside from an early hitch, Stackhouse gets better and better and it's the first time a national anthem at Barclays Center has felt like a celebration inside a club. The performance is another small victory for Stackhouse, an eighteen-year veteran, in a season of small victories.

The lights go off for Nets intros, and the arena looks like a planetarium. The BrooklyKnight, the Nets' superhero new mascot, descends from the rafters. Johnson, Evans, Lopez, Wallace, and Williams are introduced—in that order.

The team's owner, Mikhail Prokhorov, the fourth-richest owner in professional sports according to *Forbes*, stands just outside center court and greets the fans.

"I heard there is a blackout here in Brooklyn," Prokhorov says. "I came—"

There is a huge roar from the crowd. "And I came to keep the lights on."

The Nets take the court and proceed to throttle the Bulls in front of the most energetic home crowd they played in front of during the first season in Brooklyn. Lopez and Williams score 16 of the Nets' first 17 points. Wallace is a difference-maker on defense and puts up his best offensive numbers in a month. Johnson comes alive late. Reserves hop off the bench and hit timely shots. The Nets take care of the ball. It's what an $83 million roster is supposed to look like in action. In the postgame press conference, reporters are asked to identify themselves before asking questions. Nets interim coach P. J. Carlesimo, a man with basketball ties to all five boroughs, New Jersey, and most of the country, finds the request for a reintroduction silly. He begins to answer a question, but then, in jest, returns serve.

"No, I'm sorry. P. J. Carlesimo, Brooklyn Nets."

And yet, five months earlier, Carlesimo at the podium, speaking his name into the microphone, seemed absurd.

CHAPTER 1

There's No Place Like Away

No franchise mixed failure with folly quite like the one that began as the American Basketball Association's New Jersey Americans in 1967. That season ended with the Americans forfeiting a play-off game against the Kentucky Colonels because the circus had booked the Teaneck Armory and the Americans' backup home-court in Commack, Long Island, was in disrepair, with large holes in the floor and baskets off center. Still, the franchise moved to Commack the next year and became the Nets. And so, set to the backdrop of relative anonymity, a mostly infamous history—weaving absurdity, mediocrity, heartbreak, humor, and frequent relocation—was born.

The Nets sold the closest thing the seventies had to Michael Jordan in order to pay the NBA entrance fee. Their catalyst and rising star of the eighties was banned from the league for repeated substance abuse violations. Their catalyst and rising star of the nineties died in a tragic car accident on the German Autobahn. There was the small forward who made it known that he wanted out by writing "Trade Me" on his sneakers, not to be outdone by the franchise point guard who expressed his dismay by writing "All Alone 33" on his ankle tape.

But maybe it's the way the team succeeded that defines its head-scratching, sad-sack history. Nets failure went hand in hand with epic storytelling and laughingstock status while Nets success always seemed to partner fleeting happiness with the lingering bitterness of what could have been.

Consider arguably the biggest home game of the Nets' first decade in the NBA—Easter Sunday, 1984—and its buildup. The Nets were bounced from the playoffs the previous season by the Knicks, in large part because a talented young team fell apart when coach Larry Brown left late in the season. Brown was fired when ownership found out that he had flown to interview at the University of Kansas.

Said Don Unger, a member of the team's ownership group at the time, in reflection, "Whether you're Paterson, Passaic, or Bayonne, Jersey guys—like Christie said . . . 'Tell the truth, keep your word, promise something, deliver it.' And I think that resonates in Jersey. It was a sad day."

Brown, a master basketball tactician and teacher, was so close to some of his younger players that they openly wept at Brown's good-bye gathering. Power forward Buck Williams, whose jersey was retired by the Nets in 1999, could not even bring himself to attend.

"We kind of cherished the fact that Larry spent so much time with us," Williams said nearly thirty years later. "We felt a little bit betrayed, but I think what it really did, it made us realize as young players that it was a business and you had to do what was in your best interest."

Without their father figure, the young Nets regrouped in 1984 under the looser Stan Albeck, but few expected much of the team when they faced the defending champion Philadelphia 76ers in the first round. Yet the Nets stunned the Sixers in the first two games on the road, in the best-of-five series, and looked to close out the champs in game 3 after building a lead. The Nets had a chance to prove that they were resilient, that they were over the heartbreaking end of the previous season, that they were relevant.

And that's when Duncan, the team's dragon/swamp monster mascot, decided to get cute. With the Nets ahead in the fourth quarter, Duncan waved a broom—the universal sign for sweep—

near the Sixers' bench during a fourth-quarter time-out. The Sixers came back and won the game.

"It was the first time a team almost killed its mascot," center Mike Gminski said, as quoted by Guy Kipp in *From Julius to Jason*.

In front of a capacity crowd in game 4, the Nets lost again, forcing a decisive game 5 in Philadelphia. Another season seemed lost, escape from the first round of the NBA playoffs still elusive. And then Julius "Dr. J" Erving, the Sixers' forward and the greatest player in Nets franchise history up to that point, stepped up and did something as symbolically silly as Duncan prematurely waving a broom.

Erving criticized the Nets' lack of experience and said the visitors winning all three games at the Philadelphia Spectrum was so improbable, "they might as well mail in the stats."

"It just really motivated us," Buck Williams said.

The Nets had nothing to lose anyway and, led by Micheal Ray Richardson, won game 5 in Philadelphia.

"There's no place like away," Gminski said.

One player whose jersey would hang from the rafters in New Jersey and Brooklyn taking a legacy hit (Erving) while another (Williams) cemented his place in Nets lore with a series win was a coincidence befitting the Nets.

Erving's foot-in-mouth moment remains a minor blemish in an otherwise storied Hall-of-Fame career, and he remains a cornerstone figure in the growth of professional basketball. The year before Dr. J arrived, the Nets finished 30-54 and were last in the ABA in points. The Erving effect was similar to that of LeBron James getting drafted by the Cleveland Cavaliers, except with greater success on a smaller scale. Erving stuffed the stat sheet in the 1973–74 season with a league-leading 27.1 points per game piled high upon other impressive stats. Without him, his former team, the Virginia Squires, struggled their way into oblivion.

"It was like watching Baryshnikov in sneakers with a basketball," longtime Nets scorekeeper Herb Turetzky said. "He was incredible. Every night, you'd see something different, something special. What Jordan did was different; it was more athletic. What Doc did was more graceful."

Turetzky described Erving's playing style as "balletic," citing his especially long arms and fingers stretching out the classic red-white-and-blue ball, as he flew through the air, his Afro topping a figure that hovered over and around opponents like a shadow. The Nets were never particularly popular at home, but Dr. J made them a main attraction on the road.

"Wherever he went, whatever city the team went to, it was as if the Globetrotters or the Rolling Stones were coming into town," Turetzky said. "Everyone wanted to see Doc. It was unbelievable, no matter where you went. Every city you went to had a press conference for Doc."

Erving led the Nets to ABA championships in 1974, over the Utah Stars, and in 1976, over the Denver Nuggets. In between, the Nets set a franchise record for wins with 58, but lost in the playoffs to the Spirits of St. Louis. Throughout, the Doctor kept the Nets dominant.

When then coach Kevin Loughery would need his team to pick it up he would tell Erving, "Doc, I'm gonna get on your case a little bit in practice today."

"And, you know, this is a guy who is the best player in the league," Loughery said. "You get on his case, so that if you get on his case the other players will have to respond. . . . He'd go along with it.

"Of all the superstars I've been around, he was the best with people," Loughery said.

The ABA folded in 1976, its last game a Nets victory over the Nuggets at Nassau Coliseum, and the Nets, Nuggets, Spurs, and Pacers were admitted into the NBA.

"What ended in '76, started in '67, what is looked at by many, as nine years in heaven," Turetzky wrote in a poem about the ABA.

The Nets have yet to recapture that magic. They had to sell off Erving, a three-time ABA MVP, to pay for entrance into the

NBA. Without their star, the Nets went from ABA platinum to NBA scrap metal in one summer. The Nets settled out of court with the Knicks for $4.8 million following an antitrust lawsuit in which the Knicks had charged the Nets with breaching an indemnification agreement for invading the area.

NBA rules gave the Knicks "territorial exclusivity" for a seventy-five-mile radius. Fashion entrepreneur Roy Boe, who had bought the Nets from trucking magnate Arthur Brown in 1969, attempted to get the Knicks to dissolve the indemnity fee in exchange for Erving. The Knicks balked, and the 76ers bought Erving for $3 million, as the Nets paid their way into the NBA with the recouped funds. Erving immediately helped the Sixers to the NBA Finals, where they were swept by the Portland Trail Blazers after going up 2-0. Of the Knicks, Nets, and Erving, only Erving has won a championship since his sale (with the 76ers in 1983).

Selling Dr. J has been thought of as the NBA's version of the Red Sox selling Babe Ruth. *New York Times* sports columnist Dave Anderson compared Boe selling Erving to Walter O'Malley moving the Dodgers from Brooklyn to Los Angeles in the way it crushed a fan base.

On the court and the back pages, defeating Erving and the Sixers in 1984 provided the Nets only short-lived top-dog status. In game 5 against the Sixers, Albert King scored 9 of his 15 points in the fourth quarter to help propel the Nets into the next round in a game that wasn't even shown live. King was a former ballyhooed prep prospect out of Brooklyn, rated higher than Magic Johnson in the high school class of 1979.

Yet the day after King helped lead the Nets past the Sixers, his older brother Bernard scored 44 points to give the Knicks a thrilling series win over the Detroit Pistons. As the Knicks prepared for a premier series against Larry Bird and the Celtics, the Nets got set to take on the comparatively anonymous Milwaukee Bucks. Both area teams lost in the second round, but, as always, it seemed like the Knicks generated the everlasting memories. The

Nets were always the second team, the light only occasionally breaking through the Knicks' thundercloud.

Buck Williams finished his career playing for the Knicks at Madison Square Garden. "There's a certain electricity when you walk into that building," he said.

The Nets simply never had that—not in the Teaneck Armory, not in Long Island Arena (Commack, NY), not in Island Garden Arena (West Hempstead, NY), not in Nassau Coliseum (Uniondale, NY), not at the Rutgers Athletic Center (Piscataway, NJ), not at the Prudential Center (Newark, NJ), and especially not at the Meadowlands (East Rutherford, NJ), whether the arena was called Brendan Byrne Arena, Continental Airlines Arena, or the IZOD Center.

"You can talk about location," Unger said, listing problems. "You can talk about the arena. You can talk about the record. You know, but the fact was they were all correct."

He was talking about the Meadowlands, though one could argue that he was talking about almost all of the Nets' comparatively undesirable locales. When Unger surveyed Brendan Byrne Arena, he would ask marketing employees from the cheap seats, "Who's going to sit here?"

"If you didn't presell, you were dead," Unger said.

The Nets were swept out of the playoffs in 1985 and '86, the latter marred by the expulsion of talented point guard Micheal "Sugar" Ray Richardson due to three substance abuse violations. Against the Sixers in the 1984 playoffs, Sugar averaged more than 20 points, 8 assists, and 5 rebounds.

"The timing was so poor based on what we were trying to accomplish and the momentum that we had as a team," Buck Williams said.

Known for carousing and erratic behavior when he was on the Knicks, Richardson's issues were so apparent the Nets had what they called a Sugar Watch. Former Cleveland Indians great Larry Doby, who broke baseball's color barrier in the American League months after Jackie Robinson debuted with the Brooklyn Dodgers, worked with the Nets in community relations and would often check up on Sugar.

"Great kid—just had the demons, you know?" longtime Nets broadcaster Bill Raftery said of Richardson.

Drazen Petrovic did not perform or act as if anything—demons or otherwise—could stop him. The electric Croatian shooting guard was a pillar of work ethic, feistiness, and off-court kindness. Acquired from the Portland Trail Blazers in 1991, Petrovic sparked a team that brought competitiveness back to the Jersey swamp five years after Richardson's banishment and an assortment of injuries sent the Nets into a prolonged funk.

"He was such a hard worker that guys like Kenny Anderson and Derrick Coleman, who weren't hard workers, were embarrassed not to bust their tails," Turetzky said.

"He was a pretty good woofer too," Raftery said. "He didn't mind chatting on the floor. We always talk about Michael and Reggie; Drazen could give it too. I don't think they understood what he was saying sometimes."

The Nets lost in the first round of the playoffs for three consecutive seasons (1992–94), the latter two under Hall-of-Fame coach Chuck Daly. Petrovic was killed in a tragic car accident in Germany after the 1993 season and, in the 1994 playoffs, despite the Nets' taking three of four from the Knicks during the regular season, the Knicks reversed that score in the playoffs, Broadway's team defeating a regional counterpart that practiced at an APA trucking facility.

"There are times when you have to accept that the gods are not with you," Coleman said. "Every time we seemed ready to take the next step, something happened. We were putting those pieces in place to be a better team."

The Knicks went to the Finals in 1994. The Nets waited four more years to return to the playoffs. Even when Petrovic was streaking down the sidelines looking for catch-and-shoot opportunities, those talented Nets teams couldn't seem to catch a break.

During a regular-season game in March 1993, the Knicks' John Starks raked Anderson on a fast break, fracturing Anderson's wrist and bruising his tailbone. Coleman copped to feeling residual anger toward Starks.

"About two plays later, Greg Anthony drove the lane and I drove his ass right into the back of the basket. I always had bitter feelings about it, and even when I see John Starks right now I get on him about it."

Anderson missed the Nets' hard-fought series loss to the Cleveland Cavaliers in 1993. With squabbles between Anderson and Coach Bill Fitch during the '91–'92 season, Anderson's wrist injury in the '92–'93 season, and Petrovic's death before the '93–'94 season, the Nets were never able to test out their version of a Big 3 during some of their better years.

Said Anderson of Petrovic: "He just wanted to fit in and let everybody know that 'Hey, I'm an NBA player. I'm not just here. I can be one of the best.' And he did that. I wish it would have been a little bit longer because he was a good dude, a good dude."

The Nets dealt Coleman to the 76ers in 1995 and Anderson to the Hornets in 1996, ushering in another few years of losing, an era that then team president Jon Spoelstra, father of Heat coach Erik Spoelstra, said, "It was all convicts and criminals. One year we had six guys in jail. Not together, because that would have meant teamwork."

Perhaps no singular figure typified the terrible karma around the Nets more than rebounding machine Jayson Williams, who went from feel-good-rags-to-riches story and genuine in-game force, to ex-player after breaking his leg in a freak in-game collision with Stephon Marbury. Williams is now perhaps best known for accidentally killing his limousine driver while playing with a shotgun as disadvantaged children and members of the Harlem Globetrotters were in the next room being given a tour of his mansion. Williams served eight months at Rikers Island for a DUI following an eighteen-month stint in a New Jersey prison tied to the incident with his limo driver.

Williams, now sober and out of prison, was not invited to the Nets' final home game in New Jersey.

MANY POINT GUARDS

The Nets sent Robert Pack, Shawn Bradley, Ed O'Bannon, and Rex Walters to Dallas for Sam Cassell, Jim Jackson, Chris Gatling, George McCloud, and Eric Montross on February 17, 1997. Couch John Calipari held a conference call from the team plane after a loss to the Cleveland Cavaliers.

"He probably thought he had to do something," Pack told the *New York Times*. "It seems like just yesterday he was telling me, 'Hey, you're my guy.'"

The deal with the Dallas Mavericks began a process of wheeling and dealing point guards, a chain—call it Mavs Labyrinth—that would play a major part in shaping the team's future. Cassell was dealt for the Coney Island prodigy Stephon Marbury of the Minnesota Timberwolves, in the process splitting up a promising partnership between Marbury and Kevin Garnett. Marbury was eventually traded to the Suns in a deal that sent back Jason Kidd. Kidd changed the fortunes of the franchise, but was later packaged back to the Mavericks, where he began his career, in a deal that yielded Devin Harris. Harris was sent to Utah with prospects in a deal that brought in Deron Williams. Continuing Mavs Labyrinth, Harris re-signed with the Mavericks after the 2013 season.

Kidd, a pass-first leader with the court vision of a personified spookfish, brought change and winning ways to the Nets. Kidd was available in part because he was reportedly charged with domestic violence after an argument with his wife, Joumana, six months earlier.

Still, with his passing, his will, and his defensive acumen, Kidd improved his teammates drastically. Aside from lagging attendance, winning was a cure-all, as the pundits who laughed when Kidd said the Nets would be a .500 team marveled as they ascended to the top of the Eastern Conference, earning two trips to the NBA Finals, the first of which was clinched on the road in Boston in front of fans who chanted "Wife-beater!" at Kidd and sold T-shirts bearing the same message.

The Nets climbed over the Knicks during the Kidd era, at times through the air. On Friday, November 16, 2001, they improved to 7-1 and put their stamp on New York–area dominance for the next six years with a blowout win at the Meadowlands. Kidd erased lingering doubts in a first-quarter ambush when he tossed a perfect full-court bowling ball pass to a streaking teammate. The play was as awe-inspiring as it was unexpected, and it represented the kind of flair that the Ewing and Starks–era bully Knicks never had. There was a new sheriff on the outskirts of town.

For a few years the Nets were the best NBA show east of the Mississippi, highlighted by a criminally underrated defense. The offense, however, could not be ignored, led by Kidd's precision passing—baseline alley-oop tosses off of Princeton-grade backdoor cuts—and spot-up 3-pointers from Keith Van Horn and Kerry Kittles; shots that, while airborne, gave a slower counter-rhythm to the fast breaks that created them. For all their success the Nets were twenty-sixth in attendance in '01–'02, possibly owing to the fact that they played in an arena only accessible by highway.

The most exhilarating Meadowlands memory from that two-year stretch came in Kidd's first playoff series with the Nets, a double-overtime victory over the Indiana Pacers in the deciding game 5. Twice, Reggie Miller sent the game to an extra session—first with a long, banked-in 3-pointer as regulation wound down, and then with an unexpected driving dunk in the first overtime. The Nets disposed of the Hornets next and came back from a 2-1 series deficit, which featured an epic Memorial Day collapse in Boston, to defeat the Celtics 4-2. In the Finals, the Nets were swept by a vastly superior Lakers team led by Kobe Bryant and Shaquille O'Neal.

As the basketball world waited with bated breath to see which NBA team would win the right to draft a phenom named LeBron

James, the Nets shifted into another gear in the 2003 Eastern Conference playoffs, winning ten in a row against the Bucks, Celtics, and Pistons. The Nets had a chance in the Finals against the Spurs, but lost a game 3 slugfest at home and blew a double-digit lead late in game 6 in San Antonio. Bruce Ratner bought the team that summer, with the intention of moving it to Brooklyn, and quickly cut costs by trading Kenyon Martin and Kerry Kittles, two integral pieces to the team's nucleus and the team hasn't really been a championship contender since. The next season, when the Nets started 22-20, Kidd ran head coach Byron Scott out of town. Lawrence Frank guided the Nets to the second round of the playoffs. Led by a trio of Kidd, Vince Carter, and Richard Jefferson, the Nets made the playoffs in the next three seasons (2005–'07) before back-to-back thirty-four-win seasons ushered a rough three-year transition to Brooklyn. Records for futility fell in East Rutherford and the Nets finished out their time in Newark awkwardly, like a walk from Newark Penn Station to the Prudential Center when the stoplights never seemed to be in sync. Still, a bright future beckoned: a franchise point guard, a center named Brook Lopez, and a team on its way to Brooklyn.

"We were practicing at APA trucking terminal and we were playing in Rutgers," Unger said. "So where did we come from? And look at it now."

BROOKLYN JERSEYS

I don't have a strong opinion on the construction of the Barclays Center as I was not a part of the communities that fought over the arena. There have always been developers and people fighting against them. You can watch movies, read articles, or surf the Internet to form an opinion about that history. I attended games at the Meadowlands when it was named for Brendan Byrne, when it was named for Continental Airlines, and when it was named for IZOD clothing. Shaq ripped the basket down at the first Nets game I ever attended. The franchise has helped shape my understanding of basketball and the area from which I come.

The Nets in their pre-Brooklyn incarnations were circus-like, but at their best they provided an intimate sporting experience; ten guys, a ball, and your attention span. You had to want to be there, for the game, or for nothing else than the realization that you were a part of something smaller that made you a bigger part of things. It was about the option of taking something seriously. When the team's vice president of Public Relations, Gary Sussman—who doubled as the team's public address announcer for years—said, "Two minutes left to go in New Jersey, two!" as the final game in the Garden State wound down, laughter mixed seamlessly with poignancy.

So this is a story born less of an interest in Russian oligarchy or urban planning or big business backroom dealing or borough protests or corporate branding or land grabs, and more a story about basketball players, successful and unsuccessful, performing for an organization seeking—still—the rare success of winning without complications. To that end, they are both Brooklyn—shiny, relevant, new—and the Nets, fighting an uphill battle against opposing defenses and perceptions.

CHAPTER 2

Two Point Guards

The first attempt at assembling the Brooklyn Nets' roster played out like a game show. The Nets had just returned from a four-game road trip and were on a six-game losing streak. Their next game, against the Utah Jazz, was marketed mysteriously as "a night of Russian culture." The evening seemed like any other in Newark: an overmatched Nets team fighting as underdogs, Kim Kardashian blowing courtside kisses to her boyfriend, Nets power forward Kris Humphries. But at halftime, men in white hats and blue overcoats performed traditional Russian dances in front of a person in a bear costume.

At the same time another kind of circus act was playing out beyond the arena walls. Carmelo Anthony, a Brooklyn native and small forward of the Denver Nuggets, had supposedly requested a trade. The Nets would either acquire Anthony, one of the best scorers in the NBA, or they wouldn't. The Knicks were in hot pursuit as well.

Prokhorov called an impromptu press conference in the Prudential Center, and a swell of otherwise uninterested media crowded the green room. Prokhorov, a kick-boxing aficionado, financial backer of *Snob Magazine*, and the one-day hopeful for president of Russia, now had the basketball community's undivided attention. He quashed the Carmelo speculation outright.

"I am instructing our team to walk away from the deal," Prokhorov announced. "And the meeting, which was supposed to be held by our management, tomorrow, in Denver, with Carmelo Anthony, is hereby canceled."

The room, packed like an overcrowded subway car, was stunned.

"Everything was expensive," the Russian billionaire explained.

Giddy from the breaking news and looking for some other pre-game tidbits for a pregame blog, I headed over to the Jazz locker room.

I entered and found Deron Williams, then a Utah Jazz point guard, calm despite the media firestorm. I relayed the news.

"It's done?" he asked.

"Yeah," I said.

Prokhorov's press conference had tipped the first domino, and five weeks later—after a spat with Jazz coach Jerry Sloan and a deal that reportedly materialized at the last minute—Williams was traded from the Jazz to the Nets, two days after the Knicks acquired Anthony in exchange for almost half their team.

Williams wasn't on the market, so the negotiations occurred without fanfare. If the Anthony deal (and ordeal) was a full-length vanity mirror that had the NBA by the balls, the Williams deal was a small statement written on a driver's-side rearview: potential franchise players are closer than they appear.

On the night of Prokhorov's announcement, Williams scored 20 points and dished out 10 assists in a losing effort. Johnson said he wanted rookie Derrick Favors, the centerpiece of the Jazz's haul, to play with "crazy energy." Favors played perhaps his finest game of his brief tenure with the Nets (12 points, 6 rebounds, 3 blocks). Seven Nets scored in double figures, led by Brook Lopez. General Manager Billy King high-fived Prokhorov at the end of the game.

THE COMPROMISED COLONEL
AND HIS RECALCITRANT COMMANDER

On February 23, 2011, Williams was acquired for Favors, Devin Harris, cash, and two first-round draft picks (Enes Kanter and, after more wheeling and dealing, Gorgui Deng). Favors and Kanter (a power forward who could slide over to center, and a center who could slide over to power forward) were high lottery picks, important building blocks for any talent-starved franchise. Harris, acquired by the Nets in the trade that ended the Jason Kidd era, made the 2008 All-Star team in his first full season with the Nets, but he was injury-prone and more a complementary starter than a franchise player.

Discomfort was a prevailing theme during Williams's introductory press conference. The event signified the unofficial beginning of the team's transition into Brooklyn, in part because of Williams's star power, subtle though it was. In going all-in on Williams, the Nets could parade the idea that, finally, after years of embarrassment, they were a team that could be taken seriously. After missing out on LeBron James, Chris Bosh, Dwyane Wade, and the rest of the ballyhooed free agent class of 2010, the Nets finally had their superstar.

The Nets' overriding philosophy during this transition was: something to market. Brooklyn was historically boisterous, and now it was also becoming more gentrified. What do you do to make your name in a rapidly changing place before moving? Shout over everybody. As LMFAO's hypnotic "Party Rock" blasted through a half-empty arena, Marco G, then the team's in-arena MC, and former mascots Sly Fox and Mini Sly tried their damndest to make sure that on-the-fence fans felt verbally wanted—and shopped at Party City for all their party needs.

But whose team was it? Who were they marketing? The Nets celebrated Deron Williams's arrival by giving away extra Williams no. 8 T-shirts left over from Terrence Williams's rookie season.

The difference between the no. 8 Williamses was drastic. One was an ostensible franchise player, the other a recent draft pick whose career began with 18 straight losses, feuds with coach Lawrence Frank, and an incident that led a reporter to tell the rookie to "go fuck himself."

With broad shoulders and the face and smile of a hustler, nobody was going to tell Deron Williams what to do—and D-Will wasn't easily pegged, either. He was a bulky point guard not cut from any specific traditional mold. His hair confused people, meticulously stretched thin over the front of his scalp, a style that seemed to reject the fact that he was balding, even as thousands of cameras disagreed. He had the look of a guy watching a game through a chain-link fence, not the one calling the shots on the court. Basketball players were stereotyped by length; Williams was defined by width.

His game was about nuance and detail. Sometimes he'd pick up points off of an offense that utilized movement and spacing to free him. Other times he pinged around the court looking for angles to shoot floaters and leaners, or sought out open teammates. His All-Star predecessor with the Jazz, John Stockton, was a player almost wholly defined by win-at-all-costs tactics and an ability to run the pick-and-roll—basketball's most common play—better than anyone else. Williams's superstar draftmate Chris Paul often seemed to be managing a game that nine other men happened to be playing.

Williams was amorphous,* and his childhood offered a major clue as to why: as a boy in Texas he was a two-time state champion wrestler. He'd excelled in a solitary sport that puts a competitor alone on an island, balancing weight loss, body changes, and willpower, and acquiring the ability to wriggle out of trouble. Throughout his NBA career, Williams's weight had fluctu-

---

* Williams also had a postgame mannerism that was, in sound and time, amorphous. When presented with a question that deserved a thoughtful answer, Williams would let out a high-pitched, prolonged "ummmmmm," and the length of time he took to draw out that sound would change or set the rhythmic timing for the rest of the conversation.

ated, but he succeeded regardless. YouTube mixes of his exploits can take on the feel of a Deron Williams body morph movie, but the moves remain the same: the jagged quickness of his crossover dribble and the rhythm he feels when he sinks outside shots.

In a March 2012 game in Charlotte, one of the Bobcats' announcers noted that Williams—adept at posting up smaller guards—had "a little chunk to him." Williams scored 57 points that night, a career high and a league record for the NBA's lockout-shortened season.

About a month after getting roughed up in the Belgian bandbox, where reporters greet each other with European kisses on the cheek, Williams poured in 50 points in Gottingen, Germany. And that sort of summed up the diversity of Williams's game: he didn't need to score a lot and he didn't necessarily want to score, but if you gave him a list of weak defenses, he could place a thumb tack on a map and drop 50 in a pinch. From the pervasive weight fluctuations to the ruthlessly individualistic mind-set, Williams still carried the heart of a childhood wrestling prodigy. Between appreciating the personal space afforded him as the onetime face of a franchise in Salt Lake City and his stint playing abroad in Turkey during the lockout—unconcerned with the reality that an injury could have a negative impact on his financial future— Williams cemented the perception that he wasn't a garden variety NBA All-Star following the pack. Whatever he did as an NBA player, he was still the guy who temporarily moved his family to Istanbul and didn't mind playing in an arena with a 3,200 capacity. In such a small space, Williams began to understand a type of fandom not readily apparent in the land of T-shirt guns and Jumbo-Tron hot dog races. His Besiktas jersey was retired after fifteen games, and he briefly helped lead a loud crowd in a team chant before his jersey was raised to the rafters.

At the press conference, celebrating his acquisition, Williams was flanked by Nets coach Avery Johnson and General Manager Billy King.

"You don't hear any rumors, and all of a sudden . . . you learn that you just got traded," Williams said. "It's an initial shock. I didn't know what's going on. I called my agent real quick to see if he knew anything; he didn't know anything. So the next couple of minutes I got a call from Greg Miller, the CEO of the Jazz, and he told me I'd been traded to the Nets."

An acquisition of this magnitude without the guarantee of a contract extension was rare, an all-in kind of move that hinted at uncertainty.

By contrast, Anthony delayed a conference call announcing his arrival with the Knicks because he needed to complete a contract extension. Anthony's first game with the Knicks felt like a full-on party: Broadway had a new prince. Williams arrived with an eye on the future and a suitcase at the ready.

"This kind of move defines careers," *Newark Star Ledger* columnist Dave D'Alessandro wrote of the Williams trade. "[Billy] King could either be a lamentable fool or a bold-as-brass genius. We're not even sure that there is a middle ground here."

Brooklyn was all about prodigal point guards, teenage sensations with catchy nicknames such as Pearl, Starbury, and Bassy. Williams wasn't even the McDonald's All-American on his own high school team. He was part of a trio of players that led Illinois to the 2005 NCAA Championship game and didn't always need to be the primary ball handler. He had spent five-plus professional seasons running an offense predicated on interchangeability . . . in Utah.

Cannonball splash on Atlantic Avenue? Face of the franchise? In Brooklyn? Deron Williams?

He moved more like a shadow.

"I'd be lying if I didn't say I was a little nervous that I was going to a team that was seventeen-and-forty," Williams said. "That was my first process."

During a question about Williams's clash with Jazz coach Jerry Sloan, the YES Network camera panned to a side shot of Avery

Johnson stroking the sides of his jaw, as if he were preemptively strategizing a counterattack. Williams had denied giving the Jazz an ultimatum between him and Sloan, yet without provocation, Johnson jumped in to defend him, not knowing that he'd soon fall on the same sword. Attempting to sound relatable, he mentioned having been fired. After some laughter, King piped up support: "I've been fired, too."

"So did Billy, okay," Johnson said, laughing. "Thank you, Billy."

Avery Johnson is memorable for having the voice of a Baptist preacher from his native New Orleans. His accent is widely imitated. There could be a legitimate tournament of NBA beat reporters doing Avery Johnson impressions and it could probably be televised.

"Thank you, Billy" becomes Thank you, Bill-ah. The words just sort of hung in the air, resonant and memorable in their awkward simplicity.

Thank you, Bill-ah.

Johnson and King and the Nets wanted to present a unified front behind Williams, even amid widespread disagreement on the pronunciation of his name—again, *Dare-wren* not *Duh-ron* or *Der-in*. And Williams himself wasn't even sure he wanted to be the name on the marquee.

"The main thing is, this is a celebration for our franchise, okay?" Johnson said. "This is about disassembling a team that won twelve games and assembling a team that in the future can contend and compete for a championship."

Celebrating the acquisition of a player who hadn't signed a contract extension fit with the idea of embracing the greater uncertainty of relocating the team to Brooklyn. Fans didn't know if the Nets were for real and, with the move finally on the horizon, they didn't know if Williams was for real.

Sensing the uneasiness in the room, Johnson went for broke; his next comment defined the organizational transition.

Discussing how the team would assimilate with Williams, Johnson declared, "We're going to just ask him: what does he like? What plays does he like? Where does he want the ball when the game is on the line? And that's what we're gonna do."

As a point guard himself, Johnson had fed off energy on defense and making sure his teammates were happy on offense. Otherwise, he wouldn't have earned minutes. Williams both had the ball in his hands and had the talent to take a game over. If Avery Johnson's best coaching came from merging the ability to coax the extra effort out of players—a trait that defined his seemingly long-shot career—while directing traffic philosophically, acquiring a player of Williams's skill set immediately undermined him. Whereas Johnson would have done well to push the players surrounding a player like, say, Carmelo Anthony, making sure the big dog ate, Williams didn't need Johnson; he could please himself.

Johnson's speech concluded with the statement that Williams, battling a sore wrist that would eventually be operated on, could play as many minutes as he wanted in his Nets debut, and Avery Johnson received an ovation from team employees and family attending the press conference. But Johnson had just ceded control of Williams's minutes, and minutes were to Avery Johnson what the conch was to the characters of *Lord of the Flies*: a symbol of power.

In *Aspire Higher*, his motivational memoir, Johnson, who earned his degree in psychology, talks about the mental edge a coach can have over his players simply by having the power to hand out minutes.

"I can't punish them quite like I do my children, but I can take away something they value, and they value nothing more than playing time," Johnson wrote. "Losing playing time affects them in the short term (just look at any disgruntled player on the bench during a game) and the long term (contract time)."

Did it matter that the youngest player in the NBA at the time, the Nets' prized rookie Derrick Favors, played twelve minutes or sixteen minutes? The Little General emphatically analyzed the player development process, preaching what sounded like a hybrid of simple math and improvement at basketball in a rebuilding situation, as if the number of restricted minutes a player played was a determining factor in performance.

When Johnson was tapped to coach the rebuilding Nets, he brought with him from his days in Dallas a 194-70 record, the highest winning percentage in NBA history. Yet he was given a three-year contract, awkward in that it only gave him the two years in Newark and the first season in Brooklyn to turn around a team that finished the previous season 12-70 while it was understood that the Nets wouldn't be fully competitive until they arrived in Brooklyn.

Fresh off a stint doing studio analyst work for ESPN and understanding that he needed to play a little bit nicer to get what he wanted, Johnson came off as packaged. The tenacity he used to carve a lengthy NBA career out of nothing, at times, seemed muted. The Nets job—with or without Williams—was a far cry from Johnson's first coaching stop, when he stomped and screamed and nearly pushed his way to the top.

Johnson's playing career had spanned three colleges, a summer in the USBL, and ten stints with six NBA teams. Hypothetically, had he played for the Mavericks in 2004 instead of joining their coaching staff, he would have become the only NBA player to play for four different teams twice. Undrafted out of Southern University—where he set an NCAA record with 13.3 assists per game—Johnson took six years before he fully found his footing in the NBA with the San Antonio Spurs. He was treated like an undersized human pinball with an infectious twang.

Johnson signed as an undrafted free agent with the Seattle SuperSonics in 1988. After coming off the bench for approximately half of the Sonics' games over a two-year span, he was traded to the Nuggets in 1990 for a conditional second-round draft pick, and without him, the Sonics became one of the best teams in basketball. The Nuggets waived him after twenty-one games, and he finished out the season with the Spurs, before they too waived him twenty games into the next season. At one point, his career on the brink, his wife told him to quit. He wouldn't.

From 2001 to 2003 Johnson went from Denver to Dallas to Golden State. By 2004 he re-signed with the Mavericks before training camp, only to retire weeks later and take a position as an assistant coach there under Don Nelson. With the collective experience gleaned as a player under the tutelage of Gregg Popovich in San Antonio, Nelson himself, and a litany of others, it was understood that Johnson would succeed Nelson in Dallas, and he did after sixty-four games.

Avery Johnson excelled as a coach and by 2006 he'd led the Dallas Mavericks to the NBA Finals against the Miami Heat. In game 5 they lost by a point, and the Heat went up 3–2 in the series. Dwyane Wade had taken as many free throws (25) as the entire Mavericks team. In a 2-point, game 3 win, Wade had taken 18 free throws. Wade won game 5 with 2 free throws generated by a dubious call; even though he was triple-teamed, it didn't look like anybody touched him on his way to the rim. The Mavericks had lost games 3 and 4 after going up 2–0 in the series, and sixth man Jerry Stackhouse had been suspended for game 5 for committing a flagrant foul on Shaquille O'Neal, about which O'Neal said his kids hit him harder. Still, Stackhouse didn't play, the Heat got the calls, and Johnson was reeling. From the ultimate journeyman to immediate coaching prodigy, Johnson was watching a championship slip away in front of what felt like the entire world.

Dallas Morning News scribe Eddie Sefko asked Avery Johnson what his impression of the play was.

"Um, you tell me," the Dallas head coach responded, still obviously irate but trying to avoid getting fined by the league. "What was your impression?"

"Unfortunately nobody cares about my impression," Sefko said. Johnson remained adamant.

"No, but you tell everybody, you tell everybody here. You, you, you, you know; you tell us. What was your impression?"

"My impression was he got two free throws out of it," Sefko said.

Johnson called shenanigans on Sefko's use of the impartial journalist card.

"No. All right. That's a political answer. So let me ask you the question again: what was your impression on that play?"

Silence.

"We're waiting," Johnson said.

"Did he get fouled?" Sefko asked.

"I'm asking you the question," Johnson said. "What was your impression?"

"I'm done; I don't know what to say," Sefko said, defeated.

Johnson wasn't done.

"No, I want you to give everybody an honest answer. We got people from Israel and um, Minnesota. Chicago. All over. Dallas. Germany."

Sefko tried to move on. "I'll follow up with another question."

Sefko stuttered.

"Don't stutter," Johnson said.

Johnson's discipline as a player informed his coaching. In turn, his teams in Dallas were enormously successful in the regular season, but many of the same players Johnson had played with hated how hard Johnson rode them now that he was their coach. Still, he won a remarkable number of battles: first coach to win back-to-back Coach of the Month awards. Fastest coach (at the time) to fifty wins. Fastest coach (at the time) to one hundred wins. 2006 NBA Coach of the Year.

All the hard-earned dominance that came with a 67-15 record after making the 2006 Finals, including an unreal 61-7 stretch (equivalent to the best winning percentage in NBA history over a full season), was undone by one of the greatest upsets in league history, when Nelson's "We Believe" Warriors knocked out the top-seeded Mavericks in the first round of the 2007 playoffs. The Warriors lost to the Jazz, led by Deron Williams, in the next round, although Baron Davis's dunk on Andrei Kirilenko is an all-time great finish at the rim. Avery Johnson was dismissed a year later after again failing to get his team out of the first round.

"If Johnson had a fault when he was with the Mavericks, it's that he didn't listen—to his assistants or pretty much anybody else," his old friend Sefko wrote upon Johnson's hiring by the Nets. "It was his show."

Johnson had to wait six years to become a full-fledged NBA player, but he didn't have to wait six months to become a full-fledged NBA coach. The immediate, domineering liberties he took with Dallas contradicted his one-step-at-a-time, sharing-is-caring basketball upbringing. The man who started at the bottom of the NBA barrel as a player had made it teasingly close to leadership's summit, and the view must have been intoxicating.

"Sometimes I wish we had communicated a little more," Dallas star Dirk Nowitzki said during the training camp following Johnson's dismissal. "We all know Avery ran a little dictatorship here. I think this league is still a league of players, not a coaches' league."

Arriving on the job in Newark, Johnson donned his happy hat, highlighted by a megawatt smile. Nets basketball was a crash course in pride-swallowing, as the Little General fought his own frustration on a daily basis for two years. He brought his football metaphors, having given his hometown New Orleans Saints a motivational speech during training camp in 2006. He brought his conversational head bob, as if he was digesting your query inside his brain by whirling it around. Upon hiring, he brought the best winning percentage in NBA history. But the narrative shifted in Newark, and Johnson mobilized. He became a proponent of battling—specifically, the idea of battling—after tough losses.

We battled.

Guys battled.

Give our guys credit. We battled.

Johnson spent much of his time in Newark selling the idea of Brooklyn, unable to pretend that the imminent commercial breakup between the Nets and New Jersey didn't exist, which was fine because the Prudential Center was always understood to be a rental, but not fine because the day-to-day machinations of the New Jersey Nets lost meaning.

People can joke about how the Nets often meant nothing, but there's a tangible difference between a road to nowhere (2007–10) and a temporary dead end (2010–12). And so it went, sort of. Sixteen months until Brooklyn! Five equinoxes remaining in New Jersey! We need to trade for Carmelo Anthony; he is a superstar and technically from Red Hook!

Even though they'd yet to move out of their practice facility in East Rutherford, the Nets couldn't wait to get out of New Jersey. The team wore throwback jerseys from their historic Long Island days, deep blue threads with the words NEW YORK emblazoned across the front with red-and-white trim, an eye-catching color contrast with a purpose. Johnson aided the team's forward-looking marketing by making periodic appearances in Brooklyn, and his praise for the Jersey fans who stuck around to support the team often felt faxed in from Flatbush.

There was the night when Nicole Polizzi, Snooki of *Jersey Shore* fame, met Kim Kardashian courtside. It was a moment that seemed to signal the end of times. The last home game Williams played in the 2011 season before undergoing wrist surgery wasn't even televised. In the green room after the game there was only a franchise player in flux and a small group of reporters. It was nice and relatively real.

The Nets lost twice as many games as they won during the lockout-shortened 2012 season. Jeremy Lin's ascent began against Williams and the Nets at Madison Square Garden. With the Nets looking for a little transitional luck into Brooklyn, Lin's emergence—known as Linsanity—took the NBA by storm, and the Nets suffered through one of the most injury-plagued years any NBA team has experienced. The injury report—printed on sheets that the PR officers handed out—became a running joke. By June, four previously healthy Nets had injuries requiring surgery and screws in their feet. Johnson continued to coach a misshapen roster, and the Nets continued to battle. But with a new logo on its way, the team couldn't get out of the idea of New Jersey fast enough.

CANDOR'S CROSSOVER

The cameras returned on Exit Interview Day 2012. Williams's free agency was deemed the eight-hundred-pound gorilla. In a light remark that would look pretty damn prescient less than a year later, Johnson said he hoped the eight-hundred-pound gorilla had lost weight and was down to two hundred.

Mavericks owner Mark Cuban had set the tone for Williams's free agency courtship when he spoke on the Nets' future earlier in the year.

"I hope the stadium works, I hope they do a great job, and I hope the team sucks," Cuban said courtside at Madison Square Garden to a throng of reporters that the Nets wouldn't otherwise have been able to draw. Then he cackled.

Despite the Nets' going all-in on Williams, the Mavericks were seen by many as the prohibitive favorites to sign him—he spent most of his formative years in Dallas and called Dallas home, and the Mavs were only a year removed from winning a title in the post–Avery Johnson era. The cynics didn't care that the Nets could offer an extra year at a higher annual rate. There was no state tax in Texas and there was a city tax in New York. Such was the cloud that seemed to follow the Nets. Less than two months away from signing a contract on a house in Dallas, Williams said he was impressed by the progress at the transforming Barclays Center construction site.

"I mean, they've got seats in there now and it's starting to come into shape. So you can definitely tell, the locker room where it's going to be—picked out my locker for next year."

"Was it in the visiting locker room?" a reporter blurted out.

"I didn't go in the visiting locker room," Williams said.

The catharsis between subject and scribes wasn't even defined by the locker selection back-and-forth. Williams also turned his potential *sayonara*—and all of the loaded pressure that came with it—into a re-creation of a classic Seinfeld catchphrase. He was asked if he liked the media.

"Do I need to answer that question?"

We all laughed before he got around to the truth: if he could go every day without talking, that'd be great.

"No, no. It's not you, it's more about me."

While his admission was quite sane and his explanation rang true, we were flabbergasted that he went there.

To paraphrase George Costanza: You just gave us the "it's not you it's me" routine? Seriously? Nobody gives the New Jersey Nets media the "it's not you it's me." If it's anybody, it's us. We had just finished piggybacking a 12-70 campaign with two seasons spent counting Nets named Williams like sheep (Terrence, Shawne, Jordan, Sheldon, Deron) and unwittingly tracking the courtside appearances of Kim Kardashian and *Jersey Shore* cast members, as if a comparative study between Snooki's base tan and orange marmalade was in the offing.

It was crazy that he went there.

"You've never been told that before?" he added.

The NBA's most sought-after free agent at the time had just given the New York/New Jersey media the oldest breakup line in the book, and for those in the scrum the breakup had to feel real, in that it mirrored Williams's public distaste for New Jersey. It was odd: the guy whom the Nets treated like the franchise's Tony Soprano apparently wasn't a fan of New Jersey.*

---

* Worth noting regarding the Tony Soprano connection: James Gandolfini's character was a Nets fan and *The Sopranos,* which revolutionized cable television, features a mob boss with a keen sense of history having an intricate dream about ducks. The Nets left the Teaneck Armory to play in Commack, Long Island, where they shared an arena with a team named the Ducks.

On February 1, 2012, the Nets outlasted the Pistons with eight players, four of them named Williams and five of them having either Jordan or Williams in their name. Avery Johnson utilized the phrase "the Great Eight" to praise the bizarre, motley crew.

Deron Williams was asked about New Jersey.

"I love it here," he said, sounding like the point-counterpoint to a reporter who covered presidents, cop shops, and sports, a wise crank who would chime in occasionally with a simple statement about reporting on the Nets that goes: "I would rather dip my dick in battery acid than cover this team."

Yet in that same interview Williams explained his success on offense that night—his fifth straight 20-plus-point game—and joked about how shorthanded the Nets were.

"It's hard to do [a layup line] before the game with eight people," he said, both noting a universal truth and making the Nets sound like the Bad News Bobcats. "You get tired because it's just like you're going around and around."

At his best, Williams seemed on top of everything, totally in control, maybe even too on top of everything. He seemed to play for the critics, not for the people. He performed like he was an artist, as if mounting critiques and new details would only embolden him. On the night of "the Great Eight" in Newark, the only thing that number eight didn't seem to know was that he had to guard Jeremy Lin in three days. Naturally, Williams was a hard read heading into free agency.

ROLLING THE DICE

Las Vegas is the epitome of summer camp for people who take basketball seriously and people who take basketball *too* seriously. Fly into Vegas in early July and you're liable to get picked up by an unintelligible cabbie from a far-off land who somehow loathes LeBron James for not speaking well enough. You're just as liable to get picked up one day by a seventy-eight-year-old Boston native who talks about Bob Cousy dribbling minutes off the game clock before the shot clock existed. And if you'd like to shoot a machine gun instead of a basketball, just check the top of a cab for details.

Head north up the strip, past the UFC fights at the MGM; past the iconic Caesars Palace, where Jerry Seinfeld is on the marquee; past the droves of tourists; past the swanky Bellagio and the guy dressed as Zach Galifinakis's infant-toting character from *The Hangover*; past Treasure Island, which actually might just be the San Antonio River Walk with Pirate Ships . . . and eventually the Wynn, a state-of-the-art hotel that sponsors and hosts USA Basketball, twenty years after the original Dream Team, sprouts into the sky. An oasis of basketball and bullshit begins there. Wynn is connected to its sister hotel, Encore, by a super-high-end mall. If fresh air wasn't a thing, one might never want to leave.

Move farther north and the basketball bubble becomes even more concentrated because the cost of staying falls off a cliff.

Seen through sunglasses: Little boys and girls in uniforms. Players rocking slogan T-shirts ("Haters Are My Motivation," "YOLO," etc.). Tall people. Schmoozing coaches in polo shirts. More tall people. A guy carrying a basketball and a suitcase about to enter a hotel as others return to the airport.

Sin City started playing host to the NBA Summer League in 2004. The UNLV Runnin' Rebels had taken college basketball by storm in the late eighties and early nineties, under the steward-ship of iconic towel-biting coach Jerry Tarkanian. That run faded in classic Vegas ignominy when three UNLV players were pho-tographed in a hot tub with Richard Perry, a man renowned for fixing sporting events. Tarkanian was forced to resign.

Despite USA Basketball's base in Colorado Springs, Las Vegas has an allure and financial backing that Team USA couldn't deny. Players were working out there voluntarily during the summer, anyway. Beginning in 2005, when Jerry Colangelo, managing director of Team USA, hired Duke coach Mike Krzyzewski to lead the Olympic teams, Las Vegas Events, a trade and tourism group, agreed to foot the bill for every training camp through 2012. (Team USA returned, along with Krzyzewski, to Vegas in the summer of 2013.)

The agreement, priceless star-fucking in exchange for free goods and services, essentially transforms Team USA training camp into a work vacation for players already tied down by a rigorous NBA schedule at least seven months a year. In 2012, the injuries piled up before, during, and after Team USA's training camp and completely altered the NBA's playoff landscape.

The orange peel in the Vegas/USA Basketball mixed drink is that Krzyzewski and Duke defeated UNLV in the 1991 Final Four to win his first national championship. Fairly or unfairly, the Duke-UNLV rivalry—the Rebels routed the Blue Devils in the championship game a year earlier—was touted as class warfare: athletic black players representing Sin City against a private school led by a white kid named Christian. Oh, yes, and twenty-one years later Christian (Christian Laettner) is at Team USA practice, too. He'd like to get a few questions in.

The class warfare theme resurfaced again when Vegas hosted the NBA All-Star game in 2007. Attendees couldn't seem to agree on whether the Vegas All-Star Weekend was the greatest thing ever or the most dangerous event assembled by a professional sports league. Many visitors had no idea whether Sin City had been overrun with thugs or if this was what a normal weekend in Vegas looked like.

There is something for every NBA-inclined soul in Vegas, whether it's me randomly running into members of LeBron's Brontourage outside of a club called Tryst to briefly and awkwardly discuss freelancing; the giggling coed taking a camera phone picture of Kobe Bryant with the rest of the UNLV cheerleading squad; autograph seekers outside the Team USA practice facility engaging in simple idol worship; the kid chasing after the dream of going pro; or the guy on the Nets signing a $98.77 million contract extension.

On the day Deron Williams officially signed his contract to play for the Brooklyn Nets it was 118 degrees in Las Vegas, 122 if you trust the reading inside of a red Toyota Prius baking in the Thomas & Mack Arena parking lot at UNLV. If death by a sixteen-year-old's booze stash was your thing, Seagram's Wine Coolers were selling two for $8 on the Strip. On the Riviera Boulevard sidewalk between Paradise Avenue and the Strip, stray cards advertising escorts were scattered on scalding pebbles. Danielle (blonde, $99) and Carly (brunette, $69) lured passersby as they wove through the pine trees that rose up from the mulch over the pebbles. The price gap paralleled the Mavs' and Nets' opposite Deron Williams–related roster-building philosophies. The Nets were willing to do whatever it took, while Mark Cuban's Mavs allocated about 30 percent less.

Cuban would later explain how changes to the NBA's collective bargaining agreement altered the way the Mavericks needed to spend their money, but his message about Williams was simple: in the economic climate of the NBA in 2012, Deron Williams was not worth a maximum investment.

Cuban chose not to attend a free agency meeting with Williams before Williams headed to Vegas, leaving him with General Manager Donnie Nelson and Coach Rick Carlisle. Cuban was in Los Angeles filming an episode of the reality television series *Shark Tank*. The symbolism was damning. Williams was proud and aware of slights. During training camp, he compared Cuban's decision to the time he canceled a college visit when Maryland coach Gary Williams wouldn't meet with him. Williams didn't go to Maryland and he didn't sign with the Mavs.

"Probably the best feeling was when you get the phone call from Deron and he says, you know, 'I'm staying,'" King said of the re-signing.

It was 2012. Williams announced his decision by posting a picture of the Nets' new logo on his Twitter account, and he signed the contract on an iPad.

King's trump card turned out to be the acquisition of Joe Johnson from the Atlanta Hawks.

"We had pretty much agreed to the Joe Johnson deal and we kept it from you guys," King told the press two months later.

"Because when we had our meeting with Deron on, I think it was, July second, I wanted to be able to present it to him first. Because he said, 'I haven't heard that.' I go, 'Yeah, we wanted you to hear first.' Before he had gone on vacation, before our meeting, we had one last talk. I kind of got an idea of where I needed to go—not in terms of players—but in building the team to get him to commit."

Johnson was a six-time All-Star, but also the poster boy for the concept of the overpaid player. Johnson's reputation wasn't his fault. The NBA had many more maximum contracts—call them golden tickets—than they did golden ticket players. In the league's salary structure, both loyalty and years of service are rewarded with greater pay. All you need is someone to foot the bill. Johnson happened to sign a $123 million contract the same summer that LeBron James, Dwyane Wade, and Chris Bosh signed for slightly less to play together in Miami. Johnson was coming off another big contract, and the idea that he wasn't worth the money hit the mainstream as if it was sponsored by light beer.

Johnson's contract had been considered untradeable, but the Hawks had a new general manager, King's former teammate at Duke in the late eighties Danny Ferry, and Ferry wanted to start clean. King and Nets assistant general manager Bobby Marks were able to unload a number of spare parts signed to smaller, but still largely untenable, contracts. Five players (Johan Petro, DeShawn Stevenson, Anthony Morrow, Jordan Williams, and Jordan Farmar) were shipped away, and the Nets had two All-Stars to build around.

Williams and Johnson were dubbed Brooklyn's Backcourt, two golden—or goldish—tickets. The Nets were back in the playoff discussion. In essence, they traded for immediate improvement and, likely, a four-year period in which they would pay out large sums of money in player salary. Fittingly, they convinced Williams to sign an extension by making a move that Mark Cuban wouldn't have consented to, in the process acquiring a player Williams had hoped to play with before ever entering the NBA.

Williams went through a predraft workout with the Hawks in 2005 and figured there was a decent chance the Hawks might draft him, as they had just acquired Johnson from the Phoenix Suns and signed him to a lavish deal and needed a point guard. But the Hawks selected North Carolina forward Marvin Williams instead. The Hawks were terrible in Johnson's first year, adjusting to new coach Mike Woodson, but they improved every year and became an Eastern Conference postseason fixture.

Johnson began his final season with the Hawks against the Nets in Newark. The Nets had beaten the Wizards on the road in their opener in a game that featured a massive comeback and Wizards fans booing future Net Andray Blatche mercilessly. A night later the Hawks obliterated the Nets, winning by 36. It was a rare sellout crowd in Jersey, and Avery Johnson said he felt sorry for the fans.

Asked about the difference between mounting a comeback against the Wizards as opposed to the Hawks, Deron Williams said, "That was the Wizards, this is the Hawks, that's pretty much it." At the time, the subtext was as simple as stating the difference between respect (Hawks) and disrespect (Wizards).

On my last night in Vegas, I tried to walk the entire Strip—both ways. Call it the disease of being a New Yorker. I stopped short of Mandalay Bay, which is like walking most of Manhattan only to stop short of Inwood. In the MGM Grand, Scottie Pippen strolled through with his kids hanging off him.

On my way back down the Strip, I passed through the Encore Hotel en route to Wynn, just in case there was something worth seeing. My legs were Jell-O and my feet felt leaden. I walked past a club, Surrender, on my way out, only to see Jared Zwerling of ESPN

New York with a friend. Zwerling ran Deron Williams's ESPNNY blog when Williams played in Turkey during the lockout.

After exchanging pleasantries, Zwerling asked me if I saw Williams.

What?

Dude—he's right over there. Deron Williams.

I looked. I did not see him.

Zwerling pointed him out again, He acted like I couldn't see the sun; I felt like I couldn't find Waldo. Finally, through a line of partygoers, leaning against a beam trying to look inconspicuous, I spotted Williams. Apparently the people at Surrender didn't recognize him—the newly minted face of the Brooklyn Nets—and he had to wait to get into the club.

So there it is, a lasting impression of Vegas nightlife: Deron Williams, on the night of the self-indulgent ESPYS, the slowest sports night of the year, less than twenty-four hours after signing a five-year, $98.77 million contract, entering the next phase of his life by posting up incognito outside of a club called Surrender.

Rookie-to-be Anthony Davis made his professional debut, so he was the big story. Kevin Durant scored 24 points and Andre Iguodala was named player of the game.

"One of the best point guards in the world," Players Association president Chris Paul said when I asked about Williams's return to competitive action in a cakewalk win over the Dominican Republic. "It's like riding a bike."

Following a game-high 10 assists, Williams almost scooted by, but with the aid of an NBA official I managed to stop him for a brief interview.

"You would be that guy," he said.

At least he was smiling.

CHAPTER 3

White Team/Black Team

TOBACCO ROAD RUNS THROUGH IT

The odyssey begins with a Brooklyn-born basketball coach in New Jersey, the plot driven through the heart of North Carolina and Philadelphia, stopping in Kansas, San Antonio, Los Angeles, Indiana, Detroit, New York, Charlotte, and Utah before heading back to New Jersey and, finally, Brooklyn. The journey revolves around the general manager and the only coach to win an NCAA championship and an NBA title. To understand Billy King, the politically inclined GM of the Nets, one must understand—or attempt to understand—Larry Brown, a vagabond coach with a plaque in the Hall of Fame and, after fourteen stops in forty-nine years, an incredible ear for Paul Simon's "50 Ways to Leave Your Lover."

When Brown left the Nets for the University of Kansas job two weeks before the 1983 playoffs, he turned his attention toward building an NCAA contender in his image. A graduate of the University of North Carolina, Brown attempted to recruit King, a defensive-minded power forward out of Park View High School in Sterling, Virginia. King chose Duke, UNC's archrival, over Kansas.

The overlapping nature of their career paths is odd, but odd was to be expected when it came to Brown, a persnickety taskmaster with a preference for practices over games and a massive influence in coaching circles that spanned generations. Seated courtside at

Energy Solutions Arena in Salt Lake City in late March, King had just come from a meeting with an old friend, Kevin O'Connor. O'Connor traded Deron Williams to the Nets before stepping down as the Jazz's general manager. King and O'Connor worked together with the Philadelphia 76ers under . . . Larry Brown. Like King, O'Connor had experience as an assistant coach under Brown. King is fond of saying he runs prospective deals past O'Connor and vice versa.

"We scouted a lot together," King said of his relationship with O'Connor. "We talked draft. We talked trade, so we sort of, I guess, see basketball in the same way. As Larry said, play 'the Right Way.'"

Brown jumped from Kansas back into the NBA after the '88 championship, taking a job with the San Antonio Spurs that lasted three and a half years, enough time to still be pacing the sidelines when backup point guard Avery Johnson was cut. Brown hopped over to the L.A. Clippers later that same season.

King and Brown's greatest success together with the Sixers came largely by accident. A pay raise upon being traded (known as a trade kicker) in the journeyman Matt Geiger's contract killed a four-team, twenty-two-player deal, which would have been the largest in NBA history by nine players. The deal would have sent Allen Iverson packing to Detroit. The Sixers built a team around Iverson the next season and reached the NBA Finals. In a game 1 victory over the Los Angeles Lakers, the pinnacle of King's tenure with the Sixers, Iverson solidified his legend during a remarkable comeback and Geiger shot 5-for-7 in fourteen minutes, looking like a seven-foot, goateed Mr. Clean in high tops.

Again, Brown packed his bags, leaving the Sixers for the Pistons in 2003 and promptly winning the 2004 championship. King was left to run the Sixers without his mentor. In King's first two-plus years without Brown, four head coaches roamed the sidelines, but he drafted well: Andre Iguodala at no. 9 in 2004; Thaddeus Young at no. 12 in 2007; second-round steals in Kyle Korver (acquired from the Nets) at no. 51 in 2003 and Lou Williams at no. 45 in 2005.

However, King's player valuation undermined his roster-building efforts. Seven years and $50 million to retain Kenny Thomas, a middling forward, six years and $63 million to keep Samuel Dalembert, a flawed center. And then there were a number of sideways trades that brought in marquee scorers but not results. Finally, King traded Iverson to the Denver Nuggets early in the 2007 season, also his last with the team.

The draft is a risk-oriented endeavor, an inexact science. Make a few good picks and the cynics will write you off as lucky, not savvy. So King's major strength, seeing value in the relatively unknown, was overshadowed by his weakness: fiscal responsibility.

The nascent days of the Brooklyn Nets fused King's history of spending large with his deep sense of loyalty; the Nets' roster came together in part via relationships he had developed through the years: Joe Johnson via Danny Ferry, Deron Williams via Kevin O'Connor and Gerald Wallace, once an All-Star under Larry Brown in Charlotte.

With King and Brown, it always seemed to come back to loyalty and working together despite being born into rival collegiate cultures. In 2000, the Sixers played the Charlotte Hornets in the playoffs, and King spoke to the *Charlotte Observer* about his relationship with Brown.

"It's like when the United States and Russia started becoming allies somewhat," he said. "We're sharing ideas; we're working together. . . . But, hey, I'm loyal to Russia and [Brown's] loyal to the United States."

FIRST GAME: OCEAN VIEWS

Up until halftime, when trampoline dunkers went airborne set to the title track from *Space Jam*, the first official game in Brooklyn

Nets history had a distinct throwback feel, as if to honor a time when professional sports last existed in Brooklyn. The game was not on the radio. The game was not on television. Finding a working box score on press row was a chore.

The Nets were the last team to start their preseason slate because ongoing construction at Madison Square Garden pushed their preseason matchup against the Knicks back two weeks. Three months after signing his contract in Vegas, the move that signified seismic change, Williams and his teammates officially debuted at Boardwalk Hall in Atlantic City against the 76ers. When the two teams last met, the Sixers were ushering the Nets out of Newark in April.

The Boardwalk Hall gathering was also a unique moment for the Sixers, who were kicking off their golden anniversary season. Legendary Philadelphia statistician Harvey Pollack, inventor of the blocked shot statistic, was there to begin another season. Rod Thorn, in his final season as Sixers' GM, was there as well. With the Nets, Thorn built back-to-back NBA Finals teams in 2002–03, but his performance had fallen off as the years went by. By the end of Thorn's tenure, he looked like the opposite of King: unsuccessful in the draft and not able to spend money.

Boardwalk Hall played intimate host to a new beginning. Boasting a 137-foot-high barrel vault ceiling, it was said to have the world's largest "clear span space" back in 1929. The building began hosting Miss America Pageants eleven years later because Atlantic City needed to figure a way to draw tourists after Labor Day. Old-school vanity lights covered the edges of the mirror in the media room bathroom, as if Miss Maryland might show up to glance through a Sixers media guide while powdering her nose.

Banners from ECAC hockey schools (Clarkson, Union, Colgate, and a plethora of Ivy League institutions) were visible reminders of just how little the building had in terms of professional sporting events. Even the hallways leading to the Brooklyn

Nets' makeshift locker room looked like hospital corridors, not a welcome metaphor given the Nets' snakebitten Jersey past.

The hospital corridors metaphor was serving Andrew Bynum, the South Jersey native who would go on to miss the season with an assortment of knee problems, including one injury sustained while bowling. Bynum was acquired by the Sixers in a three-way trade that sent Dwight Howard to the Lakers and Andre Iguodala, the Sixers' best player, to the Nuggets. Without Iguodala or Bynum in uniform, the Sixers went from a probable playoff team to also-rans, leaving the Nets, Knicks, and Celtics to fight it out for Atlantic Division bragging rights.

The Bynum-Howard-Iguodala trade liberated Nets center Brook Lopez from a tortuous life of dealing with constant trade rumors. At Team USA practice in Las Vegas, Williams and Kobe Bryant talked about their respective teammates, both of whom were involved in Howard-related trade rumors.

"He's kind of got this 'fuck it' attitude," Bryant said of Bynum potentially being dealt. "Which is great. That's what makes him great. It wouldn't bother him at all."

(After sitting out the season because of injuries, Bynum signed a two-year deal to play in Cleveland.)

"I guarantee it's been bothering him," Williams said of Lopez. "You could tell at times that it definitely bothered him. When you're constantly getting thrown around, and your name is being thrown around in trade rumors, it's tough to deal with."

Lopez spoke of the nagging trade-rumor cloud that hung over him after Williams gave the Jersey media his stirring rendition of it's-not-you-it's-me.

"I don't know how to say this without offending you guys," Lopez said. "In the *Post* and the *Daily News*, I read whatever is on the front page, your 'headlines' or what have you. I flip through all those stories and I get to the movie reviews and comics, and then I get to the sports section and I close it."

You just ignore it all?

"I do. It's just chatter. You hear a lot of the same things every day, and then you hear wild and crazy things out of nowhere on certain days. It was best for me to ignore it all . . . I just wanted to focus on myself, and rehabbing."

Lopez did all of that work and got the best season of his young career off to a good start in Atlantic City, while Bynum clowned around on the Sixers' bench.

Before the first sporadic chants of "BROOOOOK-LYN" filled the South Jersey air—mostly generated by Nets employees who made the trip down to Atlantic City for the game—Williams walked into a sparsely populated locker room and asked his teammates what happened to the music. Nobody said anything. There wasn't any music blaring throughout the room, but Joe Johnson, iPad in hand, had been mock-crooning in front of Andray Blatche. "I know what you're saying; he got a little voice on him," Johnson said.

Blatche would later put the ball in the basket to the win the game in overtime. When I asked him after the game if the beads around his neck were inspired by the ones Jay-Z wore at the first ever Barclays Center concert, Blatche responded by making the Roc-A-Fella sign, forming a triangle with his hands. For Blatche, it was a good start to a redemptive season after years of losing and misery in the nation's capital.

AD WIZARDS

The Nets began NBA basketball in Barclays Center with a Monday-night preseason tilt against the Wizards. The place mostly sparkled, and when the press finally ventured inside the Nets' locker room something happened that brought back memories of Madison Square Garden: approximately twenty-seven reporters idling in a New York locker room with only one fringe regular available to talk—and that player, Mirza Teletovic, was a rookie coming off of a horrible shooting debut in Atlantic City. He might not have known any better. Especially in big markets it was rare for players to make themselves available before games. Between routine and a need to focus, this was understandable.

No longer aiding Nets players and the press was PR maven Patrick Rees, who had taken a promotion to join the Wizards. But it was fitting that Rees could be there for the first game in Brooklyn. He is known as P Rees. To P Rees, everyone is "brother," and when there was ever a complaint—the Nets were understaffed during training camp because of the departure of P Rees—somebody would inevitably chime in with a comment about how they missed him.

The Nets were in control most of the game, but the Wizards clawed back, forcing Avery Johnson to bring the starters back. The BROOOOOK-LYN chant finally sounded off with 3:04 left in the fourth quarter and increased after Wizards backup point guard A. J. Price flagrantly fouled Williams. Williams confronted Price, and each player was assessed a technical foul. The Nets eventually pulled away and won.

Williams sat down to begin his first Ortsbo presser at Barclays Center and called the set-up a "trial run." Ortsbo is a company that facilitates Internet chatting in fifty different languages, "Across many languages. To any Internet endpoint." The branding presented a specific vision for the future: a globalized NBA utopia, with the Brooklyn Nets and their Russian owner at the forefront, fans in China and Brazil having translated chats with second-generation yuppies in Cobble Hill and Fort Greene.

Williams was asked about the confrontation with Price.

"I don't know," he said, barely audibly. "He started talking for no reason."

"I wasn't doing anything," Williams said when the question came back to him later. "He just started talking. Kept saying, 'I'm home.' I don't know what that means. That's all he kept saying: 'I'm home. I'm home.'

"Okay," Williams said, deadpanning his on-court response, giving way to a chorus of laughter.

Someone mentioned that Price was from Long Island.

"I just don't—I'm not a tough guy," Williams said. "I just like to play basketball. I hate when people start talking for no reason. And that's pretty much what he did. He was home.

"I guess he had some boys in the crowd he wanted to impress or something like that," Williams continued. "You know, while he can—little minutes he's going to get this year."

It was, in the words of buzzing reporters, a stunning evisceration.

Asked about the crowd having Williams's back, Williams said: "It's my home now, yeah. So I told him that."

But it was an $83 million team's first game in a brand-new billion-dollar arena and Price was already up in their shit.

DOLLARS MAKE CENTS

An NBA team's payroll operates around a soft salary cap. For the 2012–13 season, teams needed to pay out a minimum of $49.3 million in roster payroll. The salary cap was set at approximately $58 million. There was a luxury tax threshold of $70.3 million, penalties of a dollar-for-dollar meant to discourage rampant spending. Teams are allowed to exceed the salary cap—using what are referred to as exceptions. The 2011 lockout reduced the players' percentage of the pie and included harsher penalties for teams that went above the cap.

Yet the Nets, backed by a Russian tycoon who didn't mind spending, assembled the second-priciest roster in the league. Of the Nets' $83 million roster, about $72 million went to the five starters. These five players wore white jerseys at practice. Coaches started referring to the second unit as the black team.

Williams's extension cost $98.77 million; Johnson had four years remaining on a $123 million contract; Gerald Wallace had re-signed for four years and $40 million; Brook Lopez had re-signed for four years and just under $70 million; and Kris Humphries had re-signed for two years and $24 million.

The Nets released the next-highest-paid player, Travis Outlaw, using the onetime amnesty provision that allowed them to remove his salary from their cap number. When the Sacramento Kings claimed Outlaw, they agreed to pay $3 million of the $7 million due to him annually for three more seasons.

The Nets spent approximately $11 million on the other ten players who filled out the opening-day roster. They scooped up Josh Childress and Blatche by submitting the highest bid in amnesty auctions, just as the Kings had done with Outlaw.

The Nets used their mini-midlevel exception to sign Mirza Teletovic, a Bosnian sharpshooter. Teletovic had to pay approximately $2.1 million to get out of his contract with his team in northern Spain, Caja Laboral (which is the name of a bank), and, per league rules, the Nets covered $500,000 of those $2.1 million to help bring him Stateside. Teletovic's total freedom fee was more money than the Nets paid to any other player on the team's bench!

Two second-round draft picks (Tyshawn Taylor, Tornike "Toko" Shengelia) and a first-round pick in his second year (MarShon Brooks) were on rookie-scale contracts. The Nets paid some version of the veteran's minimum exception to three perimeter-oriented second-unit players (Stackhouse, Keith Bogans, and C. J. Watson) and acquired the rebounding specialist Reggie Evans from the Clippers for a future second-round draft pick and a trade exception. Essentially, Evans was traded for a player who hadn't been drafted yet and a "monetary credit" that the Clippers could use in a future trade.

The enduring paradox of Johnson, Wallace, Lopez, Humphries, and Williams—the starting five at the beginning of the season—was that the Nets spent (overspent in the opinion of most) on players who, while forming a necessary on-court foundation for a winning team, actually undermined the team's promotional endeavors just by being themselves. Williams was perpetually brooding. Johnson often oozed the personality of the decoy that the Nets asked him to be on many offensive possessions. Lopez was likable but aloof. Humphries was a PR machine. Most everything he said was controlled.

Wallace was the most open of the five, but even he, the heart of the team if there was one, spoke in press conferences of being afraid of New York City and cities in general. From Sacramento to Charlotte to Portland to New Jersey, he liked the suburbs. He hailed from Childersburg, Alabama, a town of about five thousand. The Nets promoted Wallace as an off-season fisherman, and he had a two-and-a-half-acre lake built into his backyard, filled with imported fish for his own leisurely angling. So the starter whose hustle resonated with fans was fundamentally at lifestyle odds with the developing borough he was now an integral part of. It wasn't offensive—as much as the Nets tried, you couldn't force anything or anyone to be Brooklyn or be urban—but it was bizarre.

Everything revolved around Williams, but Wallace was the player whose successes provided fleeting glimpses of how good the Nets could be at full strength. Williams was the army general, but Wallace was the guy carrying the flag they were planting into the ground. And this being the first season of the paradoxical Brooklyn Nets—fifty-five years after Dodger players lived in Brooklyn—of course the land freaked him out.

Only the Lakers' starting five made that kind of money, and four of them boasted All-NBA résumés. The pricey Nets had to offset their shortcomings in charisma with flashy merchandise and a jewel of an arena.

Yet the Nets' inexpensive bench, "the black team," was filled with personalities and easy-to-root-for underdogs. Even though they maintained quiet public veneers, Keith Bogans and C. J. Watson came off as everymen, veterans on short contracts fighting for permanence. Teletovic, a favorite of the Spanish-speaking media, carried himself with class and spoke multiple languages. He had overcome the war in the Balkans as a child and was a legend in his own country, even though the Nets' marketing efforts seemed to begin and end with fans, especially little kids, mispronouncing his name on the big screen. Complicating matters, Teletovic's nickname, MTV, was probably the simplest, and perhaps most fitting, of any of the first-year Brooklyn Nets. There were constant squabbles in and around the organization between those who wanted their MTV and those who didn't; it was hard not to feel for Mirza, the twenty-seven-year-old rookie who across an ocean was a seasoned veteran.

Evans, the season's true fan-favorite success story, was in his own world and remained the most entertaining Net when things were going well. Childress was a friendly, brainy guy and probably the best Words With Friends player in the entire NBA, routinely beating me, awkward because I was writing a book.

Blatche and Brooks were criticized for not always doing or saying the right thing, but the flip side was that they had a hard time not being themselves. In locker rooms, it's always nice to talk to humans as they are. Taylor was a walking, talking Jay-Z dictionary. Avery Johnson once likened second-round draft pick Tornike Shengelia to Manu Ginobili. Shengelia, whose nickname was Toko, hailed from the nation of Georgia. We got to hear Avery Johnson say "Toko" a lot, and that alone was worth the weight of his salary in gold. A meaningless late-season comeback against the Wizards, a highlight evening for both Taylor and Shengelia, showed how much the crowd could energize Barclays Center if given underdog characters to root for.

And then there was Jerry Stackhouse. Stackhouse began his career with the Philadelphia 76ers in 1995, where, under Larry Brown, he ended up playing second fiddle to Allen Iverson, then was shipped to Detroit for two-plus seasons. He developed as a first-option scorer in Detroit with and without Grant Hill, even leading the NBA in scoring in 2000–01. From Detroit he went on to Washington, where he spent a year in the shadow of the Michael Jordan farewell tour before becoming an impactful role player in Dallas. In a league of superstars, Stackhouse always knew his role. He was the NBA's ultimate character actor, and he boasted a keen understanding of the world outside the NBA after eighteen years in the league.

We talked gentrification during the preseason, and Stackhouse understood that there were multiple sides to an issue.

"For true Brooklynites, you know what I'm saying, they probably would say a lot of that is still superficial," he said. He referenced rugged ghettos that hadn't changed much. "Brownsville is still Brownsville. As much as you still want to say Brooklyn is Brooklyn, Brownsville is still Brownsville. You can believe that."

There was a reason he was a leader in the Players' Association. Stackhouse began the season with the understanding that he would be groomed for an eventual head coaching position somewhere. He said Mark Jackson's path was his ideal blueprint. Jackson went straight from the broadcast booth—which included a brief stint doing Nets games—before becoming the head coach of the Golden State Warriors.

The voluble MarShon Brooks was being interviewed after a preseason win over the Sixers at Barclays Center, and Stackhouse interjected.

"Don't take the bait, pimp," Stackhouse said. "Don't take the bait."

Stackhouse repeated the message a few times, adding, "Leave the bullshit alone."

It was a long training camp and preseason for Brooks, a lanky, talented young scorer and the only player whose contract with the Nets remained the same from Newark to Brooklyn. Earlier in the preseason, Avery Johnson had inadvertently referred to Brooks, who had sat out much of preseason with a foot injury, as his "defunct" sixth man, and the Nets consistently made fun of his defense.

Williams and Evans took a picture of themselves next to

Brooks's car after stuffing the vehicle with popcorn, a common NBA prank. Brooks blamed himself for not bringing cocoa butter. Speaking with reporters during training camp, Brooks said the popcorn smell still crept out of his car at times.

In a sense, Brooks had to be a rookie in both New Jersey and Brooklyn. During the Nets' training camp, New Jersey didn't seem to count—especially if you witnessed the awkward chuckles whenever the Garden State came up.

During the summer lag time, Brooks was the guy the Nets trotted out to various events, appearing on behalf of the organization as a judge at a Nathan's hot dog eating contest at Coney Island and signing autographs at the Paramus Mall in Jersey. He did all of this while being subjected to daily trade rumors; speculation that saw him in Orlando if the Nets landed Dwight Howard. Ironically, he played for the Nets' summer league team in Orlando— and played poorly, trade rumors weighing on him.

In the Nets' final preseason game, an overtime loss to the Knicks, Brooks's game-tying layup spilled out and he thought he was fouled.

"He hit me!" Brooks pleaded with the referee after. "He hit me!"

The Knicks walked off the court, victorious. The rematch eight days later, the regular-season New York City basketball party that would officially mark the launch of the Brooklyn Nets, was pushed back twenty-five days on account of Hurricane Sandy. The practice court at the PNY Center flooded, forcing the Nets to temporarily abandon New Jersey, pushing them deeper into day-to-day Brooklyn life.

TRANSITIONAL HUMP

When the Nets arrived in Brooklyn, Humphries and Lopez were the only players remaining from the team's days in the Meadowlands. Humphries arrived in New Jersey in early 2010 having never averaged more than fourteen minutes per game in more than five seasons in the league. Prior to landing with the Nets in the middle of the 2009–10 season, Humphries topped out at 5.7 points and 3.7 rebounds per game.

Even though his per-thirty-six-minute numbers presaged a potential double-double player—Humphries put up his career's gaudiest numbers after being traded to the Nets—his emergence in Newark the following fall was still shocking. The first double-double (13 points, 18 rebounds) came on the road against Cleveland eight games into the season; Humphries was given the start at power forward at the last minute. After the second double-double, people started to glance around, a little confused.

Soon, a six-eight power forward who swam against Michael Phelps as a kid—and won—and who looked and played basketball like a bodybuilder would, was trending. When Humphries's rebounding prowess propelled the Nets to a few surprise wins, he was the full-blown phenomenon dating Kim Kardashian—and he had worked harder to earn his recognition than she had. The publicity began on Halloween 2010 when Kardashian showed up at the Prudential Center for a matinee between the Nets and the Heat. In the presence of Dwyane Wade, LeBron James, and Chris Bosh, Humphries was window dressing in the game, but was well on his way to dominating the supermarket checkout aisle.

Through his brief courtship and marriage to the celebutante, E! featured him in its flagship fluff *Keeping Up with the Kardashians*, thus ensuring that the non-NBA consumers would judge Humphries based on a fabricated reality TV persona. Humphries's last season as a New Jersey Net began at Madison Square Garden on December 21, the night of the last preseason game, when Knicks fans began a leaguewide trend by vociferously booing him because of his failed marriage to Kardashian. The Nets, still a second-rate franchise in New Jersey, were happy that one of their players was famous around the country. One Nets executive, when asked about Humphries ranking sixth in rebounding rate, quipped, "First on Page Six." Humphries became one of the few entertaining subplots on a losing team.

With Lopez struggling on the boards, a niche was there for Humphries. At times during his tenure in New Jersey, Humphries wowed courtside reporters by swooping in and rebounding in the clearly defined personal space of others. Watching Kris Humphries rebound back then was like watching a supremely skilled center fielder try to field all three outfield positions at once: you respected the desire and the diligence, but it was easy to get the feeling that very little teamwork was going on. The combination of his relentless hustle, increased court time, and occasional stat-padding led to remarkable statistical improvement.

Removed from a losing situation, winning trumped bullshit in Brooklyn. At the Nets' first Barclays Center practice, Humphries was asked what he wanted to achieve during the season.

"Winning games," he said. "Keeping you guys excited. Give you something positive to write about. These are good conversations. That's what I hope to achieve."

It was hard to figure out what Humphries wanted. Sometimes he came off as the midwestern meathead with a bushel of clichés for any occasion, the hunky bro chosen by the girl with the epic rump for her fame project. On other occasions he came off as incredibly media-savvy, somebody who knew exactly what he was doing. Humphries was rare in the NBA, the player who accepted his limitations and found brand recognition through other means.

He developed a decent midrange jumper and was the Nets' best pick-and-roll defender in 2012 according to Avery Johnson, which was a plaudit but also a backhanded compliment, as the team was historically bad on defense for much of the season. Through it all, it was strange to see Humphries always pushing his body to its limits on the court while spending some of his spare time participating in *Keeping Up with the Kardashians*, a show aimed at the doughnut demographic. The Nets marketed Humphries as the "Incredible Hump" on the JumboTron in Newark, an idea that seemed to both honor Kardashian's legendary posterior and Newark's status as the hump between East Rutherford and Brooklyn.

As he prepared for free agency in 2012, Humphries was asked by the *Newark Star-Ledger* about having his own reality show for his free-agency decision à la LeBron James's the Decision.

"TV special? Only if you're producing it, brother," he said.

And yet, no matter how much *US Weekly* loved him, Humphries's reality as a basketball player heading into free agency was that he was the Nets' last significant priority. Moreover, by the summer, Kardashian was involved with someone else who was threatening Humphries's future with the Nets. And that pretty much sums it up for Humphries. In less than three years, he went from averaging fewer than 4 rebounds a game to absorbing brand-strengthening shots from his estranged wife's rebound: Kanye West.

On a song called "Way Too Cold," West rapped, "I'll admit, I fell in love with Kim / Around the same time, she fell in love with him."

Humphries responded in turn with a ribald skit on the website Funny or Die called "Kris Humphries Is a Douche Bag" in which he mocked both himself and West. You could see him making a point as he dressed up like West and one of his fake representatives took away a pair of shutter sunglasses while deadpanning, "We don't want you to look like an asshole; *we just want you to look like a douche bag.*"

The funniest stuff was Humphries playing the straight man as the representatives tried to take advantage of his villain status, pitching him on ideas like a video game that consisted solely of Humphries getting kicked in the groin, and toilet paper with his face on it. Inasmuch as the skit showcased Humphries's ability to laugh at himself (when he cared to), it did a better job lampooning America's remarkable vitriol toward an incredible athlete but unremarkable NBA player.

The end results for Humphries were typically bittersweet: a two-year, $24 million contract—big dollars, but not long-term security. The Nets gave Humphries the same money with one less year, just to have more flexibility, flexibility that would end up paying off.

CHAPTER 4

Rappers, Russians, Hurricanes

On a late February night in 1995, Lamont Coleman and Shawn Carter headed to WKCR, a small radio station on the campus of Columbia University. From 1990 to 1998, WKCR was home to a weekly late-night hip-hop program that broke the first public appearances of numerous iconic rappers and groups, including the Notorious B.I.G. (a.k.a. Biggie Smalls), the Wu-Tang Clan, and Big Pun. On *The Stretch Armstrong and Bobbito Show*, two DJs with eclectic taste let aspiring lyricists with impressive flows go back and forth on the airwaves of an Ivy League campus.

Coleman, twenty, went by the stage name Big L. Even though the show was more about street cred than album promotion, Big L was repping his first single, "Put It On," from his upcoming debut album *Lifestyles ov da Poor and Dangerous*. Carter, twenty-six, was known as Jay-Z. Already involved in the rap game since the eighties, he talked of his single "In My Lifetime" getting airplay on BET.

Unimpressed record label executives had seen what they thought he had to offer. Bobbito Garcia—whose résumé includes a degree from Wesleyan University, impressive credits as a DJ, a book about basketball sneakers, voice-overs on basketball video games and at Rucker Park, and a onetime halftime host for the Knicks TV broadcast—was amazed at Carter's cockiness despite his lack of mainstream recognition.

"I used to look at him in my mind and be like, 'Why is he that confident?' It's like he knew—*he knew, he knew*—he was going to blow up. There's no denying that. There were a lot [of] artists that came to our show that were just as talented and didn't do the same. Jay-Z had a vision and he really stuck with it."

Big L made four visits to WKCR and Jay-Z made three. Since then, their '95 freestyle sessions have racked up millions of listens on YouTube and Spotify. The performances have endured as a brilliant hip-hop time capsule.

Coleman was murdered in 1999. Carter became the most famous rapper in the world. At their most famous session, each rapper took two turns on the microphone, spitting rhymes over an instrumental of "Keep It Real" by Milkbone. Big L's horror-core style glorified crime-ridden mid-'90s New York City. His highly quotable rhymes ("takes more notes than Connie Chung" is paired with "plans to get Giuliani hung") belie consistently violent imagery. He noted, "I stomp white cops 'til they life stops."

But Jay-Z pressed forward. He preached sex, wealth, and success over violence—"on the prize, my greedy eyes can't see no less."

In retrospect Jay-Z's lyrics anticipate Brooklyn's eventual gentrification: "Even if they don't let me in heaven / I raise hell, until it's heaven."

The night after the freestyle, a rookie for the Dallas Mavericks named Jason Kidd played against the Nets in the Meadowlands for the first time. Kidd, another man with impressive foresight, was the first person to suggest that Jay-Z become involved with the Nets' new ownership.

"He came to the [40/40 Club] like, 'the Nets are gonna sell; you should get into them,'" Jay-Z told a capacity crowd at Brooklyn's biggest, brightest, and newest stage in September 2012.

Blue lasers bounced through the Brooklyn sky on the evening that Jay-Z officially opened Barclays Center with a concert. The arena—a spaceship, a bronze turtle, a burned toaster, whatever you wanted to call it—felt like the center of the universe.

The interior savored of fresh lacquer: a new-car smell scaled to the more than seventeen thousand seats that ringed the shiny concourse. Workers were happy and nervous. Sponsors were everywhere. The Geico Atrium promoted the idea that one could save up to 15 percent on car insurance, yet Barclays Center's appeal was supposed to be predicated on the idea that it was a mass transit hub, where eleven subway lines, eleven bus lines, and the Long Island Rail Road met.*

The wait for Jay-Z to take the stage echoed the drawn-out anticipation of the Nets' arrival. In-house DJ Mister Cee played a snippet of the Biggie Smalls classic "I've Got a Story to Tell," the song about Biggie robbing a member of the New York Knicks after sleeping with said player's girlfriend.

Biggie and Jay-Z didn't seem to be fans of the Knicks in the mid-'90s. In fact, Biggie repped the Knicks' archnemesis Reggie Miller in posthumous rhyme, and Jay-Z's first solo video ("I Can't Get wit That") featured the rapper in a Reggie Miller no. 31 Pacers jersey. Yet the hip-hop/basketball blend brought people together more often than not; in that context, "it's all love" is a defining phrase for a reason.

There were plenty of Knicks in attendance at Barclays Center's grand opening, like Tyson Chandler, the team's best defensive player. In the concert program, former Nets coach John Calipari, the well-connected car salesman of college coaches who consistently outrecruits the competition, was featured, thanks to the fact that his Kentucky Wildcats would be playing at the arena in November.

Calipari's third season coaching the Nets got off to such a rocky start that he was fired in Toronto while Tony Robbins, the famous self-help guru, was giving Nets players a motivational speech. Calipari was not allowed back on the Nets' team plane. The lesson was, as ever, business and money have a short memory when it comes to business and money.

* Just so we're clear on what a difference a decade makes: In ten years, Dikembe Mutombo transitioned from a player making an impact in the NBA Finals during the Nets' last run at a title to the guy in a Geico commercial swatting away rolls of paper towels at a grocery store.

• • •

The concert opened with a montage celebrating Brooklyn and its history. The 1996 release of Jay-Z's debut LP *Reasonable Doubt* appeared alongside the building of the Brooklyn Bridge and other landmark events. It was Jay-Z's only self-reference in the montage. Soon thereafter, he appeared elevated above the stage, debuting the new sleek black road uniform of the Brooklyn Nets set to the glow of a few thousand smartphones, which may have said everything about how a man's life can change over time.

For his twelfth song, Jay-Z launched into "Murda, Murda," with the caveat "Don't get scared; it's only Brooklyn." Then he asked a question—repeatedly, "Can I go there tonight?" Again he was referencing *Reasonable Doubt*, almost universally agreed upon as a classic album, fifteen tracks released sixteen months after the '95 freestyle with Big L. It was a return to his roots. I watched from a luxury box my friend and I crashed.

(There's something to be said about crashing a luxury box paid for by a sneaker company to see old friends, in part because $50 tickets don't even offer a stage view of history. What had the technology generation come to? "These lights are so bright you can't even tweet in them," Myles Brown, of *SLAM* and ESPN, said outside Barclays Center.)

Following "Murda, Murda," Jay-Z launched into a passionate rendition of "Dead Presidents," and the crowd watched intently. Then, as he shifted into "Can I Live?," another *Reasonable Doubt* classic, patrons scattered around the lower bowl, and a large group of white people hurried to the bathroom.

It looked like commerce ignoring the art that laid the foundation for the pop product that made Jay-Z famous enough to open Barclays Center with eight concerts in nine nights. And so Jay-Z's statements ("Everybody's from Brooklyn"; "We need to understand our history") were played against each other. The messages were mixed out of necessity; immediately play to the bourgeois audience that helped you arrive at this moment, but try to teach them something, too.

Big Daddy Kane, the evening's only guest, arrived for an encore after "What More Can I Say?" Kane was the industry titan who gave a teenage Jay-Z the opportunity to freestyle in front of larger crowds and fuel his own fire. And if you didn't know that, Kane's presence would at least force you to Google the answer to the question. But maybe some in the audience couldn't be blamed for not wanting to join Jay on a trip to his grimy roots, back to a time when everything was on the line for him, because a large percentage of 2012 Brooklyn simply couldn't give a shit.

That Jay-Z was able to open an NBA team's new arena with a concert series said a lot about the current state of hip-hop's marriage to basketball. It started out as a sensible counterculture partnership. Michael Jordan loved R&B, but a generation of players led by Allen Iverson, Shaquille O'Neal, and Kobe Bryant loved hip-hop and recorded rap music. Shaq even had a bit of success as a rapper. When Jay-Z wasn't sounding prophetic on the '95 freestyle with Big L, he was imitating a rapid-fire style that Shaq successfully experimented with two years earlier while making a guest appearance on the song "What's up, Doc?" by Fu-Schnickens, a group from East Flatbush.

Even Jason Kidd had a rap song called "What the Kidd Did," featuring Money B, in which Kidd shouted out his hometown of Oakland, California, mentioned that he was "good on the dribble like an infant," and talked about having "more assists than a high school tutor."

Radio rap became more about flash and money in the nineties. Music videos were flooded with images of cash and floss. Thrust into a world that was losing luminaries such as Tupac and the Notorious B.I.G., Jay-Z took on the characteristics of a chameleon. *Reasonable Doubt* peaked at no. 23 on the *Billboard* 200.

His second album, *In My Lifetime*, Vol. 1—debuted on November 4, 1997, and featured Babyface and tracks produced by Diddy (then Puff Daddy), peaking at no. 3. From there, he adopted the chorus from a musical—"It's a Hard Knock Life" from *Annie*—

to top the charts with *In My Lifetime*, Vol. 2. Change and success came hand in hand. Jay-Z went from wearing NBA jerseys in videos to rapping about his button-ups.

"I think there was a period when Jay-Z and a lot of the other guys were wearing the jerseys, so a lot of NBA players tried to follow suit," said Billy King.

King was general manager of the 76ers when Allen Iverson was there. Iverson*—a tiny NBA player with a large personality and larger presence—embodied the swagger of hip-hop with his crossover dribble. Iverson's famous rookie season crossover against Michael Jordan signified a cultural passing of the torch.

NBA players during the Iverson era followed his singular lead—if not in reality then in perceived style. Baggy gear, tattoos, cornrows, and loud jewelry heightened the cultural divide between a rebellious generation and the journalists who covered it. NBA locker rooms were bastions of unspoken classism, on both sides; reporters thought players lacked class, players thought reporters were out of touch. There were reporters and players who naturally bridged the divide, but it was so abundantly clear how these two disparate worlds would never otherwise intersect.

I remember a scene in Cleveland in the middle of LeBron James's rookie season. Iverson was twenty-nine; James, nineteen. They hugged, a prolonged public embrace in an arena hallway that had the feel of a style leader meeting his successor. Iverson was the present. James, a Jay-Z acolyte, was the future. A little over a year later James crossed over, on the cover of the hip-hop magazine *XXL*. The theme of the cover shoot was that Jay-Z was the president; Kanye West, Foxy Brown, and LeBron, members

---

* The first time I watched Iverson play live was in the spring of 1998 against the Nets at the Meadowlands. Despite Iverson's efficient success in that game, the most unique memory from that night was that Bill Cosby sat near the floor, bantering with fans, watching the action. Cosby, who attended Temple University with then Nets owner Lewis Katz, would later buy shares in the Nets, back when the Nets seemed intent on committing to Newark. Katz was part of the group that eventually sold the team to Bruce Ratner in 2004. Cosby left no Jay-Z-like stamp on the franchise.

of his cabinet. The cover was incredibly prescient. Eight years later, James is a two-time champion on top of the NBA world while Jay-Z and Kanye dominate the hip-hop charts.

In the fall of 2005, the NBA instituted a dress code. Players want to look dapper. They hire stylists. They partner with fashion designers who got their start in hip-hop; the ex-wife of Jay-Z's ex-business partner, Damon Dash, did a clothing line with Amar'e Stoudemire.

Maybe the legacy of the Iverson era is that nobody blinks at the sight of tattoos or cornrows or jerseys anymore. Tattoos are normal. Players put suits over their considerably tattooed frames—body design inspired by a different era—and all people want to talk about are the suits.

The difference between Iverson and James is the difference between following your nose and utilizing a GPS. With no concrete plan, no scheme to pair with ruthless individualism, Iverson has faded from glory. The culture that propped him up as a rebel icon cries for his misfortune without much inward reflection about the perils of deification. Meanwhile, with Jay-Z as his GPS and a simple message—never stop evolving and blend the respect you demand from your craft with respect in the boardroom—LeBron seems poised to remain relevant for as long as he wants.

SANDY'S CURVEBALL

I never imagined walking six miles from Grand Central station to Barclays Center to cover a Nets practice, but when Hurricane Sandy hit, that's what happened. The subways were out of commission and the lines for buses were too long. In fact, as a New Yorker who relies almost exclusively on the subway system, it was startling to see buses everywhere. For those constantly in motion underground, buses are kind of like good songs on the radio; you're only vaguely aware that they're there, somewhere, if you remain attentive.

Shuffling south past Fortieth Street into the powerless section of

Manhattan was remarkable. The morning buzz of the big city—even after a natural disaster—and the endless line of storefronts lacking electricity brought to mind a modern facsimile of what New Amsterdam might have been like, save the cops dressed in neon attire directing traffic and a line of army tanks stationed in Murray Hill.

Down in SoHo, there was a large billboard of Carmelo Anthony looking north up Lafayette Street. The way Anthony was holding a ball, it looked like he might throw a massive bounce pass up to Madison Square Garden. The ad (for the NBA on TNT if memory serves) was just another reminder that the Nets would be the last team to start their regular season. Droves of people crossed the Brooklyn Bridge in unrelenting sunlight, some on bike, some on foot, all wearing the brave face of communal struggle.

Mayor Bloomberg had canceled the Nets' opening game against the Knicks, both the long-anticipated Brooklyn launch and an unprecedented New York City professional basketball extravaganza. The Knicks were able to start that night as the Nets waited, hosting the Miami Heat in a rematch of their 2012 first-round playoff series.

For better or worse, led by a New Orleans native with plenty of hurricane recovery experience, the Nets were Superstorm Sandy's team.

"I know for sure we're going to have some people in the building that are without power at home," Avery Johnson said. "So hopefully they can come here and get a hot dog or something and enjoy the game, and maybe just take their minds off of things for two hours."

In both New York City and New Jersey, Nets players had to deal with hurricane issues. Tyshawn Taylor had to be evacuated from his Hoboken apartment. Andray Blatche showed the NBA TV reality show, *The Association*, a program focusing on chronicling one team's season each year, how water levels had risen at his home.

At practice, Kris Humphries explained the rising water levels in Battery Park City. The disaster put Avery Johnson on a preacher's pedestal. In the sports world, the Nets were the eye of the storm.

"You've got to give folks a shoulder to cry on," Johnson said. "And then there's another level where you've still got to coach. I'm familiar with power outages and devastation. I've seen it before. Does it get any easier to watch? No."

For Johnson, to come from New Orleans and to beat the odds were to, quite literally, beat storms. Johnson's storms included: riding on the back of a hearse after being late to practice at a junior college in Hobbes, New Mexico; dealing with perceived racism at a junior college in Oklahoma, which led to a temporary social drinking problem; and biased (according to Avery) math teachers.

Displacement—the result of Hurricane Sandy—was a resonant theme for Nets fans, who had watched the team move seven times in forty-nine years. Being a Nets fan was largely predicated on sticking out life's good and bad and remaining in the area. Moving into a major hub in Brooklyn centered on the promise—publicly overlooked by an organization selling the Brooklyn brand—of merging people who understood the tristate area with those who fundamentally understand Brooklyn; a team for Brooklynites to call their own and a winner in a new home for those who had long suffered on the outside. In a way, the fan base sought to mirror the growth of Brooklyn itself—blending different people with different types of experiences and voices until the crowd would feel a new kind of real. The unifying factor of the franchise was that, from Long Island, to parts of Jersey, to pockets of New York City and the outskirts—the Nets were an organization with fundamental ties to the tristate area, at once beyond the limitations of simple geography while mostly restricted to a certain area. The branding sought to globalize a largely tristate product while increasing an urban tristate presence. It was quite the endeavor.

Of all the conversations that popped up at practices and games between those covering and those playing in the games, the idea of traffic—how to get to Brooklyn from different points on the map—was the most frequent idle chatter. Some players lived in TriBeCa, others touted certain routes, over certain bridges, to get to the arena. Canal Street seemed to be popular. Avery Johnson, who had his "Avery's Stats," recounted exactly how long it took him to get there from his hotel in Jersey City.

The larger issue wasn't that the team's players and coaches were spread out around the area—that mirrored the history of the organization, and the team still practiced in the Jersey suburbs—but that, set to the backdrop of a transit hub that offered any number of simple, comparatively stress-free alternatives, those around the organization spent their spare time as if needlessly counting their own carbon emissions.

Riding the rails is about accepting the world around you, not trapping yourself in your own tube, something Billy King inherently understood. King lived in the Philadelphia area during the first season and traveled by Amtrak. And nothing expresses elite regionalism and time to think quite like the quiet car of an Acela train passing through a coastal corridor.

New York governor Andrew Cuomo announced that subway service would be restored to Brooklyn on the morning of the Nets' opener, but the team still leased eleven buses to depart every fifteen minutes starting at 4:30 p.m. from the Port Authority Bus Terminal. Millions had been invested to reroute the city's subways through the Barclays Center, yet Nets fans would again rely on bus transport, as they had at the Meadowlands.

It felt like the opposite of a victory lap.

The issue of hurricane recovery lingered into the beginning of Prokhorov's season-opening press conference. He gave a terse speech about the situation, which felt like the right political move from a man who had recently run for president of Russia and who would turn his sights to Moscow's 2013 mayoral election before deciding against running. Prokhorov repeatedly returned to the Hurricane Sandy recovery theme, saying it was important to "express solidarity with the city," while noting that it was in the best interest of public safety to cancel the opener.

"You know, like, it's life," he said.

Prokhorov proved deft at incorporating "like" naturally in his sentences, as if he were a well-heeled eighties baby from the valley instead of one of America's richest foreign nationals.

He was asked if a fast start was important.

"Of course it's important," he said. "But what's more important is a good basketball strategy."

He said the final three words in a Russian-influenced staccato, each word rolling off his tongue—"good . . . basketball . . . strategy"—like a soothing commandment. Because Prokhorov often seemed like he was thinking through whatever he was saying, even the trite stuff had an interesting sound. Jay-Z has flow, and so too does Mikhail Prokhorov, probably to be expected from any man who doesn't use a cell phone or a computer, can do backflips on Jet Skis, and doesn't always remember where his yacht is.

ARENA IRINA

The Nets had one last bit of business before basketball: the unveiling of a mascot. As something descended from the rafters, public address announcer David Diamente ended a cheesy speech from a comic book with a breathless proclamation:

"Born from the beating heart of your Brooklyn, forged from the same steel and stone as your battleground, he's your hunger for a team to call your own, he's your passion given form; here to defend Brooklyn . . ."

Now, if those words were a hint, one might reasonably guess that the mascot had something to do with the Brooklyn Dodgers, a Barclays Center protester, or a food co-op. But the BrooklyKnight looked like the offspring of Wolverine and Boba Fett. I wasn't as appalled as many—the sleek design of his suit of armor was a nice touch.

Fans received a comic book, illustrated by the artist behind The Amazing Spider Man, written by a cartoonist with credits that included Wolverine and Thor.

"When Nets fans meet their guardian, they will immediately know that the House of Ideas has once again unleashed a hero who will soon be known all over the world for his nobility, grit, and strength," said Bill Rosemann, editor of Marvel Custom Solutions (as quoted by Comicbook.com).

Yet, the decision by the Nets and Marvel to make this guy the mascot came with all of the care of the father who buys fireworks and wonders what could possibly go wrong. *New York Times* staff writer Howard Beck joked that after walking past the BrooklyKnight, he was afraid to go to sleep. *New York* magazine took it a step further, calling the mascot "a walking nightmare."

The president of Onexim Sports and Entertainment, Irina Pavlova, saw the other side. Pavlova runs the Nets' business operations and serves as a conduit between Prokhorov and the business side of the team.

"He's smiling," she said of the mascot. "I'm telling you, he's misunderstood. People will grow to love him. He's awesome. He's strong. He's not furry. He's not soft. He's powerful. . . . You're telling me forty-year-old men are afraid of him because he's scowling at them? Kids love him! . . . They take pictures with him and high-five him!"

Her passion was remarkable. She defended the BrooklyKnight like Reggie Evans rebounded.

"Like every week, there's another superhero movie. You look at *The Transformers*—I haven't seen a single one of them—you know, how is that any less scary than the BrooklyKnight?"

"Well, it's a worse product," I said.

"What is?"

"*Transformers.*"

"Okay. . . . It's making a lot of money as a franchise. . . . So someone's buying. Someone's not afraid."

Earlier, we had been talking about business. I noted that Pavlova and I were back to square one.

"The players have the line," I said. "'This is a business.'"

"You're focusing too much on that," she said. "I'm focusing on that because it's my job . . . I talk about it too much because it's my job. You talk about it too much just because I'm talking about it."

I said I felt like I was in a Russian novel. She laughed.

When Irina Pavlova was undergoing the extensive process—more than fifteen interviews—to become Google's first employee in Russia, she would ask employees why she was meeting with them. To make sure she was Google-y, they would tell her.

"It's a very important criterion at Google to make sure people are Google-y," she said.

So what is Google-y?

"I couldn't tell you," she said. "I still don't know."

I called an interview time-out of sorts to let that sink in. Maybe Google-y is a twenty-first-century equivalent of an athletic intangible, like when a pundit says that a player has heart. Maybe Google technically couldn't prove that Pavlova was Google-y, just as you can't technically prove that one player had more heart than another—it's just something said and agreed upon based on observation.

Pavlova—multilingual, candid, and bubbly in all of her undefinable Google-yness—was born in New York while her father worked at the United Nations. She graduated from Moscow Linguistics University in 1992. She studied Marxist/Leninist philosophy and the history of the Communist Party, but majored in Spanish.

"Everything is about the collective when I was growing up in the Soviet Union," she said. "You weren't supposed to show your individuality. You will speak when spoken to. You will not go, 'me, me, me.'"

We shared a similar college major. I asked her in Spanish if we could do half of our interview in Spanish.

"In Russian," she said . . . in Spanish.

Pavlova went to Stanford for business school, and her grades were lowered for minimal class participation.

"In the U.S. you get graded on, basically, a lot of times, just hearing yourself talk," she said, the sentiment ringing true to anyone who has ever had the pleasure of attending an NBA press conference.

From her work at a search engine in an emerging market to her role on an NBA team in a changing borough, Pavlova is fond of saying that things land in her lap. Yet her success seems to bridge a Russian upbringing that focuses on the collective with an understanding of Americanized individuality. She relies on natural networking: maintaining relationships; coffee meetings, lunches, and late-night e-mails back to Russia to offset an eight-hour time difference. Work is social. She's courtside at Barclays and only bothers Prokhorov when she absolutely has to.

"I feel like I'm very independent and that's what he expects," she said. "I think if I had to call him every day for something he would not be happy."

Her world revolves around expanding the team's business, selling tickets, working with Nets marketing maven CEO Brett Yormark and, initially, Jay-Z. What tattoos were to NBA players in the early 2000s, Yormark is to corporate branding. Yormark had the Nets' locker room in Newark sponsored by Nivea for Men, as if a team's matador defense deserved to be sponsored by a moisturizer.

Jay-Z and Pavlova went back and forth about the logo. Pavlova was arguing for a BK, Jay-Z wanted a B. The B reminded Pavlova of Boston. Jay-Z argued for making the B their own.

"We sat around the table and we went back and forth," she said. "And it's not like, oh, Jay-Z said, 'This had to be a B' and everyone's like, 'Oh, okay.' But it was good discussion. It was a debate and he made some good points, and, again, looking back it was very valuable."

It was a big deal when the Nets, stuck on a hundred thousand Facebook likes in Jersey, rebranded themselves and suddenly pushed full steam ahead to Brooklyn and crossed a million. It seems like silly conversational fodder until you see people at parties rocking Nets gear exclusively as a fashion statement.

BROOKLYN BOUNCE

The mind wanders: what about those girls who thought the guys at the parties looked fly in their Nets gear and vice versa? Fashion both directly and subliminally brings people together; with a solid but unspectacular team on the court in the first year, the gear was all around, the Nets painting the people who claimed their new surroundings. In the abstract sense, the brand push was bizarre: the franchise that almost always was the antithesis of popularity—even relishing such status and playing NBA possum—had landed in the underdeveloped front yard of a Brooklyn that *New York* magazine described as "the zeitgeist's improbable golden door."

Pavlova's base, the headquarters of Onexim Sports and Entertainment, which owns 80 percent of the Nets and 45 percent of Barclays Center, is on the twenty-sixth floor of a Park Avenue skyscraper. The doorman barely recognized the company's name when I went to sign in. The space contains Pavlova's office; a desk and chair for her assistant Elaine; four chairs in a small waiting area with a plasma TV; a stylish conference room; and a nice bathroom. Oh, and there's a fancy coffee machine, assembled in Italy. Pavlova likes to joke that the machine cost more than her first car. Compared to Barclays Center, it's as close to invisible as a space can get. Pavlova, a hard hat on her head, had seen the arena from a hole in the ground and appreciated how little time, in retrospect, the construction took.

"And the team," she said. "It's night and day."

BROOOOOK-LYN

There was, finally, mercifully, basketball. The Raptors won the opening tip but Williams scored the first regular-season points in the arena on a long jumper from the wing. After the game Williams received the game ball from Avery Johnson for being the man whose decision brought all of them together. The Raptors scored seven straight points after Williams's bucket. Toronto's starting backcourt, Kyle Lowry and DeMar DeRozan, combined for 19 first-quarter points, including four 3-pointers. Lowry, built like a wide brick wall with the speed of someone slender and light, and DeRozan, whose vertical leap has been the subject of boastful rap lyrics, quieted a crowd that was ready to get riled up.

C. J. Watson led the Nets back in the second quarter, scoring 10 points, including a buzzer-beating 3 to give the Nets an 8-point lead at halftime. Watson's emergence heightened the evening's storm theme, although with a positive twist; Watson's nickname is the Quiet Storm. Unassuming and soft-spoken, he was signed as a free agent from the Bulls after being thrust into the spotlight when Derrick Rose went down with an ACL tear in the Bulls' first 2012 playoff game against the 76ers.

The Nets kept the Raptors at arm's length until the fourth quarter, when the threat of a full comeback loomed almost the entire way. Lowry drained a 3 to bring the Raptors to within 2 with seventy-seven seconds remaining. But Wallace drove the middle and found Lopez, who paced the Nets with a game-high 27 points, for a layup to put the home team up 99–95. Lopez was fouled, giving the fans plenty of time to erupt into the first fully formed version of the Brooklyn chant as he went to the free-throw line to finish off the 3-point play. The good vibes were subdued in the game's final minute when Wallace sustained a sprained ankle while landing awkwardly after attempting to block a shot.

Still, there was something unbelievable, hypnotic, and somewhat brand-affirming about watching Beyoncé mouthing along to "BROOOOOK-LYN! BROOOOOK-LYN!" with nearly eighteen thousand people. So much of the Nets' marketing push was about developing a brand voice. In the team's first big-time moment it sounded like they had one.

CHAPTER 5

Brooklyn, Home and Away

The biggest rivalry inside Brooklyn basketball pits the Boys & Girls High School Kangaroos of the Bedford-Stuyvesant neighborhood and the Abraham Lincoln Railsplitters of Coney Island. Boys & Girls has produced legends such as the ABA great Connie Hawkins, and game-changing point guards Lenny Wilkens and Pearl Washington. Lincoln High is also a professional basketball breeding ground, boasting alumni such as Stephon Marbury and his cousin Sebastian Telfair, as well as Lance Stephenson, who blossomed in the playoffs for the Indiana Pacers against the Knicks.

A night after the Nets beat the Bulls at home, I decided to check out the rivalry for myself. Wearing Under Armour pink shoes, the Railsplitters entered the gymnasium and ran around the perimeter of the court, a territorial gesture compared with the tame meet-and-greet culture generally exhibited by NBA players. Boys & Girls was coached by Ruth Lovelace, a solidly built woman in a resplendent red sweatsuit and fresh kicks. Lovelace and Lincoln coach Dwayne "Tiny" Morton looked like Brooklyn royalty. To know a Brooklyn that gentrification ignored was to know the high school basketball scene.

Things boiled over on the far sideline with 2:22 remaining in the first quarter. It happened quickly. Fans talking smack, players spilling into the stands, worlds entangled. Fans rushed the court, followed by warnings from Boys & Girls announcer Kwame Asante. The New York Police stood on the floor, and suddenly it was apparent why you needed to pass through a metal detector to watch these two teams play.

Behind the Boys & Girls bench, Lincoln big man Thomas Holley, a transfer from Christ the King and also the top-ranked offensive tackle in the state of New York, was slapped by an older man. For whatever reason, the fight and the ejections didn't seem that crazy to me, but Holley barking back at the man slapping him behind the home team's bench took the scene to a more intense level. Courtney Solomon of Boys & Girls was ejected as well, and suddenly his ouster became a family matter.

When Lincoln scored to go up 45–31, Lovelace told a referee that she wanted the game played under protest. Boys & Girls senior Wesley Meyers got ejected for clotheslining a Lincoln player going up for a dunk. Lovelace was also ejected, and the game was called with 1:15 remaining. This was the frenetic, basketball-crazy milieu in which the Nets had settled.

As I watched the game unravel, I wondered if Isaiah Whitehead, a talented Lincoln junior, would follow in the footsteps of Marbury, Telfair, and Lance Stephenson. Whitehead scored 27 points against Boys & Girls two days after getting benched for the final three quarters of a game against Transit Tech. He silenced a Boys & Girls run with two 3-pointers. He converted a huge dunk and wore a snarl on defense. His shooting form looked good and his game was effective, if not overly flashy. Whitehead's success was—and is— important in the context of the New York City basketball scene, as Brooklyn—and New York City at large—had recently struggled to produce high-level Division I players. Whitehead* was ranked no. 17 of the top 150 players in the high school class of 2014 according to Rivals.com. The next closest Brooklynite was Khadeen

---

* Whitehead signed with the Seton Hall Pirates and would look to rebuild the program once brought to the brink of a national championship by P. J. Carlesimo.

Carrington of Bishop Loughlin, at no. 108. The website Gotham Hoops called Whitehead "the last of the Mohicans," evoking the uncertainty of Brooklyn's future as a basketball powerhouse.

This puts the Nets in an interesting position. Would the new pro team inspire kids in Brooklyn and throughout the city to step up their game? And could they inspire others to dream of a world outside of New York? Does opening up a team shop in Coney Island invigorate youthful dreams or merely shape fashion?

EARLY ADJUSTMENTS

The vibe was different inside Barclays Center, placid by comparison. Despite the fun energy in the building in the first game against the Raptors, it felt like a beautiful new museum had opened up. The aim was pleasing patrons, and the organization seemed to be doing a solid job of that when the team wasn't building far too many alliances with name brands. Nets announcers on the YES Network would begin broadcasts by urging fans to log on to a social networking site called Sports Yapper and "go yap about it," pushing focus away from the product on the court and toward conversations contained within new-age technology.

The Nets choked away the second game of the season to the Minnesota Timberwolves, who outscored them 32–10 in the fourth quarter. At the postgame press conference, no one seemed overly concerned with the fourth-quarter immolation. Avery Johnson talked about "correctable errors." Williams noted that every team has a few games like that in a season.

The Nets flew to Miami on Election Day for a date with the defending champions. The game wasn't close after the first quarter.

"Nobody said we were on Miami's level," Avery Johnson said. "Never said it. We aspire to get there."

The Nets touched down in Orlando and quickly received more rough news. MarShon Brooks had stepped on Andray Blatche's ankle during a pick-and-roll drill at shootaround, spraining his own ankle. That left three Nets—Brooks, Wallace, and Josh Childress—sidelined with left-ankle problems.

For a night at least, it wouldn't matter. The blowout victory was the first of many led by Brook Lopez's assertive offense. On one play, Lopez combined a hook shot and a shotput throw and the ball went in, exemplifying that at his best Lopez's shot had the touch of silk.

The ankle injury to Brooks would alter the Nets' on-court makeup. Jerry Stackhouse, a preseason afterthought, was inserted into the lineup. He buried a 3-pointer from the corner on his second try. And then he did it again. The shot would become his signature; for a long stretch, a Jerry Stackhouse corner 3-pointer was the closest thing to legal tender the Nets' offense had. Reporters would laugh heartily when other teams left Stackhouse open in the corner. He hit 18 of 41 corner 3s (43.9 percent) during Avery Johnson's tenure.

Eleven years after leading the NBA in scoring, Stackhouse scored 11 points in only ten minutes of action. The Nets returned home to face the Magic again.

The Nets scored just 47 points in the final three quarters, but won anyway, 82–74. Despite giving a game away to Minnesota, 20-point leads are hard to consistently cough up at home. Afterward, the mood was cynical and reporters repeatedly questioned Avery Johnson about Joe Johnson's slow start to the season.

HEY JOE

Johnson was the type of player who made the difficult look simple, and his personality only enhanced a reputation rooted in style.

Rosie Perez was giving Johnson a tour of Brooklyn. "I wanted to bring Joe around the neighborhood," the actress from *White Men Can't Jump* and *Do the Right Thing* told NBA TV. "So the neighborhood could say, 'You're here. You're ours. Let's do this.'"

Rosie was always Rosie, spunky with an in-your-face attitude that was unmistakably Brooklyn. Johnson came off as the opposite; when he smiled, it was like he was succumbing to the expression.

"I said, 'My goodness, you talk slow as hell,'" Perez said. "He says, 'Yeah, you . . . just . . . say . . . whatever . . . comes . . . to . . . your . . . mind.' I go, 'Welcome to Brooklyn, get used it!'"

And then she let out that nails-screeching-on-a-chalkboard laugh.

Johnson's tour included a trip to Gleason's Gym on Front Street in Dumbo, which was once home to Muhammad Ali and Mike Tyson. Dumbo was just one more example of gentrification in Brooklyn. From the harsh reality of the streets that hip-hop documented and glorified to the land of yuppie stroller NASCAR and organic kale, much of Brooklyn was a new world. Myrtle Avenue, formerly known as "Murder Avenue," was now home to a bike shop that sold homemade vegan nut milk. The apartment Biggie Smalls once lived in while selling crack was listed at $725,000 in April. Leaving Barclays Center, a Pintrest employee could pass by 560 State Street, the apartment Jay-Z references in *Empire State of Mind* as his stash house, look up from his organic Greek frozen yogurt, and rate the neighborhood's quaintness on his smartphone.

In 1998, socially conscious rapper Talib Kweli rapped about his borough, "Killers born naturally like Mickey and Mallory / not knowing the ways will get you capped like an NBA salary." Now, after a murder rate that dropped 73 percent between 1993 and 2012, millennial Brooklynites, knowing the ways of farmer's markets and microbrews, could talk about how the Nets were well over the salary cap.

One half of the highly touted "Brooklyn's Backcourt," Johnson was the Net who most embodied that sentiment, shifting with the scenery like a well-compensated chameleon. His acquisition helped convince Williams to stay and allowed the Nets to revamp their roster.

Jannero Pargo, an NBA journeyman who played with Johnson at Arkansas, described him as a vampire: "He would sleep all day and be up all night," Pargo said. "He's in midconversation, he'll fall asleep on you."

Joe took on the personality of a vampire—and/or a narcoleptic savant—late in games, injecting life into the Nets' Brooklyn launch.

The Nets finished off the three-game home stand with two more wins, over the Cleveland Cavaliers and the Boston Celtics. The victory over the Cavs was the most entertaining early-season game played at Barclays Center. Williams and Kyrie Irving engaged in a memorable duel, and the Cavs' Anderson Varejão, the high-energy Brazilian with the corkscrew curls, scored a career-high 35 points, 17 in the first quarter. Johnson got hot late, scoring 16 fourth-quarter points, answering his critics for a night. It was the first sign that Johnson would become the Nets' de facto closer.

The game against the Celtics was the first national TV appearance of the season. Brooklyn native Marv Albert called the action for TNT. Lopez shined in the spotlight, and both Williams and Johnson managed to offset some of their shooting woes by getting to the free-throw line.

Both wins illustrated early-season trends that would continue deep into the season. Despite a 5-2 record, the Nets hadn't accomplished much. The opening-night win over Toronto was far from convincing; they blew the game against Minnesota and got crushed by Miami; two wins over Orlando were par for the course, as Orlando finished with the worst record in the league; Cleveland was lottery-bound and on the tail end of a ridiculous coast-to-coast early-season road trip; and the Celtics were playing without Rajon Rondo.

In an early season trend that would continue, the Nets frequently struggled in third quarters. Many times they came out of the locker room with a sizable lead only to give it right back. Heading into the Cleveland game, the Nets, despite playing at a snail's pace, were fourth in the league in first-half scoring and last in the league in second-half scoring. The Nets were outscored by a combined 26 third-quarter points against the Cavaliers and Celtics in the final two games of the home stand.

This reality was reflected in subdued crowds deprived of climactic moments. It took the national TV matchup against the Celtics, whose fans always bring their own noise on the road, to get the denizens of Barclays Center fired up like they were on opening night. The Nets hit the road and found interesting on- and off-court stylistic differences in California and Florida.

LIMBO AT THE BARN

In mid-November, the Sacramento Kings were in dire straits. The Maloofs, the family who owned the Kings, were in debt and had to sell. There was speculation as to where the Kings would go. Virginia Beach was considered as a possible destination. Seattle seemed like a real possibility. A move to Anaheim had been stifled the year before. All Sacramento had was faint hope. Kevin Johnson, formerly the point guard of the Phoenix Suns and now mayor of Sacramento, was leading the charge to try to keep the team from moving, and the Kings had been in limbo for eighteen months. Listening to Kings big man Jason Thompson discuss the only NBA home he's ever known potentially being ripped away from him was one of the realer locker room moments I can recall amid a sea of NBA chaos.

Said Thompson: "It's my fifth year, man, and I've been hearing, 'We're going here, point A to point B, point C,' so until someone tells me that I've gotta move and get out of my house, then—" He stopped himself in midthought. "At the end of the day, you control what you control and we're obviously not controlling what we can't control."

The only immediate connection between the Kings and the Nets was Travis Outlaw, the swingman to whom Rod Thorn (by way of Avery Johnson) gave an outlandish five-year, $35 million contract in the summer of 2010. Outlaw was the kind of last-resort signing, befitting of the Nets' first season in Newark, when they too were in a holding pattern.

The Kings got off to a great start, but the carryover didn't last. Andray Blatche, the self-proclaimed Godfather of the Nets' Bench Mob, checked in with just over two minutes left in the quarter. Blatche was in a defined role for a winning team for the first time in his life, away from the dysfunction of the Washington Wizards, and he was about to make his mark.

Reggie Evans grabbed an offensive rebound and Williams came with attention-drawing penetration, finding Blatche, who scored inside while being fouled. Blatche missed the free throw, which in retrospect seems like some sort of Jedi mind trick given what was to come. Williams was posting up on Jimmer Fredette—a mismatch—on the ensuing possession and Blatche got open, creeping by an unsuspecting defender underneath the basket, receiving the feed, and flipping in a layup among three defenders. Then Williams drove the middle and fed Blatche with a wraparound pass. Again, Blatche showed impressive dexterity and touch, converting another layup from almost underneath the rim. Williams flew into the first row of baseline chairs and landed on his arm.

From there, Blatche and C. J. Watson took over. With a behind-the-back dribble and a baseline drive, Blatche facilitated good ball movement before converting his fourth bucket with an offensive rebound put-back. The hits kept on coming: a reverse layup off a baseline cut; a drawn charge on Thomas Robinson; cutting into the lane for a short jumper; loping down the middle, without hesitation, en route to another layup (he was a seven-footer with deceptive skills and speed); a baseline step-back jumper in front of a giggling quintet of courtside traveling reporters. Then, from the same distance on the wing, he drained another jumper. You're not supposed to root in the American press box and most of us don't, but you are most definitely allowed to feel a tickled glee for someone making his mark. Blatche scored ten buckets in a row.*

Despite Blatche's heroics, Avery Johnson maintained his compartmentalized rotation, and the starters put the game away. Still, Blatche enjoyed the win, noting in the cramped visitors' locker room that he couldn't remember the last time he had been on a five-game winning streak, if ever.

Blatche's success with the Nets can partially be traced to his training with John Lucas, the former NBA coach with whom Avery Johnson is very close. Lucas looked out for Johnson when Johnson was a rookie in Seattle, hanging on to NBA life by a thread, and Johnson trusted Lucas's judgment in rounding Blatche back into form with grueling summer workouts.

LIFE OF LUXURY, LICENSE TO ILL

Kobe Bryant's legend has grown almost exponentially with age, in part because at some point he decided he just didn't give a damn. He said whatever he wanted and was absolutely fearless and polished about it. Talking to Kobe Bryant was a beat reporter's dream. You actually wanted to listen—he was either telling you an interesting truth or obfuscating in a way that demanded your attention.

---

* The Kings were supposedly taken from Sacramento over the weekend of January 5 and sold to a group that would relocate the franchise to Seattle after the season. The Kings were in Brooklyn that night, and while members of the organization were getting a close-up look at the NBA's newest arena, the Kings were getting clobbered by the Nets. Travis Outlaw went scoreless in his Brooklyn debut. Blatche dunked off a fast-break give-and-go and just stared at Outlaw in a bit of amnestied player on amnestied player crime (which is a strange sentence to type when considering the word "amnesty"). Yet the Kings stayed in Sacramento, as a majority of the NBA's owners rejected a relocation bid and Vivek Ranadive, an Indian businessman previously affiliated with the Golden State Warriors, bought the Kings. So it appears likely that Blatche—and others— will have an annual opportunity to sink ten shots in a row in Sacramento in the years to come.

Jack Taylor, a Division III basketball player at Grinnell College, had just set a new collegiate scoring record with 138 points, and Bryant was asked if he would be celebrated if he scored 138 points.

"Would people be celebrating me if I scored 138 points?" he asked after the Lakers hosted the Nets at Staples Center. "You know how it is, some people would, some people wouldn't. They can all kiss my ass, as I'm sure he feels the same way. If you score 138 points, you kind of have a license to tell people to fuck off."

Earlier in the game, Bryant had exercised his own superstar powers. Midway through the first quarter, he picked up his second foul when Wallace got him with Lopez's patented rip-through move, during which the offensive player sneakily initiates contact with his defender by shoving his arms through his opponent's space in what appears to be the beginning of a shooting motion. In the preceding sequence, Williams had connected on back-to-back 3-pointers that ratcheted up the intensity in the Staples Center.

With his superstar in foul trouble, Lakers coach Mike D'Antoni, who had just had knee replacement surgery, called for Bryant to be subbed out. Bryant waved him off and promptly drained a pull-up jumper from the top of the circle. From there, the game took on the feel of a heavyweight bout. It was D'Antoni's first game as the Lakers' head coach. He was hired to replace Mike Brown after a disappointing 1-4 start to the season in the City of Angels. Bernie Bickerstaff had done a good job filling in, but the Lakers needed a name with brand recognition, and D'Antoni had history with both Steve Nash, the Lakers' point guard, and Bryant. In replacing Brown with D'Antoni, they had chosen a coach with a sterling offensive reputation above one known for maximizing defensive potential.

"It's going to be fun," D'Antoni said before the game. "I've got the greatest job in the world. I've got the greatest players in the world."

D'Antoni, who walked away from the Knicks in part because

he couldn't deal with Carmelo Anthony, was asked if he reached out to anybody for advice on how to handle the Lakers job.

"Nah, I'm on meds," he cracked.

Before the Lakers starters were introduced, The Who's "Baba O'Reilly" blared over the Staples Center loudspeakers, and public address announcer Lawrence Tanter—the best PA voice in the NBA—noted the franchise's sixteen championships.

"The most wins in NBA history, the home team, your Los Angeles Lakers . . ."

If you can't feel the magnetism, you're jaded, a Celtics fan—the Celtics have fewer wins but one more championship—a Clippers fan, or soulless. Laker highlights are shown on a white sheet covering the JumboTron, and then the sheet unfurls, falling elegantly to the floor. The iconic Laker Girls scurry by to pick it up.

It was Brooklyn's first major road test, and they were hit in the mouth immediately. Lopez especially looked out of sorts as the Lakers jumped out to a 10–0 lead. He passed the ball to the other team, was whistled for an offensive foul, had his shot blocked by Dwight Howard, and his pocket picked from behind by Bryant. Avery Johnson called time-out, and the Nets regrouped immediately. Gerald Wallace—three steals in thirty-three seconds—was the catalyst, and Lopez, converting consecutive dunks, the finisher, suddenly brimming with confidence.

Lopez drained three consecutive jumpers, bolstering his already gaudy first-quarter scoring stats (at the time, second in the NBA only to Carmelo Anthony). But Bryant, who loves playing with fire—be it early foul trouble or streaky shooting—hadn't missed, sinking his first five shots. Tweets popped up with the inevitable jokes about the headstrong Bryant being the real coach of the Lakers; D'Antoni hadn't even enjoyed a halftime yet. These were the kinds of things that happened in L.A.; the Lakers, between magnetic story lines and raw star power, had the propensity to turn the visiting team into Hollywood scenery.

The third quarter turned into a slugfest. Howard blocked—and possibly goal-tended—a Williams floater, swatting the shot into the stands, but the call was not made and Ludacris's voice blared over the sound system, "Move, b*tch! Get out the way!"

Other than shooting 7-for-19 from the foul line, Dwight Howard (23 points, 15 rebounds) performed well as he continued to recover from back surgery. He was asked about something he was drinking that had given him more stamina.

Answer: "Orange juice; I can't tell you the rest."

It was funny in that before the game Lopez had been debating his home state's apples with the Nets' PR staff. Apples and oranges; Lopez and Howard were in the same food group, but probably never meant to play together or get traded for each other. Howard wanted to dominate a skyline; Lopez grew up sharing the spotlight with a twin. They were sort of like Romeo and Rosencrantz.

Reggie Evans overreacted to contact made by Metta World Peace while running up the court, leading to the first fine under the NBA's new antiflopping regulations—financial punishments set in place to discourage players from faking fouls, feigning injury, and generally crying wolf to referees already dealing with massive amounts of pressure.

Sometime before or after the actor Andy Garcia walked over to the visiting media section to just sort of stand there, Kobe cooled off and both teams fired up bricks, the Nets from the field, Howard from the line. The pattern continued into the fourth quarter. Howard air-balled a free throw and unleashed that megawatt smile.

The Nets held the Lakers to a single point in the first 6:23 of the final frame. Williams sank a baseline jumper, and Kris Humphries—thanklessly battling Howard all night long—was thrown to the ground, sinking a free throw to give the Nets a 6-point lead off of an unconventional 3-point play. Their biggest lead quickly evaporated.

The Nets went to the Hack-a-Howard, preferring to have the big man shoot free throws instead of letting the Lakers run their offense. It is the ultimate spotlight move against the larger-than-life personality with a weakness, and in the Hollywood glare it is a tradition most recently practiced against Shaquille O'Neal. Howard split two pairs of free throws, sandwiching a huge World Peace 3-pointer when Avery Johnson chose not to foul Howard. After hitting the 3-pointer, World Peace rubbed Avery Johnson's head on the way back up the court. For those keeping score, World Peace had played a part in the NBA's first flopping violation and rubbed the head of a coach who had a little more than a month left on the job.

The Nets' offense began to struggle. Another free throw from Kobe Bryant tied the game. The Lakers jumped ahead. Joe Johnson (another poor shooting performance) hit a runner in transition to keep the Nets within striking distance. Bryant had a chance to close the game out at the foul line, but only split the pair after a lengthy trash-talk session with Wallace.

It was 93–90 with 4.8 seconds left. The situation the franchise player lives for. Williams curled around the Nets stack inbounds set and fired up a 3-pointer that missed long. The first big-moment road game of the season was a loss, but the Nets generally showed the resolve of a veteran team in a high-pressure situation.

"I got a pretty clean look," Williams said. "It was contested. We didn't have any time-outs. I really couldn't take another dribble, there was nowhere to go."

"I like 'em," Bryant said of the Nets. "I like their talent. I like their balance. I like how Avery has them executing, and they're playing well together. They look very good to me."

I didn't follow up by asking him about the Nets possibly waving Avery Johnson off.

WE'RE MOVING IN FIVE YEARS, HOW MAY WE HELP YOU?

Stationed next to a baseball/football stadium surrounded by a massive parking lot, accessible from Bay Area Rapid Transit via a chain-link tunnel, the Golden State Warriors already have what the Nets never did in New Jersey: a rabid and loyal fan base that religiously attends games in an unglamorous locale. As the Bay Area's only NBA team, the Warriors operate as something of a Knicks-Nets hybrid, the passion and loyalty embodied by the hard-core Knicks fans fused with a base similar to any number of locations that the Nets called home — reminiscent of the Meadowlands in its multisport surroundings, the mass transit accessibility to a location across a body of water reminiscent of the Prudential Center.

The Nets headed up to Oakland the night after their hard-fought loss to the Lakers and jumped on the Warriors early before running out of gas without Gerald Wallace and Jerry Stackhouse, who were both held out as precautionary measures.

The Warriors are slated to move from Oakland to San Francisco in 2017. By moving to Piers 30–32 in downtown San Francisco, they'll become only the second NBA team, after the Miami Heat, to have an arena right on a waterfront. Media members were given an informative packet that includes an artistic rendering of what San Francisco Bay would look like in 2017, the Warriors' proposed arena jutting out into the water, under puffy clouds and a nice sunset, closer to the looming Golden Gate Bridge than the marina and AT&T Park, home to the San Francisco Giants.

Yet the game-time vibe inside Oracle was top notch, and everything lent itself to a sort of social perfection that makes a first-time visitor wonder why, aesthetically, the team would ever want to move in the first place. Barclays Center may be the home of twenty-first-century tastemakers, but Oracle Arena has stood the test of time.

California G-Funk was in heavy rotation mixed with good but understated beats that once backed the likes of accomplished lyricists Phaorahe Monche and Dead Prez. More than once, Rod Boone of *Newsday* and I spoke about canceling the game to throw a hip-hop dance party. But canceling the game would have meant drowning out one of the loudest crowds in the league. When Stephen Curry sank a 3-pointer while getting fouled, punctuating a furious Warriors comeback, it felt like the roof would lift off—no chant needed.

Although the Nets felt like they let another game slip away with another poor third-quarter effort, the Warriors spent the season proving that they were a lot better than people initially gave them credit for. Still, Williams did his part in taking responsibility for the Nets' problems on the court, something he was usually good at.

"I gotta play better," he said in the unusually spacious, if ugly, visitors' locker room at Oracle. "I played like crap today. A lot of it's my fault, especially in the second half. I was pretty nonrelevant. I don't know if it's mental. I think we're still learning. I don't know how long we can use that excuse for."

Avery Johnson was fond of looking at the season in ten-game increments and had spoken about how, at 6-4 and heading home, there were some positives to take from the Nets' first significant stretch.

"He breaks it down like that," Williams said. "I just think we're struggling right now."

Josh Childress had his best game of his brief tenure with the Nets in Oakland, scoring 8 points and grabbing 4 rebounds. The son of a health inspector and a cytologist, Childress owns a commercial real estate business based in Southern California with his brothers, flipping houses, doing renovations, and trying to repair broken-down neighborhoods. The name of the company, Adelfos, means brothers in Greek. In 2008, Childress made waves by taking a more lucrative contract to play for Olympiakos in Athens instead of remaining in the NBA.

The specific borough and neighborhood pride germane to New York caught Childress off guard.

"I don't lead with: my name is Josh, I'm from Compton," he said in a moment of levity.

JAKE APPLEMAN

LITTLE BROTHER'S BUILDING

Back from their three-game West Coast trip, the Nets hosted the Los Angeles Clippers on a Friday night, completing four straight games against the four California teams. The Clippers, like the Nets, were a little brother franchise in a big market.

For Reggie Evans, it was a matchup against his former team. Against the Clippers and then the Trail Blazers two days later, Evans, who led the NBA in rebounding rate, corralled 26 caroms in 45 minutes, becoming an instant New York media darling in the process, his winsome personality a perfect match for the growing attention surrounding him.

In the second half against the Clippers, Evans grabbed 10 rebounds in less than 12 minutes. With the Nets struggling on the boards, the crowd chanted for him before he even checked in. After a nondescript first half, he needed to pump himself up.

"Kind of talked to myself and stuff like that and just didn't want to go out like that, especially when I got my homeboy here, my brother here," he said. "['Cause] I knew if I played soft I've gotta go home and hear they mouth and stuff like that. So I ain't have time to be hearing that from them."

Evans talked about the crowd appreciating blue-collar players and noted how the Nets wouldn't pop champagne bottles if they beat the Knicks. Just like that, he won over everyone in the locker room. Newspaper profiles popped up about his rough upbringing, selling crack-cocaine and quitting when his cousin was sent to jail, Evans staring at a life he didn't want from the public side of a glass divider. It was the classic American success story: Evans transitioned from a contact-loving rugged man weaned on a hybrid of football and streetball to a rebounding specialist with value in the pros. Former teammates were comparing him to The Thing from The Fantastic Four, and he spoke with a style and a rhythm that would otherwise be foreign to those dealing with him.

Voted the league's dirtiest player multiple times by a player's

94

poll conducted by *Sports Illustrated*, Evans first gained attention as a rookie for taking a steroid test at halftime. "Cleaner than Pine-Sol," he proclaimed when the test came back negative. Evans later became a household name by grabbing Chris Kaman in the testicles while boxing him out during a game in 2006.

Evans usurped Kris Humphries in the starting lineup after eighteen games and became the only unquestionably underpaid player in the starting lineup. In Brooklyn, Evans was the underdog. "Reg-gie!" chants often echoed through Barclays Center. Evans grabbed defensive rebounds at a greater clip (38.7 percent) than any player in NBA history. But his offense was so nonexistent that his record-setting season also included the daily reminder that the Nets were often playing four-on-five on offense when Evans was on the floor. On the same night in March when Williams set an NBA record for 3-pointers in a half, Evans was so flummoxed at the foul line that the crowd decided to urge him on, deliriously and therapeutically chanting his name. Evans stepped to the stripe and sank both. For the majority of those in the arena, hitting 5-for-16 with thousands of eyeballs on you felt relatable.

Before the Clippers game, NBA.com stats guru John Schumann asked Avery Johnson if he was surprised the Nets ranked last in the league in pace, that they played the league's slowest brand of basketball.

"It does," Johnson said. "It does. I don't think we'll be in the top ten with our team, but I think we'll improve in that area, especially in the third quarter. In the second halves, we see a drastic change in our pace. Normally, our pace in the first quarter is pretty good. I think you'll have to tell me where we rank in the first quarter, if we took just the first quarter as a sample. But our pace goes down, downhill as the game wears on."

Schumann said he'd tell Johnson after the game.

"As promised, I looked up your pace," he said. "You're last in first-quarter pace although it is your fastest-paced quarter of the four."

The Nets had a good second half, notching their biggest win of the young season. But the team had failed to register a single fast-break point. The Nets, it seemed, were effective but slow, like a safety-first Volvo. There was an annoying contradiction in there somewhere, and after Avery Johnson was fired the team would speak consistently about pushing the pace even though its roster lacked speed.

MAGIC CONFIDENCE

Gerald Wallace is a brick wall, six feet, eight inches of refined, defined muscle, and his voice—hard to understand at times—is the opposite: a deep baritone, soft, nasal, and reflective. Talking with Wallace felt less rehearsed than talking with the other three members of the Nets' Core Four. He wore baggy clothes reminiscent of the Allen Iverson era, and the scars covering his chiseled frame were visible, distracting at times. Wallace's voice and body both gave off clues to his injury history, the rugged abandon with which he played, and that added another dimension to the interviews he conducted in his corner of the locker room.

"I don't think," Wallace said. "I can't play thinking. Just whatever happens, happens."

As far as Wallace was concerned, any play, any team, any assignment was a screen he could plow through en route to a steal, or a loose ball that he could save by hurdling over spectators.

"LeBron is LeBron," Wallace said, with a matchup against the reigning MVP on the horizon. "He's just like everybody else."

After losing that game: "What gap? I think we're just as good as them."

Gerald Wallace came off like a confidence cousin to Kobe Bryant. No matter how many times Wallace would say he thought the Nets were as good as any elite team, it rarely came off as arrogant or ignorant because Wallace was so relentless on the court.

On the last day of November, Gerald, who otherwise shot 26

percent from long range on the season, got his groove back, sinking five of six 3s. Wallace and Joe Johnson led the Nets to their third victory over the Orlando Magic in a month. The Nets overcame a mediocre first half with good energy and great shooting after intermission.

The Amway Center, a palatial arena that opened in 2010, is adjacent to Hughey Avenue in downtown Orlando, a short walk from the police department. A little farther down is Orlando's Florida A&M law campus. If you got arrested at a Magic game, you could probably find a good legal expert within walking distance.

Orlando, the sparkly yet generic condominium development of the NBA, has seen its fair share of superstars, from Shaquille O'Neal and Penny Hardaway to Tracy McGrady and Dwight Howard. Located a short distance from Disney World, Magic fans were always on the lookout for the next franchise player.

With Brook Lopez out with a sprained foot, Reggie Evans and Kris Humphries actually saw court time together, immediately fighting each other for a rebound. Shortly thereafter, Evans found Humphries down low with a beautiful pass, but Humphries missed, lending credence to the idea that the two had all the chemistry of two positive charges. Still, the Nets chalked up another victory on the road.

Johnson's impressive November run would garner him a Coach of the Month award, but he couldn't savor it. The Nets had a date with the Miami Heat the next night, a battle for the best record in the conference. Johnson showed little interest in celebrating what would be the penthouse moment of his Nets coaching career.

"We just haven't played well against the Heat," he said. "I want to see if we can take a step in the right direction. I want to see a little bit of how far our defense has come and I want us to, um, play really good offense. We haven't played good offense either. If it was football: defense, offense, our special teams, we haven't played in any of those departments."

It was honest, but a little strange to hear from the man who preached positivity so thoroughly when things felt dire in Newark.

Williams was asked if it was the sign of a good team that the Nets turned their focus up in the second half to beat Orlando.

"Huh?"

Intentional or not, it was the timeless trope, the comedian making an attention-deficit joke by not paying attention. Laughter enveloped the circle around him.

He clarified: "I didn't mean it like that. We just weren't happy with the way we were playing."

DOWN BY BISCAYNE BAY

If Avery Johnson's speech after the Nets' victory over the Magic represented the pinnacle of his time with the Nets, the game in Miami spoke to the tenuous nature of his position.

The Nets built an early lead. Stackhouse hit an improbable fadeaway jumper and blocked Dwyane Wade at the rim. Heat coach Erik Spoelstra was incensed and drew a technical foul. At the end of the second quarter Stackhouse summoned his surprisingly spry vertical leap, drawing a foul as he dropped the ball into the basket. It was a glorious old-man dunk. Wade finished with 10 of his then season-high 34 points in the period, attacking the rim relentlessly. Wade's persona was the opposite of Williams's. He could always smile when called upon, and puff pieces about his love for his kids, or relationship with his mother who battled addiction in Chicago, seemed to follow him wherever he went. He projected the kind of aura and embraced the kind of publicity that enticed the casual fan. Spoiled by the exploits of LeBron James, the Miami media tended to take on Wade's persona: nonchalant unless needed and seemingly unimpressed by anything, almost like a major network was ready to pick up a sitcom about five guys who—as a unit—dress casually, get paid to go to basketball games, and sigh a lot.

The Heat* picked it up and the Nets wilted in the second half, their fifth game in seven days. The last two games were without Lopez, whose presence in the paint gave the Nets the option of slowing the game down as his opponents double-teamed him.

"They're a really good team," LeBron James said. "Well coached. Have some great players. They're going to continue to get better."

The future sure looked good for Avery Johnson. "You would hope you would be in this position," Johnson said before the game. "Nobody had a crystal ball."

After a hard-fought, entertaining home loss against the Western Conference champion Oklahoma City Thunder, the Nets thought they were what they were, a good team with room for improvement, still finding its way in an ever-evolving NBA. But their legitimacy had all the ironclad permanence of a real estate market in recession.

"The good teams, they get up for the great teams," Johnson said of the consecutive games between the Heat and the Thunder. "The great teams get up for everybody.

"It's a challenge. It's one we embrace. At one time, it would have been a horror film."

In between the Nets' three early-season victories over the Magic were a pair of wins over the Celtics, a close one at home and a dominant performance on the road. The highlight of the latter victory was a confrontation between Rajon Rondo and Kris Humphries near the baseline. Earlier that evening, Joe Johnson had executed a dribbling maneuver around Paul Pierce so slick

---

* The battle for first place in the conference wasn't even a sellout. Miami is a wonderful place, a happy place one might even argue, but the in-arena experience remains remarkably subpar. I wonder if a Reporter's Experience Package (like a Florida-based baseball fantasy camp) would help sell more of the seats, in which fans could—as I did in Miami—pester Mario Chalmers about being name-dropped on *Saturday Night Live,* watch players debate referee decisions in college football games in the home locker room, and listen to team executives tell stories over dinner.

that legendary Celtics broadcaster Tommy Heinsohn likened it, intentionally or not, to a snake eating a mongoose, the same reference used by a nature channel in a program Will Ferrell's character watches in *Stranger than Fiction* before a wrecking ball is accidentally taken to his home.

CHAPTER 6

The Battle of the Boroughs

LITTLE BROTHER FRANCHISES

Along with the inferiority complex that comes with second-class standing, the Mets and Jets feed their respective neurotic fan bases with the dreamy nostalgia generated by miraculous championship triumphs—victories and teams that have come to define sports during some of the most hedonistic times in American history. The Miracle Mets and Broadway Joe Jets were championship bedfellows that closed out the sixties in symbolic style. In 1986, the swaggering, cocaine-addled Mets dominated baseball, but they relied on ridiculously implausible late rallies against the Astros and Red Sox to win the World Series while Lawrence Taylor of the Giants and Mark Gastineau of the Jets turned vicious hits into an art form.

In their various home arenas in New Jersey and Long Island, Nets fans had neither a legitimate inferiority complex (usually, you need to be able to fill your home during times of success to be able to claim that), nor an NBA championship memory to fall back on, just simple solitude and occasional success. It's hard to feel like a little brother when the only child in town never wanted you born in the first place. Giants and Yankees fans have been forced to recognize their Jets and Mets counterparts, little bro looking up and tugging on their shorts, begging and wailing, wanting to play too. It's never been like that for the Knicks, thanks to indemnity and inaccessibility.

What Nets fans—past, present, and future—had with Knicks fans was a different kind of hybrid rival. The Yankees and Giants are flagship franchises that have succeeded throughout their history, earning the respect that winning demands. Their fans preach that winning is all that matters from what seems like fandom's massage chair. Before they shared a stadium, Jets fans responded by making more noise inside of a stadium named for their co-tenants. Mets fans responded to Yankee success by consistently chanting, "Yankees suck!" during and after games against opponents that aren't the Yankees, and waxing poetic with ideas like, Yankees fans like winning; Mets fans like baseball.

Pre-Brooklyn, Knicks-Nets was a rivalry a few notches below. The Knicks are a flagship franchise whose results mirror the miscues of the Mets and Jets. Team owner James Dolan is George Steinbrenner without the confidence derived from self-made status, the free-market sport, or the road map. The Knicks had been, perhaps, the worst-run major-market franchise in all of sports for much of the aughts. Yet the Nets' lack of cultural resonance empowered Knicks fans, who habitually made the Nets' arena their own in East Rutherford and Newark with a sea of orange-and-blue and what felt like a transplanted sound cloud. Just when you begin to hear yourself think, Knicks fans show up for dinner, thrilled by the unclaimed place mats and the cost-effectiveness of the experience.

With the Knicks now poised to be playoff mainstays and the Nets on the rise, professional basketball in New York is in an unprecedented situation: the Knicks and Nets have the chance to shape a rivalry, local and intensely combative, for generations, something unlike anything the NBA has seen.

TWO POINT GUARDS (REPRISE)

On media day, a hundred-plus reporters milled around Barclays Center, cavorting into and out of the Calvin Klein Courtside Club and a practice court below the arena's Starbucks. Flashbulbs sang. Junior's Cheesecakes were fashioned for each Brooklyn Net. Smooth jazz passed through the plush, silvery surroundings. The Nets were cool and new and the New York press couldn't get enough, lapping it up like a golden retriever in front of a water dish.

Although he opened with a statement, Avery Johnson spoke slowly, without the lingering awkwardness that comes from being the designated mouthpiece for a franchise in waiting. Johnson discussed shifting from failure-based insomnia to the sleepless stirring generated by having good problems.

"I've been waiting for this kind of pressure for two years, where there's pressure on us to win; expectations are a lot higher," he said. "This is what we want. This is what we signed up for: where we get really, really criticized when we don't win. And then, when we win, the players really get celebrated. That's what it's all about."

Late in his press conference, a man sat down in the front row and raised his hand.

"Your name . . . ?" Johnson asked.

"Deron Williams from the *Deron Williams News*."

It was a simple gag, but the press corps giggled.

"I think the question everybody wants to know is, uh: who is the best team in New York? Has that been asked?"

"You're about the millionth person that has asked me that question," Johnson said. "I have answered that question a million times. Here's what I'm going to say: it's not about having the best team in New York."

Then Johnson started talking about Deron Williams like he wasn't in the room. "My point guard, he often talks about being the best team in the NBA because he's a two-time—two-time— gold medal winner and he wants to bring that same spirit to the rest of the roster because he wants to be an NBA champion. And that's what I want for him. So what's going to happen this year; he's going to average about eighteen points a game and eleven assists and help us achieve our goals of winning an NBA championship and not just the city championship."

It was fluff. Nobody clapped.

DELAYED HYSTERIA

The score was tied at 84 in regulation, and the shot clock was turned off. The play was live, but the players stood almost completely still for more than ten seconds before springing into action. It was the first meeting of the Brooklyn Nets and the New York Knicks, and it was, as Knicks coach Mike Woodson was fond of saying, "nut-cutting time."

Standing near the far sideline, right next to the Barclays Center logo, Raymond Felton dribbled the ball idly, waiting for the action to begin. Watching him closely was Williams, his longtime rival. The two came of age competing against each other in summer camps and tournaments. Felton was the most ballyhooed point guard of the 2002 high school class and arguably its best player, the other candidate being Carmelo Anthony. Williams was its forgotten star-in-the-making.

Williams and Anthony, the intertwined franchise players at their first competitive New York crossroads, got to know each other playing for the United States at an amateur tournament on Island de la Margarita, Venezuela, the summer before they began college. Humphries and other future NBA players Chris Bosh, Andre Iguodala, and Aaron Brooks played on the team. Williams was the starting point guard in part because Felton wasn't on the team. His coach on the team, Ernie Kent, then the coach at the University of Oregon, told Williams that he could be a great player if he improved his conditioning.

Kent praised Williams's Illinois teammate Dee Brown as the

best player on that team. The Jazz drafted Brown in the second round of the 2006 draft, one year after taking Williams with the third pick. Brown has spent most of his career overseas.

Williams's mother wanted him to attend the University of North Carolina, but Carolina wanted Felton, a McDonald's All-American, so Williams went to the University of Illinois and they faced off in the 2005 National Championship game. Felton hit a dagger 3-pointer over Williams, winning their most important matchup, but Williams was drafted higher and had gotten the better of Felton in the pros.

In the corner closest to Williams and Felton, Joe Johnson watched the Knicks' J. R. Smith. Both Johnson and Smith were notoriously streaky shooters, but Johnson was a smooth, soft-spoken All-Star who liked to blend in. One of the NBA's most unusual personalities, Smith mixed raw effervescence with a mind-boggling shot selection. His body could serve as a tattoo catalog; Smith had more ink than most newspapers, and he was seen around town with Rihanna during the playoffs, his late-night habits intensely scrutinized.

At the foul line, there were six players about to be set in motion. Keith Bogans had checked in for Jerry Stackhouse. Bogans looked like Laurence Fishburne's Morpheus from *The Matrix* and dressed like a personal trainer. His teammates jokingly called him by his middle name, Ramon. Bogans was a cool customer, a man who always seemed to know his role. He liked jokes, but he'd look at the carpet before he unwillingly altered his mood. Devin Kharpertian of the Nets blog The Brooklyn Game nicknamed Bogans "Role Star Hip-Hop" after the website World Star Hip-Hop, which merges hip-hop and shock value. Bogans was to stick with the Knicks' 3-point marksman Steve Novak.

Meanwhile, Reggie Evans had subbed for Lopez, who had tied the game by splitting a pair of free throws. Evans was to guard Tyson Chandler. Both were incredibly physical men with rugged beards and who loved rebounding. Chandler had scored a career-high 28 points, while Evans, who had proclaimed the day before that he wouldn't be popping champagne bottles like he had won a championship if the Nets beat the Knicks, had snared 14 rebounds in only eighteen minutes.

Chandler stepped in front of Bogans, and Novak curled away from the scrum. Chandler then freed Carmelo Anthony with a screen, Gerald Wallace in pursuit.

It was the last play of the intracity Knicks-Nets premier that could be drawn up in a huddle. Barring a sleight of hand, it was Anthony's ball and a narrative that the Brooklyn-born, Baltimore-raised Anthony shared with Williams. From coveted by the Nets to publicly rejected by Prokhorov to traded to the Knicks, the game was in Carmelo's hands unless Wallace could come up with a not-yet-invented form of ball denial. Trying to keep Anthony from shooting was like trying to keep America from foreign oil. Anthony received the ball on the left wing. He drove left and drove hard. With Wallace covering him well, he lofted a midrange jumper that clanged off the side of the rim.

"That's the look I wanted," Anthony said. "I'll take that shot all day. I got a perfect look at it. I missed that one, but that's the look I wanted."

The shot gave the Nets a chance to break the 84-all deadlock and win the game at the buzzer. Williams took a 3-pointer from inside half-court but missed. The first ever Battle of the Boroughs was headed to overtime. Hurricane Sandy had sapped drama from the Nets' Brooklyn launch, but the cancellation allowed for an interborough rivalry to simmer.

It was the first time since 1977 that the Nets had hosted the Knicks in New York State, and the first time ever that both teams entered the matchup with a winning percentage above .600. The Nets' 6-1 home record was the team's best since an 18-1 start in 2002–03, and it was the first time in fourteen years that both teams had a winning record going into a matchup.

The Nets won going away in the extra session, sending their fans—about 50 percent of those in attendance—home happy. With the win the Nets were five games over .500 for the first time since the end of the 2006 season and tied for the best start after thirteen games in the franchise's NBA history.

Williams said when the Nets pitched him on re-signing they spoke of nights like this. Hotly contested rivalry games would foreground the franchise's push to mainstream prominence. There was a reason why Nets CEO Brett Yormark, the marketing maven partly responsible for NASCAR's early 2000s mainstream surge, pushed so hard for Knicks-Nets on opening night. Two teams within New York City limits playing basketball, the city game to many, had enough untapped potential to shape a rivalry for generations.

There were many heroes for the victors. Williams's 14 assists tied the entire Knicks team and added a layer to the Williams-Anthony preferred franchise player debate, for a night at least. Williams starred opposite a struggling Felton (3-for-19 shooting), who looked lost without an injured Jason Kidd next to him. In scoring 22 points, Lopez worked well with Williams and came up with 5 huge blocked shots. Wallace hounded Anthony into a mediocre shooting performance and scored 16 points. Evans was everywhere.

"The city's under new management," Jay-Z said in a rare tweet. It was a fun proclamation that kept people talking, but really, what the Nets and Knicks would prove by playing four games in less than two months was that they were perfect foils for a budding rivalry. There was no landlord. It was more like an on-court co-op.

"We didn't win the championship of New York," Williams said. "We won a game against a division rival and it was a great game for us."

REVENGE,
A DISH BEST SERVED FROM DEEP

The Knicks and Nets had gone in different directions after their first encounter. The Nets won two in a row, only to lose four straight after that, three defeats to legitimately good opponents—

Miami, Oklahoma City, and Golden State—before wearing their Sunday worst against the Milwaukee Bucks, who deflected forty passes by Avery Johnson's count. The Knicks, meanwhile, had gone 7-1 since losing the inaugural Battle of the Boroughs.

"Nobody's in a crisis mode," Johnson said at practice the next day before launching into a detailed, if imperfect, definition of crisis mode.

The silver lining was that the Nets had been losing without Lopez, sidelined by a foot sprain he sustained against the Celtics. The Nets were clearly a better defensive team with their big man slowing down the pace on the offensive end and providing a shot-blocking presence.

It was strange to see Lopez standing there at practice, looking healthy, raring to go. Despite the losing, we were becoming accustomed to career nights from Blatche on the offensive end. Although Lopez was pain-free for more than a few days, he said he needed to get his explosion back and be able to put his full body weight on his foot before he could play again. He also needed to complete the team-mandated recovery plan, which sounded like an obstacle course: practice; talk to the media; recover from practice; participate in shootaround; recover; get cleared to play by the doctors. When he came back later in the week, Pistons coach Lawrence Frank said he was willing to offer Lopez four free Disney passes not to play. It was a tempting offer; Lopez kept a Goofy figurine in his locker in Newark.

"People who haven't really seen him play or been around him: his size is immense," Frank said. "He's a huge guy. Got great hands, great touch. Unorthodox player. He's got part European; I think he may have went over to Serbia when he was twelve 'cause he's got some of the stuff that you don't see in a lot of American players."

Lopez was technically half Cuban, but it was that "part European," the unconventional shot-making, that made him such a skilled anomaly.

• • •

One of the blissful things about covering the NBA is the ability to walk around a quiet arena and simply observe pregame. To the passionate diehard, the devil is in the details that come before the cacophony of noise, before the chants, before the T-shirt cannons, the moments you might otherwise miss while catching up with a friend in the stands or taking a later train to the game. So it was with a modicum of head-scratching bemusement that I watched Dave Hopla, the Knicks' new shooting coach, receive on-the-money passes from Nets ballboys and drain 3-pointer after 3-pointer two-plus hours before the game. When Hopla hit the left wing, Aretha Franklin's "Respect" fittingly blared over the JumboTron.

The Nets held the Knicks to 6-for-21 shooting from behind the arc in the previous meeting. The Knicks, the most prolific 3-point-shooting team in recent memory, on pace to shoot more 3-pointers than any team in NBA history, were averaging a staggering 29 attempts a game and almost 12 makes, 3.5 more than any other team. To put that in simple math: the Knicks scored over 10 points more per game than any other team from behind the arc. And the Nets were best in the league at preventing long-range bombing. Something had to give. Thinking about Hopla, the middle-aged shooting coach, sinking seven in a row, I took the question to Avery Johnson before the game.

"It's not that easy, especially with another three-point shooter like Kidd in the lineup," he said, a statement that would sound prophetic after the fact.

Johnson noted that it came down to "what you're willing to live with," the implicit reality being that what you're willing to live with can also kill you, as a quarter of the way through the season, the Knicks had the fourth most efficient offense of the past thirty-six years. Along those lines, in holding the Knicks at bay in their first meeting, the Nets had lived with giving up a career-high 28 points to center Tyson Chandler.

Chandler picked up his first foul on the Nets' first offensive play, and Blatche—with quicker reaction timing inside than

Lopez—deflected away a lob pass intended for the Knicks' big man on the ensuing possession. Less than a minute into the game, the Nets had set a tone demanding a full-out response from Anthony. And so it became a game that swung very much on a 3-point pendulum, with five plays and sequences defining the Knicks' comeback.

THE THEME SETTER

With the Nets up 5–0, Ronnie Brewer intercepted a Reggie Evans pass. The ball moved swiftly, from Brewer to Felton to Anthony to Kidd—wide open from the wing—and the Knicks were on the board. Kidd then grabbed a Blatche airball and pushed upcourt. Joe Johnson pointed at someone to pick up Kidd in transition, but as Johnson floated over to Felton nobody stepped up to Kidd, who fired a straightaway 3-pointer. The shot missed and the Knicks wouldn't have the opportunity to take the lead again until early in the third quarter. A tough fadeaway from Johnson began a 16–2 Nets run that featured them attacking Kidd through Johnson.

THE SIX-POINT SWING

Up 47–33, Williams curled around a screen and took a 3 from the wing that went down halfway before spilling out. Kidd grabbed the rebound and whipped a pass upcourt to Felton, who found Anthony trailing. Anthony pulled up in rhythm and drilled his second 3 of the quarter. The third would bring the Knicks within 4 by halftime.

Heading into halftime, the Knicks' lyrical announcer Walt "Clyde" Frazier called Anthony's second-quarter performance "Melo Mania." Indeed, Melo Mania had brought the Knicks fans out with greater force, a force not yet known to most Brooklyn Nets fans. This left a Nets fan to label Melo "a black hole" when the Nets were up big, only to fall silent and become insecure when the Knicks' ace scorer started asserting his will on the game.

"This place is too quiet!" he shrieked. "Say something somebody!"

"Carmelo was hitting 2s, 3s, 4s,* seemed like 5s," Stackhouse said. Anthony finished with 45 points, 5-for-7 from behind the arc.

THE "WAIT, REALLY?"

The Nets rode Williams to a 6-point lead midway through the third quarter, forcing Mike Woodson into a time-out. Steve Novak entered the game. In his first real opportunity, Novak came around a Tyson Chandler screen, received a Kidd pass, took one dribble, and clanged a wing 3-pointer off the side of the rim. It was his first—and only—shot of the game, a remarkable feat given that the Knicks sank 14 of their 28 attempts. Doing so without a successful contribution from Novak, the NBA's leader in 3-point percentage a year earlier, was like a pitcher tossing a shutout without utilizing his blistering fastball.

THE INJURY DELAY

With the Nets up 91–88, Blatche tossed up an off-balance shot that rimmed out. In going for the rebound, Evans aggressively knocked J. R. Smith out of bounds. As Smith lay on his back, players moved back up the court. The pace of the game slowed. As Smith limped ahead, grimacing, Felton caught the Nets off guard with a cross-court bullet pass to an open Kidd. Kidd was standing just where Dave Hopla stood before the game when he hit his seven in a row. The shot went in. Anthony gave the Knicks their biggest lead,

---

* When asked why he shot plenty of 3s instead of more high-percentage shots, Paul Pierce's former frontcourt running mate on the Celtics Antoine Walker famously opined, "Because there are no 4s."

2 points, with a tip-in on their next offensive possession, after Blatche was called for a questionable (and game-changing) basket interference penalty.

NO KIDDING

With the game hanging in the balance, Tyson Chandler back-tapped J. R. Smith's long-range effort, and the Knicks had one more possession. The ball went to Anthony. Three passes later, after a sequence that had the Nets scrambling to help and recover like madmen, Felton found Kidd on the wing, a few feet from the Hopla spot. Spike Lee's hands were raised high. Kidd buried the 3-pointer while getting fouled by Stackhouse. Kidd missed the free throw but Wallace and Williams missed potential game-tying 3-pointers before the buzzer sounded.

Lee pranced along the sideline, overjoyed. It really was a special night for the filmmaker. The player who had rendered the Knicks second-class on the court for much of the 2000s (Kidd) hit the shot to give the Knicks a victory a few blocks from the filmmaker's office. The moment was tense, so turbocharged with adrenaline, on the court and in the vicinity of the court, that it was impossible not to feel the development of a budding rivalry.

Adding to the drama: Kidd kicked his leg out on Stackhouse, technically committing a foul according to the Reggie Miller rule. After the fact, the league confirmed to the Nets that a foul should have been called. Incredibly, something controversial involving Reggie Miller had managed to benefit the Knicks. Yet the Nets raced out to a 26–9 lead and, in their minds, the game probably should not have come down to the need for bailout call, a tricky slip of the leg from a player renowned for his savvy.

Avery Johnson also said that in a perfect world the Knicks would have made seven or eight 3-pointers instead of fourteen. Of course, when you're going up against a team that is historically good at something, the very idea or hope of a perfect world contradicts reality.

END OF THE WORLD AS WE KNOW IT

Three days before the Mayans had predicted the end of the world, it began to feel like Deron Williams might beat them at their own game. Williams's world was in disrepair. Heading into a matchup with the Jazz, Williams created a controversy by saying he preferred the flex offense the Jazz used in Utah—based around predesigned cuts, spacing, and interchangeability—to the isolation-heavy system utilized by the Nets. It was a tricky thing to say because Williams's pretrade clash with Jazz coach Jerry Sloan suggested the opposite.

Saying that he was always a "system player" was also an easy way for Williams to devalue himself as a superstar in the one-on-one limelight (real or imagined) of the NBA. And it was a swipe at Avery Johnson, who not only installed a lot of the Jazz's system in New Jersey, but also practically knelt down to Williams when he was first acquired: *we're going to ask him what he likes.*

Williams downplayed the sudden controversy before the Nets faced the Jazz, but Johnson was visibly annoyed.

"We're in this, like I always tell you guys, this microwave Twitter age, right?" he said. "So everybody wants everything instantly. Nobody really wants to wait. And sometimes things just take time. And when you say that, then you come off as making an excuse. That's just the way it is. For us, we've got to start making our wide-open shots."

Johnson's point was well taken. Williams's statements came on the heels of his extended shooting slump. Coach and player were at loggerheads, which might not have been an issue had Williams been able to play without pain and perform well. Williams's shooting struggles had never been more evident, and pain in both ankles didn't help. He had only shot the 3 with less success in the twelve games he played for the Nets after being traded by the Jazz, but back then he was prepping for wrist surgery.

Williams was also making a career-low number of shots at the

JAKE APPLEMAN

rim. Whether it was that the system didn't offer movement off .the ball for easy opportunities near the rim, adjusting to new personnel, or Williams's reluctance to take the ball to the basket hard while already playing banged up wasn't clear.

Three hours later, the Nets had recycled another double-digit, first-half lead and the Jazz were on the attack. Another atrocious third quarter had the Nets backpedaling, Williams struggling through another mediocre performance. Mo Williams pulled up in transition and drained a 3-pointer from the wing, his defender, Deron Williams, nowhere near him. The Nets came down the other end and Lopez attacked the rim. He was met, midair, by Derrick Favors, who had matured a bit since his Newark beginning. Favors emphatically rejected Lopez, one of many brilliant plays from the twenty-one-year-old. On the ensuing possession, Favors drove past Kris Humphries, converting a layup on an impressive drive. After a pair of Lopez free throws, Mo Williams hit a jumper over Deron Williams, and a relatively subdued affair turned tense.

The teams traded 2 points once more, before the Nets finally got a stop, Deron Williams corralling the rebound in traffic. But Deron was whistled for a charge seconds later, elbowing Mo (who may have flopped). Fighting himself, searching for answers after the game, Deron said he did not believe the elbow warranted a charge call. Despite a frantic last sequence where the Nets stole the ball and had two chances—first to win and then to tie at the buzzer—the Jazz escaped victorious. The Nets' fifth blown double-digit lead of the season was also the Jazz's first road victory over a winning team on the year. The Nets headed into their third matchup against the Knicks facing apocalyptic meaninglessness, the very sporting definition of "meh": a .500 record.

At least Humphries was funny. His brief marriage to Kim Kardashian allowed Knicks fans the opportunity to start a near leaguewide trend of booing him.

"They love me," Humphries said. "The boo is, 'I love you.'"

• • •

BROOKLYN BOUNCE

The Nets' first trip to Madison Square Garden, on December 19, was to be the franchise's last game if the Mayans were correct and the world ended two days later.

Per usual, Knicks history, in every form, was readily visible. Spike Lee, whose semi-autobiographical film *Crooklyn* had aired that day on HBO, was omnipresent at his courtside seat before the game in an oversized Bernard King jersey and an orange and blue Knicks Christmas hat. King, who had played almost the same amount of games for the Nets, was always remembered as a Knick, his everlasting contribution the 60 points he poured in during a Christmas Day game in 1984. (People tend to forget the Nets won that game.)

On their roster, the Knicks listed Carmelo Anthony as a game-time decision. Avery Johnson did not believe for a second that Anthony would sit out. Johnson was right. It was nothing more than a psychological ploy. Right out of the gate, Anthony jacked up three shots—including a 3-pointer from almost thirty feet—and snuffed out a Humphries baseline drive.

Whereas the Nets and their new home were all about space and accommodation, the Knicks were bound by a unifying claustrophobia. Fans are adjoined by the circular shape of the Garden, and vociferous unity coalesces almost at once with the aid of architecture, history, passion, and beer.

It wasn't a particularly loud night at the Garden, but the vibe was still special because it almost always is. Fans received free bright orange hats sponsored by Foot Locker, giving the arena the look of a circular citrus field.

The game stayed true to the first two meetings, with the lead changing twenty times before the Knicks ran away with a victory in the fourth quarter. As the Nets headed into intermission, YES Network sideline reporter Sarah Kustok spoke to Nets assistant coach P. J. Carlesimo. Carlesimo said the Nets needed to improve shot-making inside, take care of the ball, and close out quarters well. They did none of those things.

Williams came out aggressively in the second half, firing—and hitting—from the outside, but Lopez was frustrated inside by the Knicks' defense and a loosely officiated game; the Nets turned the ball over four times in the third quarter compared to zero for the Knicks; and the Knicks closed the period on an 11–4 run.

Unlike the Brooklyn Nets, the New Jersey Nets were known for their use of the alley-oop. In the early-to-mid-2000s, Jason Kidd could put the ball anywhere near the rim and his high-fliers—Richard Jefferson, Kenyon Martin, and later Vince Carter—would go get it. Even though the Nets really relied on a staunch defense, and their offense had the propensity to bog down, the prospect of such aerial excellence made the Nets the darlings of the *SportsCenter* Top 10 countdown. In sweeping the Knicks 4-0 in 2004, the Nets asserted their dominance with the alley-oop and turned Madison Square Garden into their own personal playground.

The Brooklyn Nets did not have the personnel to throw many alley-oops. Lopez, for all of his unparalleled shot-making excellence, was a creature of sedentary habit. He often finished short-range alley-oops as layups instead of dunks, and he used such little elevation on his midrange shots, it's conceivable that ants could survive underneath his sneakers on most attempts. Humphries could put one down occasionally, but he wasn't a lithe fast-break finisher. He dunked most on put-back attempts or short-range lobs. Reggie Evans was ground-bound effort in the flesh. Gerald Wallace, whose nickname was Crash, was known less for his aerial prowess and more for his aggression. The Nets made fun of Bogans for not dunking in games, and Williams, once a sneaky surprise as a high-riser, admitted in mid-February that he couldn't dunk even if he tried.

In winning the third Battle of the Boroughs, the Knicks, backed by Kidd, turned the tables in the third quarter by making perfect use of basketball's most acrobatic play. The Nets took a 4-point lead on a pull-up jumper from Williams, and Mike Woodson called a time-out. In defending a screen, Williams switched on to

Anthony. Wallace and Lopez both committed to the ball handler (Felton), who threw an easy alley-oop to a streaking Chandler. Described by *Sports Illustrated* as a man who celebrated alley-oops as if he'd just "slain a Bengal Tiger," Chandler's dunks energized Madison Square Garden in the most euphoric and direct sense; there was little anticipation, just carnage. Williams airballed a 3-pointer on the next possession.

The Knicks scored again, and the Nets called time-out. The Knicks used their first possession to strike with the alley-oop again. Williams again switched on to Anthony—two franchise players alone on an island away from the action—and this time Joe Johnson was the lost wingman trying to contain Chandler on a beautiful reverse alley-oop dunk. The Nets had inexplicably triple-switched on defense—Williams to Anthony, Lopez to the point guard, and the wing player to Chandler—and it was possibly the most ill-timed strategic move of Johnson's tenure because it demanded that wing players, not experts by trade at defending the pick-and-roll, try to contain it. The move undermined Johnson as a tactician and underscored a relentless tinkering approach that unnerved Johnson's players. With the outcome all but decided—Knicks up 14 with three-plus minutes remaining—the Nets defended the play the traditional way. Fouled by Williams, Chandler got two free throws instead of an open dunk.

If it felt like the bottom had fallen out on the Nets after the second-half collapse, that's because it had. The loss had come after a series of close games. Prior to the Knicks' second visit to Barclays Center, the Nets had built double-digit leads in three of every four games and had only occasionally been involved in a close finish. That had all changed.

CYCLES OF THE SEASON

There was something off about Avery Johnson talking about trust on a day when Billy King gave Deron Williams the day off from talking to the media. Nets players hung back on the practice court while Johnson and Johnson, Joe and Avery, opened up to a handful of reporters, conference room table style, in the press workroom at the PNY Center. Despite the sense that Avery's job was in jeopardy—a rumor mostly bandied about by impatient fans on the Internet—the potential decision seemed extremely premature. To some pundits, the Nets weren't actually that good, so a team hovering a game over .500 after a disappointing stretch early in the season just didn't feel all that surprising. And given the Nets' disappointing track record in New Jersey, it shouldn't have warranted rash action. After five years, the Nets finally had a winning record.

Joe hit leadoff. Like any media-savvy pro athlete, he was a lot more up front in talking to smaller numbers—the smaller, the better. In front of large hordes, swells of tape-recorder-wielding humans like he rarely saw in Phoenix and Atlanta, Johnson turned up the volume on "Definitely, man" and went on his way, usually cordial in stopping for anyone who wanted a moment on his way out the door.

Johnson was a chameleon who occasionally wanted to blend into his surroundings, so if blending required keeping it real, he occasionally kept it real. When Johnson found out he was traded to the Nets in real life, he traded himself to the Nets in NBA 2K12 for Xbox or PlayStation. In NBA 2K13—a game technically "produced" by Jay-Z—there is a press conference after every game in the create-a-player mode. Reporters ask typically clichéd questions, and those controlling the player can pick between four-phrase excerpts from possible answers, ranging from the obvious platitude to controversy-generating selfishness. Suffice it to say, Johnson knows the difference between pressing square and pressing X.

In real life, however, he shocked everyone with his candor. He was the video game character come to life whose answers—according to the game—would boost his popularity but hurt team chemistry.

"We have so many breakdowns defensively, we don't even give our defensive schemes a chance to work," he said. "So we don't even know if they work."

He talked about unnamed teammates who weren't having fun and asserted that NBA players have the best jobs in world, that there was no excuse for not having fun.

"It's a new chapter in my career," he said. "There's no way I'm going to take a day for granted and not come in here and have a good time, so I know I don't show it, express it a lot, but that's just my demeanor, it's just who I am."

He also backed Avery Johnson. It was the Nets' first practice in East Rutherford since Hurricane Sandy, and in marched the coach, ready to take on another storm.

Avery Johnson loved talking about the cycle of the season. On December 21, the winter solstice, Johnson implied that a harsh coaching winter begets a reborn coaching spring. It was a self-affirmation that savored of hedging. Johnson was getting out in front of the closed-door discussions that would ultimately determine his fate with the Nets.

He started citing examples. The Spurs almost fired Gregg Popovich during the lockout-shortened 1999 season, but they kept him on, and the Spurs won the championship. The '99 Spurs began with a worse record than the Nets had under Johnson. He also cited the Houston Rockets when Rudy Tomjonavich took over for Don Chaney. The team had given a chance to a coach facing adversity, and they went on to win a championship too.

Johnson had a strong argument but was ultimately powerless in the last year of his contract, and he knew it.

"Coach of the Month, or 'the coach should be fired,' whatever it is, it's all fair," he said.

MATINEE IDOLS

The Nets and Knicks met for the last time in the regular season in the annual Martin Luther King Jr. Day matinee at Madison Square Garden. The Knicks had hosted a game while honoring Dr. King every year since 1986, with the exception of 1999, when the season started after MLK Day. It was also the day when Barack Obama was inaugurated for a second term, an event that featured the Brooklyn Tabernacle Choir, a group from the largest nondenominational church in downtown Brooklyn, performing "The Battle Hymn of the Republic." They shared the stage with Beyoncé, then the first lady of the Brooklyn Nets, who sparked a controversy for lip-synching the national anthem.

Joe Johnson had mostly struggled to make his mark against the Knicks in the first three matchups, but sank a trio of 3s in the game's first seven minutes, although Brooklyn's Backcourt was quickly relegated to the bench late in the first quarter with two fouls each.

Kris Humphries didn't quite make his mark against the Knicks until their final meeting, either. He battled Amar'e Stoudemire and Anthony, aggressive with his second efforts, rebounding the ball after stopping his man. He also made good use of space, flying out of nowhere for a rebound that led to a 3-point play. When he ran a delayed pick-and-roll with Johnson, the result (a dunk from Humphries after Johnson drew the attention of the defense) was the epitome of what went right in the game for the Nets.

The Nets seemed comfortably ahead, but the Knicks scored 10 straight points to take the lead, helped by back-to-back turnovers from Johnson and Humphries. With bragging rights suddenly on the line and the Knicks suddenly ahead, the intensity amped up to another level. It wasn't pretty, but it was meaningful and powerful, like something out of a Knicks game from the early '90s.

The Nets caught a break early in the fourth quarter when

Bogans hit a 3 that bounced off the rim, off the top of the backboard, and in. From there, Johnson, who had virtually disappeared after his strong start, took over. He found Watson for a 3. Then he drilled a pair of 3s on back-to-back possessions, and sank a top-of-the-key jumper after the Nets had failed to take advantage of an extra possession provided by Humphries's offensive rebound. Johnson's flourish staked the Nets to an 83–77 lead, and the Nets wouldn't score again until the ball found its way to Degree of Difficulty Joe, with the Nets down by a point, five minutes later.

Johnson dribbled the ball through his legs like the cocky kid at the playground, drove right, and made a hard stop, sequencing into a beautiful fadeaway, the only shot that can feel like it is slowing time down as you glide away from the basket. Like most of Johnson's MLK Day buckets, the shot hit nothing but net. Johnson gave the Nets the lead for good, having scored or assisted on 13 straight points.

"That was a big shot," he said. "I was holding my breath. I had to exhale a little bit." Johnson admitted that hitting a game winner against the Knicks meant more than hitting one against the Wizards or Pistons, which he had already done.

A few stalls over, Humphries, whose ability to remain on the floor was predicated on doing a good job on Carmelo Anthony, was wearing a mischievous grin.

"People were heckling me, walking in and out of the tunnel," he explained. "I asked them on the way out, 'Why are you so quiet?' So it's a good feeling. It got quiet in the Garden tonight!"

What were they saying?

"Come on. Everything under the sun, brother."

An underrated aspect of the Nets victory, seemingly as always, was Lopez. Lopez allowed Williams the opportunity to ice the game at the free-throw line by making a dexterous save of a rebound along the baseline after Anthony missed the potential game winner. Lopez seemed to be in great position all night, seeking out rebounds and timing runs. He made two huge fourth-quarter blocks, casting an imposing shadow in the lane. In victory Lopez also bettered Chandler, his fellow All-Star, for the first time in a borough battle. In limiting the Knicks to only 6-for-21 from distance and holding Chandler to 7 points, the Nets had succeeded where they had previously failed. The game was only close because the Nets were sloppy (19 turnovers) and the Knicks weren't (5 turnovers).

Gerald Wallace was happy. Not only had the Nets earned their revenge at Madison Square Garden, eking out an 88–85 win, but Wallace had just been informed that Deron Williams had snapped a streak of consecutive free throws made at 52. In a locker room of even-keeled men of status and role players running the personality gamut, Wallace was the Nets' emotional barometer. He said fuck when fuck needed to be said. But now Wallace was happy, notified that Williams had made 52 straight free throws, tickled by the news of the streak.

"What?!"

Yeah, he made 52 in a row, until a late miss gave the Knicks a chance to tie at the buzzer.

"Damn, D-Will! Where he at? . . . Seriously."

Wallace started half singing, half yelling. "Dar-ra! Dar-ra!"

(Dar-ra! was my second favorite pronunciation of Williams's name after "Dar-row Weeeel-yo!" as exclaimed by a group of Flemish teenagers in a Mons, Belgium, hallway on the night Williams and his Besiktas teammates were eliminated from a European competition during the NBA lockout.)

Wallace was informed that Williams was in the shower.

"He trippin'," Wallace concluded.

Standing at the free-throw line, all alone in front of twenty thousand people—just you with yourself and your thoughts—is the ultimate measure of repetition and self-control. Williams often found himself there, alone on his island late in the fourth quarter, icing games. Late in his streak, the feat was compared to a no-hitter.

"I'm still mad about the one I missed," he said. "It felt good. Looked good. Wiggled out."

Obama was ushered in for a second term, and the first regular-season chapter of the Knicks-Nets rivalry was complete—four games in less than two months thanks to Hurricane Sandy. Before and after the game, talk of a potential playoff matchup—see you in May . . . right? . . . this is inevitable, right? . . . because this is just one of those things that has to happen—was all the rage. It was the kind of tantalizing prospect that even the staunchest hipsters wouldn't try to dismiss.

The Nets would finish the season half a game out of third in the conference. The Knicks finished second. Had the Nets finished third, neither team would have needed to face the Miami Heat in the second round, and it would have set up a possible Battle of the Boroughs playoff series. That prospect, a stretch of basketball that would have done more for the Nets' brand than any promotional endeavor, remained something for New York basketball fans to ponder.

CHAPTER 7

From Christmas Coal to Carlesimo

The NBA's annual Christmas slate kicked off with the Nets vs. the Celtics. Interestingly, Avery Johnson and Celtics coach Doc Rivers were former teammates. They'd both played as point guards for San Antonio twenty years earlier, under Larry Brown. The former teammates remained friends and dining companions.

The Celtics (13-13) and the Nets (14-12) were together for the first time since Rajon Rondo earned a two-game suspension for his role in a late November melee in which Kris Humphries held Rondo in a modified headlock. Both teams were struggling relative to preseason expectations, but the Celtics had been there before. They started the 2009 season 27-2 only to lose Kevin Garnett—and a good shot at a repeat championship—to a knee injury. The next year, they came within a game of winning the title. They understood the significance of the regular season, which to many casual fans began on Christmas.

"When you put this jersey on, it comes with responsibility," Garnett said in October after the Nets beat the Celtics in a tune-up at Barclays Center. "Whether it's preseason, you fucking around, chillin', one-on-one, twenty-one, whatever it is, it comes with responsibility and we don't take that lightly around here."

"I've never seen a team rebrand themselves in six months," Rivers said. "It's like this is a whole . . . this is a whole new franchise. . . . It feels like they just plucked this team out of space and all of a sudden they've got a hell of a team in our division that wears black uniforms. It's unbelievable."

The Nets had already beaten the Celtics twice, but Rondo, the player supposedly responsible for carrying the Celtics' vintage veterans, had not played a full game against the Nets. Rondo was sidelined with an ankle injury during their first matchup, then thrown out of the second two weeks later. The Nets won that second game, and it was the high-water moment of a record-setting November.

The teams wore special holiday uniforms, coal black for the home team and evergreen threads for the visitors, highlighting the idea that this was a matchup worthy of holiday drama: friends and former teammates roaming the sideline; struggling star point guards; a recent fracas. And so it was a Charlie Brown Christmas in Brooklyn: a botched national anthem, fireworks at noon, the menacing BrooklyKnight descending from the rafters, and Garnett pulling an imaginary chair out from under Lopez in the third quarter.

The game tipped. Rondo missed a jumper, and Williams turned the ball over. But both players responded quickly, scoring and finding teammates in the right spots. Lopez found an early groove taking and making shots that would look ridiculous if hoisted by any other human. The Nets got a pair of vintage fadeaways from Jerry Stackhouse as well, fitting as Stackhouse had been the longest-tenured NBA player to never have played on Christmas. Stackhouse's play up to that point most resembled a Christmas gift to the Nets.

Stackhouse was the one player who was consistently engaging and forthright, an eighteen-year veteran who brought wisdom to every conversation. He would subtly bring reporters into discourse by narrowing his eyes on the person asking the question before shifting into an answer naturally, like a driver in total control of a manual transmission. In a season that shifted drastically for him as a veteran leader—he transitioned from a surprisingly large role to a man who disappeared to a surprising role in the playoffs—he took it all in stride, at times with remarkable openness, whether talking about family or later the admission after nearly two months away from the wear and tear of game action that "it's almost like they're protecting me from myself."

FORT GREEN(E)

The Celtics owned the second quarter, outscoring the Nets 34–18, in part thanks to two big plays from Rondo, a savvy offensive rebound leading to a 3-pointer (Boston +8), and a driving-and-1 conversion (Boston +15). Rondo dominated the third quarter's most important sequence as well. He stopped the Nets' momentum by drawing a charge on Joe Johnson approximately sixty feet from the basket. It was a cheeky play, the kind of thing that would start a fight on the playground, and Rondo made sure to say "thank you" to the referee while lying on his back. After a stop, he slipped a slick pass to a cutting Jared Sullinger for a layup, then punctuated the quarter by pulling up and nailing a 3. Williams was practically invisible on the court.

Tempers flared early in the fourth quarter as Wallace got tangled up with Garnett, grabbing Garnett's jersey as Wallace tried to break his fall. Wallace pulled Garnett close to him. Garnett smacked his hands away.

Garnett's side of the story: "He just kind grabbed my shorts and I helped him up, you know, whatever, make sure he didn't fall. And then he just kept grabbing my shorts. And I asked him what he was doing and he didn't respond and I looked at him like, 'What are you doing?' and I tried to smack his hand away. It wasn't nothin'. He just jacked my shorts up. I didn't know what he was doing. . . . This whole thing, it's like a movie. People get caught up into the shenanigans and all the bullshit. That play was over when it started. We was just trying to make sure each other was safe, and that was it, and then I don't know where in America you can jack somebody's pants up or shorts up. I don't know what the hell was going on."

When I asked Garnett if something like that could linger, he passed.

"Next question, man."

The answer wasn't a scolding and it wasn't quite a tacit acknowledgment of bad blood, but it was the second time I had been directly or indirectly reprimanded by the Boston Celtics on Christmas. Prefacing a question before the game about the Nets and Celtics both finding themselves below expectations, "under-performing," Rivers quipped, "You know that it's Christmas and you're going to ask that question, but that's okay." He then made a salient point about how both teams were in "search mode."

When I asked Rondo if the charge he drew on Joe Johnson so far away from the basket was a rarity, he disagreed, but politely spared me further interviewer scrutiny, subtly acknowledging my status as a visiting reporter, perhaps a familiar enough face. Another reporter wasn't so lucky. He asked Rondo about Pierce leading the team in assists and Rondo leading in scoring, if that was a plan.

"No, we designed it," Rondo deadpanned.

Few NBA players seem to care less for the day-to-day NBA media than Rondo, who briefly interned at *GQ* magazine over the summer, wearing chic clothes and performing menial tasks like carrying lots of things at once, delivering the mail by throwing behind-the-back passes, polishing a company logo, and photocopying his hand. Media Rondo is like a combination of Williams's ornery side and a terse, blunt LeBron. Rondo remained adamant about the joke, unflinchingly trying to convince the reporter on his way out the door that the Celtics designed a bizarre role reversal game plan where Pierce would lead the team in assists and Rondo, then the NBA's per game assist leader, in scoring. It was funny if you had a cast-iron stomach.

The Pierce-Garnet Celtics had a different media style than any other NBA team. They were green royalty. Their stars were veterans, men of status, who dictated the terms of engagement regardless of the vaunted reputation of their town's sports media. It was easy to see that "search mode" was something the Celtics, who could fuck with you or the team you were covering at a moment's notice, knew would fade at some point.

For the second consecutive trade deadline, rumor circulated that the Nets were eyeing the Celtics star Paul Pierce. It was easier to envision Pierce, then a lifetime Celtic, sending his GM Danny Ainge a text message like "There's a missile aimed at your house LOL" than it was to imagine him a Net. (At least it was at the time.) There was a code in Boston built over time. The Celtics were a stock you held on to. The Nets, meanwhile, proved that their coach couldn't survive the ramifications of Garnett stepping on Lopez's foot up in Boston.

"I love our team, man," Garnett said in October 2012. "I love our team. Our team is dope. I like us a lot."

Meanwhile, Wallace, the day after his little brouhaha with Garnett, lambasted his teammates for losing in Milwaukee. The Nets had lost ten of thirteen and he was "fucking pissed."

Lopez summed up the Christmas Day blowout loss and a lot of the Nets' problems well. He said the Nets went away from what was working. What was working was Lopez.

FALLING AXES

The Nets did not give Avery Johnson an opportunity to rebound from falling to .500. After the loss in Milwaukee the day after Christmas, in which Williams suspiciously sat out with a sore wrist, Johnson was fired the next afternoon.* True to his own

---

* I was not briefed by the Nets about Avery Johnson's firing. I had watched the game in Milwaukee on television the night before and found Johnson's postgame mannerisms strange, awkward even by Johnson's overly pronounced standards. The Milwaukee game was the night after a Christmas in which all of my family was out of the area, so I woke up alone the following day—with no customary email or text message confirmation about the move—and turned on the TV to see that a press conference was about to start. Johnson approached the dais wearing

form but awkward given the circumstances, Johnson met with the media after Billy King and fielded questions.

"I don't think it's fair for anybody to hang this on Deron," Johnson said. "He's one player." Whether or not Williams influenced management's decision to can Johnson, his play—something Johnson couldn't control—was the primary reason for Johnson's dismissal.

The Nets were nearly 6 points per 100 possessions better than their opponents with Williams off the floor and 3.4 points worse with him on the court.

It was remarkable that the Nets had been a worse team statistically when their franchise player played. For all the talk about their offensive sets and Williams's career-worst shooting numbers, the defense also suffered when Williams was playing, some of it because of lineup permutations—Williams and Humphries were especially poor together—but a lot of it fell on a lack of effort and execution by the team as a whole.

Johnson's teenage son, Avery Johnson Jr., ripped off a series of unhappy tweets, utilizing the word "outrage" and blaming the Nets' inability to make open shots for his father's ouster. Junior wasn't exactly wrong. Lopez's stretch of missed games because of the ankle injury helped put the Nets in a tailspin, but the three other members of the Nets' Core Four had struggled too. Williams was listless or subpar relative to his own standards; Wallace's shooting made him an offensive liability; and Joe Johnson went through rough stretches with his shot. As much as Avery Johnson wasn't the perfect (or even right) man for the job, the players collectively and individually had to face the reality that their simplest shortcomings had also facilitated his demise.

Johnson said he was caught off guard by the firing and thought

a button-down shirt that I'm pretty sure I own—that or I own its cheaper look-alike. To recap: Wake up alone two days after Christmas. Amble over to television to find out that the second biggest character of this book has been more or less removed from the narrative and said character is wearing something that is—or looks almost exactly like—fabric hanging in the closet a few feet away.

he'd at least have his third season to begin to see change through. He said he was meeting with Billy King that morning to discuss potential trades the Nets could make beginning on January 15, a date when Humphries and Lopez became trade-eligible. Johnson said it was ownership's decision and that King fought for him.

However, admitting that he was meeting with King to discuss two recently re-signed players who would soon became trade-eligible highlighted how Johnson had lost the locker room. Lopez and Humphries were the longest-tenured Nets, dating back to the team's days in the IZOD Center. Humphries had finally earned a large contract, but Johnson, grasping for something that would work when things were going wrong, replaced him with Evans in the starting lineup and decreased his minutes. Johnson was publicly criticizing Humphries's and Lopez's defense as early as the team's sixth game, against Cleveland, when he said that Evans and Blatche were doing a better job. It was a damning criticism and it revealed a double standard. Evans was arguably the least offensively inclined player in all of basketball, but that was a given, which meant no public reprimand. Lopez was the hub of the Nets' offense, but his shortcomings on the other end of the floor were fodder for public critique.

Lopez especially was sensitive to Johnson's criticisms. He was the team's best player throughout most of the regular season, and his emergence highlighted how much better the team would have been had he played more than five games the previous season in Newark. He was an improved defender, an improved shot blocker, and an improved rebounder. He had added post moves that no other seven-footer in the NBA had. Yet from the beginning of training camp, Johnson went public with his desire for Lopez to focus on "attempted rebounds." It wasn't that Johnson didn't praise Lopez when Lopez did something well; it's that Lopez was needled while other veteran players, namely the other three members of the Core Four, were almost impervious to criticism.

Consider it from Lopez's perspective: A recently re-signed All-Star on the rise does all the work, fights through the perception that he's more than just trade bait, and never publicly says anything controversial. Of all the Nets, Lopez was the most likely to feel like he was being talked down to. He was a creative writing major at Stanford. He had studied character and conflict; if he wanted to write comic books or anything else as a side career, which was a consistent rumor among the media, it was his job to be keenly aware of cause and effect, how hurtful words could easily lead Batman, one of his favorite superheroes, to unleash a can of whoop-ass.

Johnson noted how much energy it took to re-sign Williams and called the Nets' 3-10 mark in December up to that point "a bad patch." He also went out of his way to note that he'd been fired on his wife's birthday.

"That's the human side of this," he said.

Mikhail Prokhorov would reveal the next night that he decided to fire Johnson a week earlier, around the time of the embarrassing collapse against the Knicks at the Garden, which was preceded by an embarrassing loss at home to the Jazz.

"I just know when the coach comes in, he's going to have to be able to do it his way," Johnson said. "Hold everybody accountable, coach true to his style. That's the way it's going to have to be."

P. J. Carlesimo sat in front of the New York media, unsure of whether he was just an interim coach or on the road to something greater. It was the fourth NBA head coaching stint for the raspy-voiced guy with the static beard. Carlesimo looks like the college professor you'd appreciate more with age, which makes sense; Carlesimo had coached at Wagner on Staten Island, Fordham in the Bronx, and Seton Hall in northern New Jersey. He recruited all around the metropolitan area. He was familiar with the gyms at Boys & Girls High School and Lincoln. His father, Peter A. Carlesimo, had a distinguished career in sports, which included serving as the athletic director at the University of Scranton and at Fordham, before serving as the executive director of the National Invitation Tournament from 1978 to 1988. Peter A. Carlesimo even appeared on *The Tonight Show Starring Johnny Carson*. He was apparently slated to be on for six minutes and he stayed for twenty-three. He passed the gift of gab on to P. J.

"Your head's spinning a little bit, you're trying to think of all the things that were second nature," P.J. said at the dais during his first pregame interview session. "I'm old but hopefully I haven't forgotten."

The Nets' locker room was surprisingly relaxed. Josh Childress and I engaged in a conversation about our most recent Words With Friends match. Childress was noting the fact that I was junking up the board, making larger plays harder; call it Defense With Friends. For the umpteenth time, the Stanford grad had come back with a word seemingly materialized out of nowhere— perhaps something barely in the English language, as if Childress stored rarely used words in his giant Afro. Childress's greatest NBA-related Words With Friends challenge came from Grant Hill, whose mother roomed with Hillary Clinton in college. Hill didn't stand a chance against Childress.

Childress didn't seem to understand why I was complaining, as I was actually ahead in the game.

"We all know what happens around here when you're winning," I said, a reference to Avery Johnson's dismissal.

"Low blow!" Childress exclaimed.

Two days later, with no really defined role on the team, Childress asked the Nets to release him from his contract.

The Bobcats were riding a sixteen-game losing streak and the Nets were excellent against mediocre opponents, so their next matchup seemed like the perfect time for P. J. Carlesimo to gain favor with his moody players.

It was a strange dynamic, but the first rendition of the Brooklyn Nets was generally the epitome of wolves blanketed by sheepskin. They took on the personalities of their point guards. The Brooklyn Backcourt dynamic between Williams and Johnson played out like the interplay between Marlon Brando and Johnny Depp in the film *Don Juan DeMarco*. One acted cool and coy, clutch under pressure, like the ultimate ladies' man, while the other sat back and listened and watched like a therapist, coming home to a caring wife who implicitly understood the vocation. Williams's wife, Amy, was known throughout the organization and those that covered it for posting pictures of their children on Twitter and updating her followers about exercising in New York City.

The Nets' other point guards played their parts in oozing a generally disinterested vibe. C. J. Watson was probably the only guy who could claim and carry out a vow of silence unless approached, only to turn around and tell Alyonka Larionov, the team's savvy in-house reporter and daughter of an NHL player, about attending space camp and the joys of raising a young daughter. And Tyshawn Taylor, for all of his raw energy, was rarely the story, like sobriety at a bachelor party.

Of course, the reporters played their part too. Nets basketball had long been a crash course in learning the NBA ropes, whether tabloid reporters with personalities seemingly plucked out of a sitcom; four-sport reporters learning a little bit more about the game; assorted Internet-based media judging players by the money they made; or an author learning on the job.

Against the Bobcats, the Nets jumped out to a 19–7 lead behind Lopez, Bogans, and Williams. In a 33–18 first quarter, they turned the ball over once, and when they did miss shots, Lopez was there to tip them in. Williams scored 17 first-half points, including a trio of 3-pointers on 6-for-13 shooting, not exactly the type of play representative of someone whose wrist was under recent scrutiny. MarShon Brooks, liberated from a coach who thought little of his talents, saw rare first-half action.

At halftime, Prokhorov met with the media for the first time since the season's first home stand. He had been on vacation, heli-skiing in British Columbia, relishing the fresh powder. Back in Brooklyn he was in full-on deflection mode, seemingly there for no other reason than to provide in-the-moment support to

Carlesimo. Prokhorov spoke accented English, but the one word he always enunciated clearly was "championship." An infamous bachelor, Prokhorov famously vowed to get married if the Nets didn't win a championship in his first five years as owner.

Standing in front of the white wall off to the side of the Ortsbo media room, surrounded by a bulging semicircle of reporters, Prokhorov pledged his undying loyalty to the idea of a "championship."

His goal? "Just to win a championship, that's all."

He said he would be personally involved in the coaching search. Very?

"Very." The way he said "very" was so seductive, something out of the Most Interesting Man in the World playbook. There was a name, floating in the wind, a man with eleven rings, who was an ideal candidate to helm the Nets: Phil Jackson.

Prokhorov tried to coyly deny even knowing who Jackson was and endorsed Carlesimo for the time being.

In a follow-up about Jackson, Prokhorov gave a confusing response: "I will meet tomorrow with P.J."

Saying P. J. Carlesimo or just Carlesimo could have spared some real head-scratching. Yet Prokhorov seemed to be behind Carlesimo for the time being. Answering a question about expectations, Prokhorov stayed on point. "It's not very high, only championship, that's it. Not more, we're only human beings."

The Nets won easily that night against the Bobcats. Williams spoke of finding his aggression and a change in mentality.

"I thought we just played with more energy, honestly," Lopez said.

Asked about the difference with Carlesimo on the sideline, Lopez gave a classically Lopez answer: "Um, you know, I don't know if I can really pick out the differences, you know. But he was very vocal, you know. He helped us focus, you know. He got us together, you know. And he gave us a few bullet points—you know—on what we wanted to focus on, you know: getting out there, trusting each other, being energetic, you know, and just really trying to play faster."

"That's the best I've seen Brook Lopez pass the ball in two years," Carlesimo said, before turning on his trademark self-deprecation.

"Honestly, I mean, if I had a choice of somebody else getting the job or me," he said, "I'll think about it, but I'll probably pick me."

Asked what he hoped to get out of his meeting with Prokhorov the next day, Carlesimo deadpanned: "I think a lunch, we're going to a restaurant so hopefully a lunch."

Carlesimo, a renowned foodie around the league to the extent that family dinners have been written about in the *New York Times*, described the lunch the next day. "The vegetables were incredible, the sliced zucchini. The food was really good. I couldn't really eat a lot because it's hard to eat before a game and I couldn't drink wine, which really disappointed me."

Carlesimo was able to explain both his situation and the tough situation that Johnson found himself in.

"I think very few coaches in this league have the, I need to think of the word—media help me . . . it's not support . . ."

Power?

"It's kind of power. There's a word that I'm forgetting. I'm sorry . . . I'll think of it."

"You want to phone a friend?" Nets vice president of public relations Gary Sussman asked.

"You had it in college . . . we got to the point in Seton Hall where I had it."

"Carte blanche?"

"No, I'm slow, I'll think of it. But where the players knew I was going to be there regardless of what happened. [Gregg Popovich] has that. Phil had it. There are very few guys in the league that have that. If you don't have that, which very few do, it's infinitely better to have many years on your contract and hopefully at a good number 'cause that does make you a more effective coach, no question."

Carlesimo didn't have a uniquely elite coach's special leverage, but he did have a personality that could win people over—both on the court and in the media room. Early on, he prefaced or concluded some of his rambles by telling us he wasn't "being smart" or "blowing smoke" when the situation called for such a clarification. In doing so, he acted as his conductor for his own train of thought, extremely funny when funny and incredibly boring when some in the room sought printable news and there wasn't much there.

That behavior spoke to a fundamental difference between Carlesimo and the man he replaced. Whereas Avery preached down, P.J. looked up, like the good boy in Sunday school. Johnson received a psychology degree and went as far as to write that he would have been a psychologist had it not been for basketball. Carlesimo was smart enough to marry a sports psychologist, Carolyn, now retired and raising their children in Seattle. Johnson received a media packet every day that he perused; Carlesimo was said to not have read the written coverage. And while Avery came prepared with the injury updates for reporters, P.J. usually professed to knowing little about player injury specifics. "I'll have to ask Timmy," or something along those lines—a reference to longtime Nets trainer Tim Walsh—was a popular refrain less than ninety minutes before tipoff.

The next night, the Nets held off the pesky, undermanned Cleveland Cavaliers down the stretch behind 35 points and 11 rebounds from Lopez—both season highs—and hit the road for what Carlesimo called "The Daily Double."

THE P. J. CARLESIMO WHIRLWIND ALUMNI TOUR

The Nets and San Antonio Spurs will forever be linked in two ways. First, by their shared ABA history, best captured by their sleek, high-flying superstars—Dr. J of the Nets and George "The Iceman" Gervin of the Spurs. And second, by the grind-it-out 2003 NBA Finals, won by the Spurs. That's pretty much where the similarities end. The Jason Kidd era notwithstanding, the Nets in Jersey were NBA bottom feeders while the Spurs have been the most consistently successful NBA franchise of the past twenty years.

Peter Holt, the Spurs' owner, began investing in 1993. Holt's sterling military track record (Purple Heart, Silver Star for a one-year Vietnam tour) and practical business success (growth in expansion of the family business, Caterpillar tractors) are both representative of San Antonio, a small military city, and imprinted all over the Spurs. David Robinson, the player who turned the franchise around, graduated from the Naval Academy with the nickname The Admiral. Avery Johnson eventually became his point guard and thus The Little General. Spurs coach Gregg Popovich has an air force* background and considered joining the CIA. Not surprising, Holt manages the franchise with military precision.† As a point of reference, Mikhail Prokhorov would owe approximately Holt's net worth in luxury tax payments heading into the following season. Not surprising, the quickest way to a head coaching or general manager job has seemingly been through the Spurs' system.

When Carlesimo was in exile after a stint coaching the Golden State Warriors that will always be remembered for Latrell Sprewell choking Carlesimo at practice, it was Popovich who brought him back into the league as an assistant. Carlesimo stayed for five years, from 2002 to 2007, and the Spurs won three championships.

The Spurs have an organizational maxim, Corporate Knowledge, embodying the idea that if a group of people stick together long enough, principles and philosophies become second nature and redundancy is avoided. Additionally, the Spurs spend extensive time researching the personalities of the players they bring in and put a premium on having a good sense of humor and solid self-awareness, traits that portend one's ability to fit in with others.

---

* Popovich graduated with a degree in Soviet studies (he reportedly speaks Russian) and some even think he served as a spy. His air force yearbook entry notes two things of interest: (1) "He came to these nondescript hills from Merriville, Indiana, with his ways and his ball. Ball has continued to capture Popo's time during his visit to the Academy." (2) "His future plans include happiness."

† The Spurs rarely overspend, and Tim Duncan even took less money to keep the Spurs' books in the black after the season. In doing so, Duncan went from being the NBA's third-highest-paid player to the fourth-highest-paid Spur, allowing the Spurs to reload for the 2013-14 season in a fiscally responsible manner.

In San Antonio, a wing defender who understands comedy's rule of three trumps a volume scorer with a fancy crossover dribble.

"With one exception, he usually doesn't hire people that aren't good people," Carlesimo said of Popovich, and jokingly referring to himself as the exception.

Carlesimo stated that the Spurs would sacrifice talent for a "good person," and the statement seemed to damn American youth basketball, as more than half the Spurs' roster was composed of internationals.

Surrounded by a semicircle of fawning reporters at All-Star Weekend, Popovich made a joke about sitting out a few games and letting one of his assistants coach. The joke referenced the controversy he created by resting four of his main players against the Heat in a national TV game in November.

One reporter wasn't quick on the uptake.

"You didn't laugh; you couldn't make the team," Popovich half-joked.

Popovich, or Pop, is widely regarded as the best coaching interview in the NBA for his wry and dry humor. He also boasts a unique ability to prolong discourse by dragging follow-up questions out of media members by staring at them after a classic Pop one-word answer leaves them dumbfounded.

Seeking levity, he noted, "San Antonio, we don't talk much. We pretty much keep it in the locker room, keep it to ourselves. We don't care who you are or anything, we just don't give a shit."

It was the simplest, cookie-cutter questions that always seemed to bring out the don't-give-a-shit in Popovich.

For example: "What has [Spurs guard] Danny Green brought this year?"

"Danny: Shoot ball."

Popovich paused for effect. "If Danny has the ball, he should shoot it." (Green set an NBA Finals record in 2013 with 27 3-pointers by shooting the ball.)

Pop was happy to elaborate on what he felt it took for a team to be successful without taking a dig at his protégé's former players.

"Are they enjoying each other? Can they root for each other? Do they have the character to be happy with teammates' success? Can they support teammates? . . . The more character there is, the more selflessness, the more they have the ability to get over themselves and care more about the group will determine the rate at which something like that comes together. And I don't know those guys well enough to figure that out."

Does a coach need power in that situation?

"A coach can't change people. They are who they are. No matter what team you're talking about, a coach can be observant and try to put his team in situations both on and off the court where some of that can develop, some of the camaraderie sorts of things. But you can't change people. So hopefully the group has those good character qualities where over time they'll come together. I just hope they don't like each other tonight. . . . Then they can fall in love, I don't care. Do whatever they want, I don't care."

The Nets didn't like one another on New Year's Eve when the Spurs obliterated them in one ridiculous third quarter (the worst quarter of the Nets' season), winning the frame by 30–5.

Up 8 coming out of intermission, the Spurs put on a clinic running a play that called for Williams to chase Tony Parker around a Tim Duncan screen, only for Parker to turn around, rerouting Williams around Duncan. Parker had been exploiting the Nets' defense throughout the first half, and the play ended in a short bank shot from Duncan off a feed from Parker.

In a way, the image of the Nets' franchise player chasing after one perennial opposing All-Star while being impeded by another represented the chasm between the two teams. For anyone looking for a message, a simple one was blatantly obvious: teamwork trumps the individual. The sequence singled out Williams, alone on a defensive island, helpless to stop two future Hall of Famers.

On the ensuing possession, Parker, who had any Net that guarded him on skates, drew extra attention and fed Tiago Splitter for a layup. The Nets failed to score again and a beautiful passing triangle among Parker, Splitter, and Duncan led to a Duncan dunk. An 8-point lead became a 14-point lead, and from there, the year was ostensibly over. The Nets ended 2012 on a low note, and Carlesimo suffered his first loss as Nets coach in the home of his greatest NBA successes.

REBIRTH

It was a new year, and Oklahoma City felt like a new world. There was an invocation before the game, which finished in most of the crowd saying "Amen" together. In God's country, the Thunder fans cared deeply, taking the idea of basketball as religion to a more literal level. They stood as the Thunder mascot, a bison, banged on a drum and clapped in rhythm. Participation was mandatory and displayed the unified feeling that Barclays Center had lacked beyond the occasional "BROOOOOK-LYN" chant. Thunder fans chanted "O-K-C" on the first possession and only sat down when the first point was scored on a Kendrick Perkins free throw.

Oklahoma City was also Carlesimo's most recent stop as a head coach. He coached the Seattle SuperSonics in their last season in the Pacific Northwest and lasted only thirteen games into the franchise's transition to Oklahoma. Along with Nick Collison, Kevin Durant, a rookie under Carlesimo, was another Seattle holdover. Durant had grown into the game's second-best player, a scorer with impossibly long limbs. Durant's arms were so long, he looked like he might be able to wrap downtown Oklahoma City in a big hug. But in reality he destroyed his opponents efficiently, methodically, and without emotion, like the NBA's Grim Reaper.

Carlesimo had left, but Thunder general manager Sam Presti, also an alumnus of the San Antonio Spurs and Corporate Knowledge, stuck around and built a championship contender, drafting stars in the making during the rebuilding process and filling out the roster with players who acted as like-minded soldiers.

The Thunder was 16-2 at home, but something—maybe that

clichéd "sense of urgency"—had gotten into the Nets, and they jumped out to a 14–5 lead behind Williams, Johnson, and Lopez. Their main three scorers would account for the Nets' first 27 points. Johnson, fresh from a morning of yoga in a downtown with few distractions compared to New York—or a borough inside New York—was clutch down the stretch and finished with 33 points. Yoga had also left Johnson extra lucid. At the morning shootaround Johnson spoke candidly to *Newsday* of Carlesimo's impact. "If you ain't playing worth a shit, then he's going to tell you, you ain't playing worth a shit."

Led by Johnson, the Nets drew twelve Thunder fouls in the fourth quarter, earning early trips to the free-throw line that killed the Thunder's ability to establish a flow and frustrated Durant into the first ejection of his career. Seeing the cold and calculating Grim Reaper of basketball go after an official in a show of raw emotion was stunning. It took a lot to rattle Durant, who has never fouled out more than once in any season, and on this night the Nets had the rare antidote en route to their season's biggest win.

The Nets went into halftime with a 16-point lead that seemed ripe for collapse, as they hadn't beaten a team with a winning record in more than a month. Indeed, the Thunder clawed their way back into the game, but the Nets never wilted.

Afterward, they were a happy bunch. Williams would tell anyone who was listening that it was a new year. Evans interrupted Joe Johnson's postgame interview session to sing bits and pieces of "Rudolph, the Red-Nosed Reindeer."

Wallace contributed by focusing on guarding Durant hard, so that Johnson could rest on defense and take over on offense, his shot-making and fresh legs helping to spur his teammates. It was throwback logic in the age of advanced metrics, but it worked.

Playing the right way, this was surely a sign of what the Nets could do.

"What do you think?" Wallace asked rhetorically.

Jason Kidd pushes the ball up the court against the Indiana Pacers in game 5 of the first round of the 2002 playoffs. A thrilling overtime victory set the Nets on course to represent the Eastern Conference in the NBA Finals for the first time.

Nets center Brook Lopez addresses the crowd at Newark's Prudential Center before the Nets' final home game in New Jersey. Lopez was the Nets' most consistent player during the team's first season in Brooklyn.

People who helped bring the Nets to Brooklyn (*left to right:* Gerard LaRocca, Bruce Ratner, Marty Markowitz, Jay-Z, Irina Pavlova, and Brett Yormark) attend a press conference in September 2011.

Barclays Center lit up before the Nets' opening night game against the Toronto Raptors.

The first head coach of the Brooklyn Nets, Avery Johnson, calls out a play during a preseason game against the New York Knicks at Nassau Coliseum.

Assistant coach P. J. Carlesimo took over when Johnson was fired two months into the season and compiled a 35-19 record.

Nets general manager Billy King chats with Deron Williams, the central figure in the team's transformation from doormat to winning team, before the Nets hosted the Chicago Bulls in game 1 of the 2013 first-round series.

Joe Johnson composed "Brooklyn's Backcourt" with Williams and redefined late-game excellence during the season, although (seen here) he struggled in an elimination game against the Bulls.

Always interesting off the court, big men Reggie Evans and Andray Blatche exceeded on-court expectations in 2012–13.

Unlike Evans and Blatche, Kris Humphries (right) sometimes found himself out of the rotation. Like NBA player Lamar Odom (left), Humphries was more known at times for his tabloid marriage to a Kardashian sister.

Gerald Wallace and Kevin Garnett during a Christmas Day dust-up at Barclays Center. Wallace, who often struggled in the Nets' first season, was included in a deal that brought Garnett from the Boston Celtics after the season.

Kobe Bryant dunks between Wallace and Humphries, as Williams looks on. The iconic Lakers guard said it was as if the Red Sea parted on the play, so he "felt a little like Moses."

Brooklyn's Backcourt Heats up
Vol. 1: C. J. Watson and Joe Johnson
celebrate Johnson's game-winner
against the Milwaukee Bucks with
a delirious Barclays Center crowd.

Brooklyn's Backcourt Heats up Vol. 2:
Williams celebrates one of his eleven
3-pointers (including an NBA-record
nine in the first half) against the
Washington Wizards in March.

King, owner Mikhail Prokhorov, and Kidd, hired to be the team's coach, welcome new Nets Paul Pierce, Kevin Garnett, and Jason Terry to Brooklyn.

16

The greatest player in the Nets' NBA history, Kidd, is joined by the team's 2013–14 starting lineup of former All-Stars at media day before the second season in Brooklyn: Johnson, Pierce, Garnett, Lopez, Williams.

CYCLE OF THE FOUR SEASONS

Andray Blatche looked giddy at practice on January 7. Joe Johnson's double-overtime game winner in D.C. three days earlier won Blatche's first game against his former team in front of fans who loathed him. The next night he helped the Nets blow out the Kings at Barclays Center. To top it all off, Blatche's contract had become guaranteed on January 7 for the rest of the season. He was crossing that sacred line from unpredictable commodity to protagonist in a tale of redemption.

The Nets boarded the team bus after practice and headed down to Philadelphia for a game against the 76ers. I was on a Bolt Bus headed to Philadelphia to write about the game when the news reports trickled in. A late-night incident had occurred at the Four Seasons in Center City, involving a sexual assault and a member of the Brooklyn Nets. I recall specifically thinking that it would be really bad for stereotyping if Blatche ended up being the Net in question because of his history of negative press. Blatche had even been carjacked in Alexandria, Virginia, shortly before his first training camp with the Wizards. But he quickly revealed himself with a tweet—"I'm ok and I didn't do anything jus was n the area when it happened"—that was quickly deleted.

His statement was backed up by Philadelphia police chief Charles H. Ramsey, who admitted that Blatche was in the area but not involved in the incident. Ramsey also said one of the more damning things in the history of recent sports scandals when he opined to the *New York Times* about the alleged victim: "She was so intoxicated. She is not going to be a very good witness."

Before Blatche was known as the Net in question, Philadelphia TV reporters tried to feast on whatever they could at the Nets' morning shootaround.

"You don't want to talk about what happened last night?" a reporter asked Williams.

"I don't know much of anything that happened last night," Williams said.

"Deron, how did the Philadelphia police treat you?" the same reporter asked.

It took Williams, who obviously wasn't in the room or questioned at the Philadelphia SVU unit, a little while to come up with the appropriate response, but he found it.

"You're a tool."

The media room at the Wells Fargo Center was surreal. Televisions were fixed on different local news channels, all reporting heavily on the Blatche situation. Soon, in a bit of life imitating the early-evening news, non-basketball reporters and those covering the Nets closely converged on Carlesimo in an ugly hallway, leading to the most bipolar pregame presser of the season.

The first question came from YES Network sideline reporter Sarah Kustok about the 76ers' recent struggles. Carlesimo empathetically cited their difficult recent schedule and wondered if the circus coming to the arena forced the tough road trip, not unusual in the NBA world.

There was a pause.

A news reporter jumped in. "Coach, how did the allegations at the Four Seasons affect tonight's game?"

"I'm not going to comment," Carlesimo said. "We issued a statement about that. There are no allegations."

The reporter followed up. "The police are investigating, and the investigation involves one of your players' suites."

"Right, and I'm not going to comment on that."

Kustok asked if Evans was still starting for Humphries. Carlesimo confirmed.

She followed up with a question about the rotation. Carlesimo discussed five big men who needed playing time, and the Sixers' Thaddeus Young being a tough matchup as a small power forward, a situation that might call for Wallace to slide over to guard him and for the Nets to go small.

There was another pause.

"Coach, police tell us that the date rape drug was found inside Blatche's suite. He has pictures of the girl on his cell phone. If you're not even commenting, but to have those—if those facts are true—one of your players has the date rape drug in his suite, that has to bother you as a coach."

"You're right about me not commenting," Carlesimo said. "That's correct."

Carlesimo confirmed that Stackhouse was not available because of personal issues and finally received a Blatche question, from a Nets reporter, that he could answer.

"Anything you can say about Andray at all?" Stefan Bondy of the *Daily News* asked. "Where he's at right now?"

"Andray's going to play," Carlesimo said. "He's been playing well. And I expect him to play well tonight."

The interview session was like dueling banjos, except one of the banjos was actually an elephant trombone. A Blatche controversy putting Carlesimo in the line of fire less than two weeks after he took the job was ironic in that Blatche had toed the line and flourished under Avery Johnson. His last tweet prior to the incident at the Four Seasons—since deleted—was to Avery Johnson's son: "man I wish yal was still here."

As if making a statement, Blatche had been late on the first day Carlesimo took over. With Johnson gone, Blatche's alleged group of rabble-rousing friends suddenly came into focus, and poor choices were easier to make. The very tactics that rubbed some of the Nets the wrong way were Johnson's calling card among his reclamation projects such as Gerald Green, who, under Johnson's tutelage, eventually turned a ten-day contract in 2012 into a three-year, $10 million deal with the Indiana Pacers. This isn't to say that Blatche stayed completely out of the news during Johnson's short-lived time as coach, although if I'm being honest, I feel partially responsible for that.

It was November 26, 2012; pregame at the inaugural Battle of the Boroughs had been sadly uneventful. Despite their cliché-addled interviews leading up to the game, players knew the magnitude of the first incarnation of Knicks-Nets, and most of them deeply cared. Getting close to a bursting throng of reporters probably wasn't the best idea. The visitors' locker room was packed to the point of qualifying as a fire hazard, such was the circus that followed the Knicks.

Back in the Nets' locker room, a place so devoid of intrigue that Bogans's phone ringing qualified as noteworthy, Blatche entered. Blatche saw us, and a look crossed his face that read: Uh-oh, do I talk to them? Playing well, with his reputation on the upswing, he decided it was okay.

Merely seeking to be entertained, I asked Blatche to tell us a story. He looked past tall tales, fables, guy-walks-into-a-bar jokes, and went straight to basketball. He asked me to name the top three teams in the East.

"Miami, New York . . . is it Brooklyn?"

"You know Brooklyn's in there!" he said with excited innocence. "Don't do that." He was jovial and defensive and engaging all at once. We were passing the buck with Blatche, and pregame had suddenly become something more than an abject waste of time.

"Last time I've been top three?" Blatche added. "High school." A few snickers came from a small cluster of reporters.

Then he did it.

"Hey, anybody seen how them Wizards was doing lately?"

He laughed.

"I was wondering how the Wizards was doing; I was just wondering," he repeated as he walked away.

He kept talking. "How they doin'? They win yet?"

The Wizards had not won yet.

Josh Childress, the Nets' other amnesty claim and very much Blatche's diametric opposite in life and basketball, asked if the countdown clock in the locker room was correct, to see if it was time to go to chapel.

"Come on," Blatche said. "Let's go pray for the Wizards."

Like Bugs Bunny listening to Daffy Duck prattle on about minutiae before Daffy inevitably turned his beak around, Childress was stupefied by Blatche's bragging. With good reason. Reporters would tweet Blatche's comments out to the masses, leading Blatche to appear the next day on a show hosted by sports radio jockeys Holden and Danny on 106.7 FM in Washington.

Blatche volunteered to go on the show, and its hosts aired all of his dirty laundry: Wizards fans booing him; his solicitation of a prostitute; Lapdance Tuesdays, an event Blatche hosted at a club; refusing to go back into a game; cutting up Gilbert Arenas's suit during a prank war; and more. Blatche's primary gripe was that nobody in D.C. ever seemed to have his back. He harped on brotherhood, something he had seemingly found in Brooklyn with a coaching mentor in Johnson and somebody, also an amnesty claim, to attend chapel with in Childress. He was neither as guilty as the over-the-top hosts made him out to be—seemingly the entire Wizards' organization was an embarrassment for years—nor as innocent as he would like to have come off. The jarring duality of the interview was the ability of Holden and Danny to thank him profusely for joining them and then to cut him down in the same breath.

In a highly competitive world of shysters and false prima donnas, Blatche just wanted to be liked. And whether it was calling into a sports radio show to deal with people who wanted nothing more than to chew him up and spit him out, or firing off a tweet about an incident in the Four Seasons, voluntarily putting himself at the scene of a crime, he would inadvertently stumble to clear his name. He was like a seven-foot Don Quixote. He had never had the chance to benefit from going to college and was still in many ways a developing adult.

The Nets crushed the 76ers on the strength of a 35–14 third quarter. An "in the zone and stuff like that" Reggie Evans grabbed a then-career-high 23 rebounds. Yet Sixers fans gave Humphries a harsher greeting (for being Kris Humphries) than Blatche (for dominating the local news) or Evans (for dominating the game). Blatche, as if nothing were wrong, scored 20 points off the bench.

He was everything on the court that he was supposed to be, but he wasn't made available to talk.

For all the controversy, Carlesimo gave a resonant speech about Blatche's performance: "Players are very, very resilient. I just think that one of the traits of NBA players are they come at seven or seven thirty and they play, and they really don't bring any other, any outside interference into the game normally. I haven't seen that very much at all. Guys come and they play."

Wearing a navy blue hoodie, Blatche spoke for a little under three minutes two days later, often surveying the rest of the practice facility in the distance, past the group of reporters huddled around him. It was a gloomier place a few days after his precontract extension practice and a different look for a guy who was so often goofy and engaging earlier in the year.

"Right now it's still under a legal matter and I can't really have any comments about it," he said. "I feel like everything will resolve and everyone will know exactly what's going on sooner or later." Blatche was cleared in July 2013 of any wrongdoing.

What wasn't up for debate after Philadelphia, however, was that even though he wasn't Carlesimo's guy, the organization and his new coach still had his back.

The Nets won three straight home games after Blatchegate, running their New Year's win streak to seven before falling in Atlanta on the night of Joe Johnson's homecoming. After the seventh win, Williams happily wore a shirt that read "Running Sucks." The protagonist of the NBA's slowest team and his mates seemed to be settling into a groove under their new coach, and there didn't seem to be much anyone could do about it; the Brooklyn Nets were riding high again.

"You know what I'd like to know?" Williams asked at practice. "How the Philly police are treating me."

CHAPTER 8

Stars—Reluctant and Otherwise

The Nets came back to earth, 4-3, following their seven-game winning streak. That stretch included the Martin Luther King Jr. Day matinee win over the Knicks and a victory the following night in Minnesota, after which C. J. Watson admitted that he flopped to give Minnesota guard J. J. Barea a taste of his own medicine. But a three-game trip against Western Conference teams ended poorly. The Nets were blown out in Memphis and run out of the gym by the NBA's pacesetters in Houston.

The All-Star reserves were announced the night before the games in Memphis. No Net was selected, and Lopez was seen as the biggest snub. The Nets had struggled in the seven games he missed from late November to early December, a stretch that included losses that augured Johnson's dismissal. On TNT, Charles Barkley argued that the Eastern Conference coaches—who voted for the reserves—were standing up for Avery Johnson by not voting in any Nets.

Lopez began aggressively against the Grizzlies, but the Nets were no match for Memphis, also boasting a snubbed center. Marc Gasol was the ultimate team player, the Defensive Player of the Year, an excellent passer and efficient scorer. Gasol got the better of Lopez, hitting 10 of 14 shots in the first half as the Grizzlies built a 30-point lead. Reggie Evans complained about Grizzlies coach Lionel Hollins leaving his regulars in too long after the outcome had been decided.

Houston, home to Avery Johnson and host to the 2013 NBA All-Star Weekend, made for interesting timing the next day. Despite banging knees with the Grizzlies' Darrell Arthur while fighting through a screen, Williams came out gunning against the Rockets. The Rockets started Jeremy Lin opposite Williams at point guard. Lin's ascension to global sensation began against Williams's Nets less than a year before. It was trumpeted that Williams couldn't stand Lin and that Linsanity was born on Williams's watch. Lin did score 25 points and dish out 7 assists in his coming-out party, but the Nets were a bottom-three defensive outfit in the lockout-shortened 2012 season.

While half of his field goals came with Williams guarding him, Lin's signature maneuver left Williams on his back, and the playground-like euphoria that engulfed Madison Square Garden left little doubt as to who would have to answer most of the questions about Lin. It was a strange position to be in for a man once considered a top-two NBA point guard: on his ass, looking up, as an unheralded Ivy Leaguer waltzed by. Williams was used to doing the pointing—on and off the court. Five weeks later, Lin was the most popular athlete in New York according to an ESPN.com poll. For a New York minute, a kid from Harvard brought heart back to the World's Most Famous Arena, dropping 25 as Pearl Jam's "Jeremy" blared in his honor.

The Knicks chose not to match the Rockets' backloaded contract offer, and Williams, now with a more talented crew, had to wait until after playing the Knicks four times in *less than* two months to face Lin. He didn't waste much time, scoring 20 points in the first quarter on 7-for-7 shooting, but he aggravated his leg injury and managed to get ejected for jawing with a referee. He was tossed while arguing something at the free-throw line during the fourth quarter following a call that went in his favor. Williams did not speak to the media after the loss.

The Nets licked their wounds from Memphis and Houston. They returned to Brooklyn and soundly beat the Magic for the fourth time, pushing their record against teams with losing records to 17-0, hoping not to lose against a LeBron James–led team for the seventeenth straight time.

CROWN HEIGHTS

In training camp, Avery Johnson was asked if he was worried about the Nets being subjects of NBA-TV's annual reality show *The Association*. Johnson said he wasn't worried; the Nets had final cut. Pressed on the issue, Johnson said that he would not be interested in participating in a show like HBO's *Hard Knocks*, which gives a relatively honest up-front look at an NFL team's training camp.

One of the narrators for *The Association*, Brooklyn-born actor Michael K. Williams, etched himself into television lore with his portrayal of Omar Little, a shotgun-toting, gay stickup boy in *The Wire*. On the JumboTron at Barclays Center, Williams frequently reveled in one of his famous lines from the show, "Come at the king, you best not miss," before adding "Brooklyn, baby!" for effect.

Before his first visit to Barclays Center and last of three games against the first rendition of the Brooklyn Nets, James walked through the slim hallway leading to the visitors' locker room screaming rap lyrics, or just screaming. It was hard to tell. Reggie Evans had been trash-talking LeBron at shootaround, and when James had learned of Evans's comments, he tweeted, "Just keep throwing rocks at the throne, don't matter 'cause nothing can break my zone."

James had the 2013 NBA superstar alpha male routine down pat: emphatic gestures and booming noise in combination with nonprescription eyeglasses and tightish clothing that made the baggy jeans of the Allen Iverson era seem like forever ago. From his perch, he slammed the Nets for firing Johnson.

"It sucks that Avery had to take the hit for them not wanting to play at a high level."

"I think that LeBron, as much as or more than anybody, is entitled to his opinion," Carlesimo said.

He added: "I'm certainly not going to disagree with LeBron before we play him, but, you know, no one liked the situation and we all felt like we were a part of it."

James, the two-time reigning MVP, shared the evening's spotlight with a literal crown-wearing public figure: Mallory Hagan, recently crowned as Miss America, was the evening's national anthem singer. Nets broadcaster Ian Eagle introduced Hagan. The pair had brief banter. Hagan seemed caught between an obligatory public relations style and an actual desire to showcase more than the stereotypical crown-winning persona.

Hagan moved to Brooklyn from Alabama. Before Miss America, she was Miss Brooklyn. Hagan said she chose Brooklyn because someone close to her family offered her a place to stay and she didn't want to leave. Since moving to Brooklyn, Hagan changed addresses six times in four years. She listed off the neighborhoods in rapid succession. As a transient adopted Brooklynite, Hagan embodied qualities of the Nets, past and present.

"The average New Yorker came from somewhere else . . . and Brooklyn has been really receptive to me," she said.

Hagan spoke fondly of living in Windsor Terrace and Bedford-Stuyvesant (because of its proximity to Clinton Hill). Here was a blond Miss America winner—more than a Barbie Doll but less than a global agent of change—speaking fondly of living in Bed-Stuy. It was a huge coup for the evolving borough.

The Heat's Shane Battier, who was making his first trip to Brooklyn in almost fifteen years, also sensed the changing landscape. Battier lived in the Cobble Hill area while working on Wall Street during summers away from the Duke campus.

"It was sort of before urban revitalization was *en vogue*," he said after the game.

"They've come a long ways, obviously, with the restaurants and the cultural scene that's in Brooklyn now. It's easier to rise from sort of just urban decay to a center of new culture and so the potential was always here."

Fans were treated to the rare highlight bonanza. In taking a 5–2 lead, the Heat ran the fast break as if the Nets weren't on the court. James made a steal and—moving at full speed—casually flipped the ball to Mario Chalmers with his off hand. Chalmers passed it back to James, who rolled a mini–bowling ball to Dwyane Wade for a simple dunk. It was understated poetry in motion.

The frequency of awe-inspiring flair from the Nets in response was surprising. A few possessions later, Joe Johnson sent Chris Bosh flying in the other direction with a crossover dribble and step-back jumper. James scored underneath against two defenders, eluding a double team like a ballerina. James wore a defiant snarl on his way back up the court. Wallace rejected Udonis Haslem at the rim and threw down a ferocious dunk off a baseline drive.

As the Nets mounted a second-quarter comeback, the bench got in on the act. Blatche posterized Chris "Birdman" Andersen with a one-handed dunk. C. J. Watson flung a long pass to Johnson, who, in one motion, caught the ball and moved it on to Blatche, streaking down the middle for another dunk. Watson crossed up Norris Cole and hit a floater. And Williams converted a ridiculous scoop shot high off the backboard. Between Johnson in the first quarter and Watson in the second, the Nets had done a fine job honoring the crossover dribble, the quintessentially New York playground move, often mastered by New York City point guards who went on to play for the Nets in New Jersey, such as Pearl Washington, Kenny Anderson, and Stephon Marbury. Williams had one of the best crossovers in the NBA, but he was under the weather.

For the third straight time, the Heat beat the Nets on the strength of a dominant second half. James had 24 points, 9 rebounds, and 7 assists. Reggie Evans had no rebounds. James noted this.

"You can't just come out and say something like that versus a champion," James said. "No one knows what it takes unless you've done it."

It was an ideal Brooklyn debut for James. He and his mates kept play close for a half, feeding the crowd its Gladiator-worthy "Are You Not Entertained?" moments before seizing control.

Getting to James for quotes—or even into the visitors' locker room—was almost impossible. There was a line in the tiny hallway leading into the entrance that was like that of a nightclub. Eventually, after doing interviews, Wade and Heat big man Udonis Haslem entertained a visitor: Jamie Hector, the actor most well known for his portrayal of Marlo Stanfield, the young drug lord, on *The Wire*.

James and Wade were not gangsters like the characters portrayed by Brooklyn natives Michael K. Williams and Jamie Hector on HBO. Instead the Heat's leaders were trendsetting style mavens in line with the borough that the Nets sold as a stylized brand. On their way out of the arena, James and Wade posed for a picture to run in a *GQ* article about the style of NBA stars.

The Heat followed up their Brooklyn debut with a loss to the Pacers, then reeled off twenty-seven straight wins, the second most in NBA history. You could put a crown on an adopted Brooklynite, call her Miss America, and watch her nail the national anthem. And you could plop a perfectly cast ghetto kingpin into the visitors' locker room. But the NBA was about rare star power. You couldn't just put a crown on a prodigal basketball player and call him LeBron James. He was an original.

The Nets had more pressing concerns. Carlesimo had finally lost as a head coach at Barclays Center after eight straight wins, and the Nets had dropped three of four overall.

"We didn't actually lose those games," Wallace said. "We got our ass kicked in all three of those games."

A PREVIEW AND A DUNK

The Nets bounced back two nights later against the undermanned Chicago Bulls. The Bulls were missing their superstar point guard, Derrick Rose, sidelined with a torn ACL. Rose tested his knee before games in opposing arenas, a bizarre tease for fans. The Nets were in the middle of a seven-day stretch against the Heat, Bulls, and Lakers—all premier franchises—that served as a mid-season reminder that basketball was back in Brooklyn. The games invited hard-core fans from large fan bases into Brooklyn to mix with casual fans who just wanted to see LeBron, Rose, or Kobe. In an atmosphere that contained three different crowds, any play could generate noise, and the decibels didn't always make sense.

The Bulls were without starters Joakim Noah, Carlos Boozer, and Kirk Hinrich, but Coach Tom Thibodeau was known for riding players hard and usually getting maximum effort regardless of who suited up. Thibodeau played four players at least forty minutes, including Nate Robinson, a point guard whose contract had recently been guaranteed for the remainder of the season. Robinson's electric offense came and went like summer lightning and he struggled with his shot in his first game in Brooklyn.

With *Forbes* magazine watching with Mikhail Prokhorov for a cover story, the bench, led by Brooks, Blatche, and Watson, sparked a comeback, tallying 25 of the Nets' 30 fourth-quarter points. Matchups often decided whether Brooks would play. As much as he had in any game since Avery Johnson's dismissal, Brooks looked comfortable in the flow of the offense.

"P.J. called my play a couple of times and thank God things went well for me tonight," Brooks said.

At the time, with both teams sitting on twenty-eight wins, it seemed hard to gauge how the Nets and Bulls stacked up because the Bulls were playing without key contributors and the Nets were banged up.

"They're real physical, no matter who plays," Brooks said. "I don't care who plays; their coach could play. It's going to be physical on the defensive end. They'll make you work for everything."

Kobe Bryant brought the ball back near half-court on the left side. Gerald Wallace was checking him. The game was tied at 80, with less than three minutes to play. Bryant earned a little separation on his way to the middle, Wallace still on his tail, and Williams offered little resistance.

"I was pretty shocked that the lane was so wide open," Bryant said. "I think that everybody's been drinking the Kobe-pass Kool-Aid, so everybody kind of stayed on the perimeter with the shooters."

Bryant said the lane "parted like the Red Sea; so I felt a little like Moses."

He rose. Wallace and Humphries elevated with him—Wallace at first, Humphries a split second later. Like a golf ball passing through a mini-golf windmill, Bryant squeezed through the space with impeccable timing and crushed the dunk home. Humphries and Wallace gave each other what looked like an air high five. The crowd roared. Bryant had been battling pain in his elbow, and he admitted it hurt to dunk so hard.

"After a play like that, you really can't—you can't grab your arm," he said. "It messes up the swag of the moment. So you've got to kind of suck it up for a while."

Lopez responded to Bryant's dunk with a remarkable 3-point play, but the Lakers reeled off 10 straight points to end the game.

Bryant's season ended sadly with a torn Achilles, trying to maneuver around the Warriors' Harrison Barnes, but he was every bit the aging but springy athlete in his Brooklyn debut. He sank fadeaways after making hard fakes, beat his man with razzle-dazzle dribbling, and played eager, aggressive defense. He had the energy in his legs to go up with a second effort in traffic after missing an alley-oop layup and converted a powerful one-handed dunk off a steal. He was still singular and brash on the court, fulfilling the role of both hero and antihero for the masses.

BROOKLYN BOUNCE

As always seems to be the case with the Lakers, there were interesting subplots. Dwight Howard was finally in Brooklyn, wearing a suit, gazing into the crowd. Pau Gasol was hurt late in the game, altering the course of the Lakers' season. Earl Clark stepped up against the Nets, the team he rooted for as a kid, and was the difference-maker.

The Lakers were on a roll, winners of six of seven. Battling food poisoning, I barely had the strength to make it to the game, and the Nets themselves were also feeling sick or not up for the game: Blatche (illness), Stackhouse (stiff neck), Brooks (sprained right ankle), and Watson (sprained left ankle) were all made available by Carlesimo, although he said Brooks was the least likely to play. So the Nets were back to being ordinary around interesting competition. The loss snapped the Nets' streak of seventeen straight wins against teams with losing records (at the time of the game). Fittingly, the streak—consistent fodder for media room conversation—was broken by a team considered a championship contender at the beginning of the season.

POP, INTERRUPTING

Gregg Popovich, the San Antonio Spurs' head coach, was candid about his team's win over the Nets under Carlesimo on New Year's Eve. "We kicked his ass," Popovich said. "We just drilled him. And we loved it . . . I don't know what the hell [Carlesimo's] doing. I didn't know what the hell he was doing when he was with the Spurs, but we sure had a good time together and he was very important to our program."*

When the Nets visited San Antonio over New Year's, Avery Johnson's firing was still too raw for discourse. Six weeks later, Popovich called the move "a little shortsighted or a little bit impa-

---

* With Popovich and Carlesimo both known as foodies, it's easy to imagine the two coaches discussing intricate basketball strategy and extolling the virtues of garlic in the same quick-witted conversation.

tient." His friend had been fired and his other friend had been promoted.

"You make one phone call to one and then you call the next one," he said. "Strange feeling. I love 'em both."

The Spurs withstood a 35-point first quarter from the Nets. They feasted off Nets turnovers and turned the game on its head in the second half.

"This ain't the first time we've unraveled in the third quarter," Wallace said.

Pop interrupted a familiar French reporter before the game.

"You're one of those French guys," the coach and wine connoisseur said, taking on a mockingly pedantic tone. "Tony Parker's great. We. Love. Tony. Parker. Hello France. I hope everybody's good. Have a good year in the vineyard."

Parker shredded the Nets for 29 points and 11 assists. Williams was helpless against him. Both Williams and Parker cut different figures on and off the court. Parker was formerly engaged to TV star and tabloid mainstay Eva Longoria, and was hit by stray glass during a bar fight between the entourages of musicians Chris Brown and Drake. On the court, he was a poised leader of a tried-and-true system. Off the court, Williams had four kids. His family often traveled with him on the road. But Williams was difficult to work with. The disparate perceptions around the two point guards highlighted the reality that few cared about your purported lifestyle integrity if you disappointed on the job.

Parker was so good and the Spurs' continuity so evolved; they hammered the Nets without Tim Duncan or Manu Ginobili. The Nets had lost six of nine. A month later, in an expletive-laden reflection, Williams complained about how hard it was to walk up stairs.

To ease his pain, Williams received platelet-rich plasma (PRP) therapy in both ankles and a cortisone shot. Billy King called the injury synovitis, an inflammation of the joint linings in his ankles. Williams had already undergone two rounds of cortisone shots, including one after the Olympics, and battled pain because of a bone spur in his left ankle.

"It's not like I haven't wanted to be aggressive," Williams said two weeks later. He talked about his ankles wearing down as the game went by.

"I push the ball [in] the first quarter. And in the second quarter a little bit. Third quarter not much. Fourth quarter it's hard to."

The PRP was to speed the healing process. In an age where Kobe Bryant went to Germany for a new-age knee procedure—he might have been the bionic man when he executed his Red Sea–parting dunk in Brooklyn—Williams was just another athlete pushing ahead. Other athletes, such as Jose Reyes, Tiger Woods, and Hines Ward, had undergone PRP.

The procedure entailed taking blood from the body and separating the red blood cells, white blood cells, plasma, and platelets with the aid of a centrifuge. The plasma, chock-full of platelets with bioactive proteins, sped up the recovery process. The process allowed science to reinsert the very best of Williams back into Williams. Over All-Star Weekend, Williams also partook in a juice cleanse, which allowed him to remove the very worst of Williams from Williams. It was time for the point guard—the once prodigal child wrestler—to drop a few weight classes.

THE REPLACEMENTS

The Nets rebounded the next night in Indiana, doing their Jekyll-and-Hyde dance against one of the Eastern Conference's best teams. Watson started for Williams and struggled, so Tyshawn Taylor, a Hoboken native who played high school at fabled St. Anthony's Prep in Jersey City and college at the University of Kansas, pitched in 14 points. Taylor possessed raw speed and kinetic energy that was as unpredictable as it was fun to watch—and rare on the Nets. Joe Johnson forced overtime with a runner in the lane. Lopez scored 25 points. Evans grabbed 22 rebounds. It was an inspiring win.

The Nets kept the good vibes flowing heading into the All-Star break with an impressive performance, hanging a season-high 119 points on the Nuggets at home. The offensive explosion, in which the teams combined for 28-for-44 from behind the arc, honored their shared ABA history. It was the Nets' third straight game against a former ABA team. For the first time since 2005 all four ABA transplants—Spurs, Nets, Pacers, Nuggets—were headed to the playoffs.

Watson and Johnson combined for 51 points and 15 assists. It felt like they were just taking turns spotting up from behind the arc and letting fly, easy and free. For the first time in six years, Johnson wasn't selected to the All-Star Game.

"I want us to be a tough team," Johnson said. "At times, I think we're a little fragile when teams make runs on us, hit us first. We have a tendency to, maybe, not come back so strong, so we have to develop that tough edge, that mental toughness in the second half of the season."

Brook Lopez was named an All-Star replacement before the loss at home to the Heat. The media were chomping at the bit, needing to file early stories on Lopez's selection. With the locker room about to close to the media and Lopez reportedly needing treatment, a Nets PR flak tried to play a purportedly prerecorded sound file. Our recorders were capturing nothing.

The situation was mildly embarrassing for the Nets, but it felt right. Lopez never gave the media anything to chew on. Why would a statement about making his first All-Star team, arguably snubbed, be any different? In big situations, he was a machine of put-on "you knows" and quick exits. Occasionally when he didn't play well, especially on the road, he just left without talking before the locker room opened.

The jarring duality of Lopez was that, while his media persona kept folks at arm's length, he was goofy and engaging off the court. Lopez took playwrighting, screenwriting, and short story classes at Stanford. His final for playwriting culminated in a table read. He labeled his play's genre "humor adventure." He brought former Stanford teammates—including his twin brother, Robin, now of the Trail Blazers and Landry Fields, now of the Raptors—to read.

"There were some dark ones," he said of other classmates' plays. "I just—I don't get some of those . . . I listened, but it was dark for the sake of dark." It made sense, then, why cynical sportswriters weren't up his conversational alley.

Because he was reportedly working on writing a comic book with his brother, people looked at him (by NBA standards) as a writer of sorts. He and Robin then were regarded as the writer and illustrator, respectively. Of trying sportswriting, Brook said: "Hey, it's writing, you never know." Sure it sounded dismissive, but he actually said it.

Lopez's first visit to an All-Star Game interview began with him being scolded for his attire, for wearing a vintage Sonic the Hedgehog T-shirt, and it concluded with a question whether he would ever wear a pink Speedo. The Sonic the Hedgehog snub seemed to unnerve him a little bit.

Lopez generally stuck to the principle of demonstrating knowledge when a topic piqued his interest. It felt like the superheroes he referenced had narrative meaning in his life, whether name-dropping Batman, Captain America, or Hawkeye. He displayed a thorough and categorized knowledge of comics and cartoon culture childlike in its brilliance, the opposite of his futuristic combination of size and shotmaking.

An ESPN reporter with a big microphone, apparently arriving straight from Lopez's Wikipedia page, started asking him same-old, same-old questions tailor-made for what Lopez's personality was supposed to be. With Valentine's Day having just passed, another reporter asked him if he'd seen the film *Love and Basketball*. He had not.

"Am I missing something?"

"Yeah, you're missing love. And basketball."

"Sounds great!" Lopez deadpanned.

He was asked what he would give up for Lent, countless super-hero questions, and whether he considered the Thunder's Russell Westbrook more of a dog or a cat.

"Dog."

"You say that confidently. Why would you say that?"

"I'm a cat person."

He was informed that his friend Ryan Anderson of the Hornets had said Westbrook was more of a cat-dog. After the fact, Lopez riffed that he thought the mixture of a cat and dog was a fox.

Yet in a perfunctory one-minute span that yielded almost nothing, Lopez talked about cartoons, Carly Rae Jepsen, *Cool Runnings, The Mighty Ducks,* Jay-Z, and Kanye West.

With all that madness, Lopez's table still appeared to be the least heavily trafficked in the room. A sweaty throng clung to Carmelo Anthony a few tables down. Tyson Chandler held court with class. Kevin Garnett and Joakim Noah oozed intensity. LeBron was LeBron. Dwyane Wade could smile. Indiana's Paul George could fly high. Even Heat coach Erik Spoelstra drew a bigger crowd.

Lopez did have a few unique experiences to offset the weekend's tedium. He attempted half-court shots with the diminutive legend Muggsy Bogues as part of the Shooting Stars competition and cooked ceviche with Aquiles Chavez, a celebrity chef with a handlebar mustache and dreadlocks. Again, instead of Brook he was trotted out as Lopez. In broken Spanish, Chavez encouraged liberal use of olive oil. I asked Brook if it was his most intimate experience with ceviche because one rarely gets the chance to ask a seven-footer about his most intimate experience with ceviche.

"Yeah, it was," he said. "Didn't know what to expect going in, but it was a lot of fun though."

All-Star Weekend solidified its salacious reputation with a condom giveaway outside Barclays Center days earlier that promoted both safe sex and the upcoming festivities; the name of the condom brand was also the name of the media hospitality hotel in Houston (ICON). There were competing vodkas—large Ciroc cutouts versus a party at the House of Grey Goose—and groupies spilling onto street corners. Michael Jordan celebrated his fiftieth birthday in style.

It wasn't tailored to Lopez. BROOOOOK-LYN'S first All-Star had a "quiet fire," as Kevin Garnett put it. Reporters might have looked at him more like one of the popular kids if he cared to play the media game. Or if he jumped high. Or if he was a Nets hat instead of a seven-foot person. But Brook Lopez was complicated and withdrawn, a dude with a brain, not always keen on sharing it. Maybe for the best.

CHAPTER 9

New Stats, New Energy

There were nights in the Brooklyn Nets' season bereft of narrative pull. In an eighty-two-game season, this is bound to happen. I would find myself at Barclays Center for a game that would play out like so many before it. The Nets would throw the ball into the post to Lopez early in the first quarter. He would do impressive and efficient things. Wallace would either hit his shots and add another dimension to the Nets' offense or throw up bricks and cramp the team's style. The bricks came with alarming frequency; Wallace was the NBA's worst shooter, just under 28 percent (minimum 200 attempts) outside of 16 feet in 2012–13.

Sometimes attention shifted to guys such as Blatche, Bogans, and Evans to provide interesting subplots. When reserves didn't stand out, my eyes wandered over to Joe Johnson. No matter the weather, no matter the background, you can always count on the chameleon for details. Degree of Difficulty Joe kept my mind engaged on cold winter nights. Johnson wasn't about speed or gaining separation; he sank shots in rhythm while a member of the opposition clung to him like hipster garb. It was fun to watch and fun to wait for, although sometimes it never came, hence Decoy Joe,* a nickname bandied about on Twitter and in the media room. But when Johnson was getting into the lane, wind-

* The Nets were 20-3 when Johnson scored 20 or more points. As such, Decoy Joe wasn't all that helpful.

ing his way below the free-throw line, it felt like the Nets were doing something right. The defense was drawn to him, options opened up around him. Still, Game-Winning Joe was redefining clutch, taking headlines, and dominating the highlight reels.

According to the *New York Times*, "In those tense moments of desperation, Johnson is a virtual power station, capable of sending a massive jolt through the atmosphere and thousands of fans into happy delirium with a casual flick of the wrist."

MANO A MANO

In the Nets' return from the All-Star break, Johnson scored 24 points, grabbed 5 rebounds, and handed out 5 assists against the Milwaukee Bucks. He took 18 shots and made 10.

Johnson was mostly guarded by Luc Mbah a Moute, a rugged forward who defended multiple positions and even gave scouting reports to ESPN's basketball blog during the 2011 playoffs. When Johnson turned over his right shoulder and lofted a fadeaway, Mbah a Moute was right there with him. The shot, propelled at a rainbow trajectory, went in anyway.

When Johnson beat the much smaller Monta Ellis to the middle, he did so by backing into Ellis before spinning into space and getting a friendly bounce on a floater. The whistle blew. He was fouled and did a modified version of his giddy-up trot. The trot was normally reserved for major moments. Maybe it was foreshadowing.

A charge on Williams put the Bucks in control, but the Nets got the ball back, down 3 with 6.7 seconds left. On the season, Johnson was setting new precedents for late-game excellence, 6-for-7 with less than thirty seconds remaining. Thoughts ranged from *They have to go to Joe* to *He can't possibly do it again, can he?* Johnson inbounded the ball to Williams and looked to break free. Blatche used a solid screen to impede Mbah a Moute's progress long enough to spring Johnson, and as Mbah a Moute was running at Johnson, Wallace stuck his ass out to slow him down. Johnson caught the ball behind the arc, fading away, Mbah a Moute still flying at him. Johnson landed on one foot, and the shot swished through the net. Barclays Center erupted.

Overtime, game tied at 111. Keith Bogans, who hit the game-tying 3, inbounded the ball. Johnson, with Mbah a Moute all over him, created a small amount of space with a slow, through-the-legs crossover dribble. The move was clunky and looked like something out of a dribbling obstacle course. Johnson maintained control, faded with barely any separation, and lofted the shot. The ball hit the net. Delirium.

"I totally read the man who's guarding me, how he's playing me," Johnson said.

Johnson called the late-game isolation situations, "mano a mano, man against man and there's no help." But Johnson came out on top. In the freeze frame immediately after the shot is released, it looks like Johnson and Mbah a Moute are holding hands.

It might have been the most fun evening of any in the Nets' first season, in-arena bedlam mirrored by the rare raw emotion Johnson expressed in incredible moments. The win snapped a thirteen-game losing streak against the Bucks. Johnson struggled the next night in Milwaukee, but the Nets, sparked by excellent bench play, won again anyway.

Johnson shot 3-for-14 in the second half of the back-to-back, and was suddenly suffering from plantar fasciitis, a painful inflammation on the sole of the foot.

Back at home, Watson started for Johnson against the Rockets. The helter-skelter Rockets coalesced around ball-dominating superstar shooting guard James Harden in a fast-tempo offense, based on freelancing, spacing, and with high-value shots. The Rockets' torrid pace was such that Carlesimo compared the Nets' ability to avoid getting blown out for most of a game in Houston a month earlier to the story of the little boy in Holland putting his finger in the dike.

On paper, much of the Rockets' roster looked like a spread from a college alumni magazine promoting diversity: the Asian American Ivy League point guard (Lin); the superstar shooting guard with a famous beard (Harden); the second-round draft pick looking like he came straight from a J.Crew catalog (Chandler Parsons); the tricky Argentine with a buttery jump shot (Carlos Delfino); and a big man from Turkey who did everything reasonably well except shoot free throws (Omer Asik).

The trading deadline had just passed and the Rockets had made another deal. With old players already out the door and new ones waiting to get cleared by doctors, the Rockets pushed the tempo and beat the Nets without a traditional power forward. Billy King met with reporters before the game to talk about the Joe Johnson injury and standing pat at the trading deadline. It might have been hard to find two more different general managers than King and the Rockets' Daryl Morey. King was entrenched in the basketball establishment, a part of a network of former college and pro players familiar with old-school politics and faded on-court glory. Morey started a highly popular stats conference and advocated the death of the box score.

CARD COUNTERS AND BUZZ FEEDERS

February had turned to March. The Dallas Mavericks were in Brooklyn. Mark Cuban was in Boston speaking on a panel called Revenge of the Nerds, with Daryl Morey. This entailed Cuban telling MIT students and business executives about the importance of job preservation to the NBA general manager; how making a splash and avoiding mediocrity trumped rebuilding and winning it all.

At the MIT Sloan Sports Analytics Conference—SSAC, or Sloan for short—the voice of *Sport Science*'s John Brenkus echoed through the halls of a convention center overlooking the Boston seaport. You may know Brenkus as the guy who has appeared on the ABC/ESPN halftime show to give a full scientific demonstration of LeBron's dunk-related torque, as if LeBron were a car driven by Vin Diesel. SSAC is where, with a $295 basketball that measures 360 degrees of force and an app, you can learn how to split two defenders with a 5G dribble. Hopefully, it's the only convention where the schwag is a thermos.

Founded by Morey in 2006, the annual conference in Boston has basically doubled in size every year since its inception and it has had a hand in slowly but surely pushing moneyball into the basketball sphere. Attendees range from the most powerful front-office types to high school kids trying to get ahead. SSAC is about data evolution in sports. It brings together sports agents, media, team employees, and business school students.

There are thesis paper presentations, after which viewers form a line to ask questions, usually lauding the work first—subtext: "We are all smart here, good job"—before probing hard into the nitty-gritty of the data and what it represents. There are high-profile sport-specific panels too. The Basketball Analytics panel—featuring high-level team executives Mike Zarren, Kevin Pritchard, and R. C. Buford as well as former Magic and Heat coach Stan Van Gundy and Zach Lowe of the ESPN website Grantland—entertained a packed auditorium of people with influence. The Nets were used as an example.

Lowe recounted a November Celtics-Nets game in Brooklyn when Avery Johnson, with the Nets up 4 with twenty-three seconds left, intentionally fouled Paul Pierce.

"All of us were like, 'What is Avery Johnson doing here?'" Lowe said. "What's going on here? You're giving the Celtics two points."

Zarren, the assistant general manager of the Celtics, interjected. "Well . . ."

Lowe self-corrected. "One point five points."

Laughter sprinkled through the crowd. It was one of those dorky moments when everybody realized that on average two free throws yield approximately 1.5 points. Lowe recounted

Johnson noting that Pierce had hit a pull-up 3-pointer earlier and that the Nets didn't want to get burned again like that.

"There might be some mathematical explanation justifying what Avery Johnson did," Lowe said. "That is not it."

More laughter. Avery Johnson had what he called his "Avery's Stats," but most of the kids from MIT, the Kellogg School of Business, and *Bleacher Report* didn't seem to know that.

Pritchard, the general manager of the Pacers, presented an executive's viewpoint.

"As a general manager, the thing is, I just don't want to be surprised about those kind of things," he said. "And there's a big reason because in two minutes after the game, the owner's going to ask me."

Van Gundy made sure the panel didn't get too consumed in *Revenge of the Nerds* stylings. He explained the other side of not rushing shots in two-for-one situations at the end of quarters, arguing for the emotional aspect of the game and the interconnectedness of plays and sequences, all undermined by players "jacking up horseshit shots" in the name of math and messing with the culture that the coach worked so hard to build.

"You're not gonna sit in that locker room and have a forty-five-minute session of analytics and numbers," Van Gundy said. "What we need to figure out is what we need to do to win this game. And we'll come to that by numbers, by filmwork, by everything else. And then we communicate that to the players."

A NETS STAT

When the Nets gave Public Relations manager Calder Hynes the keys to the PR department's Twitter account, fans and reporters were treated to a level of enjoyable snark that defined the team's Jersey days, when mounting losses (financial, on-court) could only be countered with humor. The Nets were personable in Jersey, a mom-and-pop shop for fans. Surrounded by rows of empty seats, reporters could learn the ropes of the NBA under less pressure.

Hynes had taken to ribbing reporters from @Nets_PR and posting silly jokes, especially after wins. Heading into All-Star Weekend, the Nets were "undefeated after Brook Lopez gets a haircut." When the Nets started 2013 on a seven-game winning streak, Hynes reminded reporters daily of the team's success with the consistency of a verbal alarm clock. When Joe Johnson worked his game-tying and game-winning magic on February 19, Hynes stepped up his game to match; "#Nets now 32-0 when out-scoring opponent this season," the tweet read. The message went viral and global. "God Bless the Brooklyn Nets' PR Staff" was the headline on Deadspin. Most people got it. Some didn't. The new business-oriented Nets were sensitive to the spotlight, to new-age criticism. And so, Quirky Hynes was replaced by Business Hynes after thirty-two wins and a single magical tweet. It didn't change the fact that, once upon a time, the Nets were 32-0 when leading after four quarters.*

"You can look at numbers and make numbers say whatever they want," Carlesimo said less than two weeks before the Sloan Conference. "I don't know what the stats were—we have more wins than I think this franchise has had in a bunch of years at the All-Star break. We're playing in a new building with new teammates. We were—I don't know how many games we won last year for the whole year."

"Not many," Gary Sussman said.

From the Nets' vantage point, you couldn't blame Carlesimo for making the case.

"When we were still in Jersey, I went on the West Coast trip with them when I think we lost four of four games and it's tough," Irina Pavlova said. "It's like, you can't say, 'We'll get them next time' when you're pretty sure we won't. I loved the feeling; this year, like, every game I felt like we could win. We always had a chance."

For all that is made of the NBA's statistical advancement—

---

* Hynes was so magical that the Lakers hired him after the season.

some of it justified—the game is still a soulful dance; ten men moving in some variation of harmony. The ball still moves and bounces in unpredictable ways. Every possession can be endlessly scrutinized, and there are almost two hundred possessions a game. Players can change rapidly from game to game, week to week, month to month; the micromanaging of advanced stats can border on a reality akin to a dog chasing its tail.

"And like I'm saying, 'What am I missing?'" Carlesimo asked. "You know, I think from the outside world people would say things are okay in Brooklyn and Deron has a lot to do with that. Deron's basically been the single most important factor in transforming the franchise, so like, what?"

He understood—the franchise player had disappointed on the court—but the Nets were having a solid season. Carlesimo was deep into another speech about Williams. He paused. Then sighed.

"He's a pretty good player."

Here were three simple stats about Williams that mattered: three cortisone injections, one juice cleanse, and a round of platelet-rich plasma therapy.

YOU DOWN WITH PRP?

On Twitter and in person, Tony Allen fascinated. The defensive specialist and his Grizzlies teammates had just defeated the Nets. Allen and his mates stopped Williams down the stretch. I asked Allen if Williams's injury recovery and issues were noticeable.

"I don't know his injury history, tell me about it," Allen said. "What's wrong?"

I told Allen about Williams's platelet-rich plasma therapy and cortisone shots.

"I didn't know that. You just told me that. He had twenty-four points."

Indeed, he played well. Without Joe Johnson, Williams scored a third of his team's points against a stout defense and shot the ball efficiently. Still, I tried to follow up and see if Allen could tell that Williams was playing through pain.

"I mean, he had twenty-four points. Ain't no excuse."

"My game is up and down," Williams said in the home locker room.

The Nets went 29-22 before Williams underwent his platelet-rich plasma therapy and 20-11 after, 17-11 in games in which Williams played. On a singular level, Williams was one of the best players in the NBA after the All-Star break, probably top five. He averaged a shade under 23 points per game to go with 8 assists. He shot more than 48 percent from the field and 42 percent from behind the arc. He pushed the pace more and more as the playoffs neared and the Nets blew teams out. His turnover ratio fell in March and then April. The collective performance had the Nets looking like an offensive juggernaut. After back-to-back losses to the Mavs and Bulls to open up the month of March, Williams and the Nets dominantly won three in a row.

In front of legendary point guards Nate "Tiny "Archibald and Eric "Sleepy" Floyd in Charlotte, the Nets opened the second half on a 16–3 run against the overmatched Bobcats. Williams knocked down a few big 3s from the left wing, holding his form for a moment, looking like he was in a zone. Williams returned home and set an NBA record against the Wizards with nine 3-pointers in the first half. He was like a kid all alone in a driveway, launching 3 after 3, and the makes came in quick rhythm, like waves spraying a shoreline. Williams broke the Nets' season high for 3-pointers in the game's first 4:42 with 6 and staked the Nets to leads of 16–0 and 22–2.

"It happened so fast," he said.

Williams shot 11-for-16 from distance; the rest of the Nets were 1-for-11. He admitted his sixth make was a heat check.

"I think I should have shot another one after that, too. Joe told me I should have when I came to the bench."

Evans said Williams was "hot like fish grease" and compared the performance to watching Ray Allen when Evans and Allen were teammates on the Sonics. Williams's eleven 3-pointers were a Nets franchise record and a career high. Williams was aware of the crowd's growing buzz. He was a single 3-pointer shy of tying an NBA record held by Donyell Marshall and Kobe Bryant. Bogans decided against giving Williams a final crack at the twelfth 3 during garbage time. When Bogans shot it instead, fans got mad.

"He didn't want it," Bogans said. "He was tired. He wanted to get ready for tomorrow, so I was trying to screen for him myself and he was like, 'Nah, never mind.'"

The next night, in Atlanta, Williams cooled off, scoring 17 points, but the Nets still turned in a total team performance. The bench made a big difference. A night after inciting the ire of Brooklyn fans, Bogans made a couple of big 3s of his own and Joe Johnson had his revenge in Atlanta after the Hawks trapped and confused him in his return to Phillips Center in January.

Over about two months Williams dropped fifteen to twenty pounds and looked like a different person. Literally, there was more space when he moved past in the locker room. Among a group of guys with impressive physiques, Williams stood out early in the year as an out-of-shape anomaly. Wallace was cut like an Adonis. Johnson, Evans, and Bogans didn't seem to know what body fat was. Brooks and Taylor were sinewy, Shengelia and Teletovic in great shape. Lopez had transformed his body during a year spent mostly away from NBA action, and Stackhouse was keeping ready. Finally, Williams looked like the leader of this troupe, and he played like it, a weapon that the guy coaching him earlier in the year didn't have at his disposal.

RECYCLING OF THE SEASON

On one of those days that remind you that spring is just around the corner, students filtered through Huntsman Hall at Penn's Wharton School of Business. In a classroom adjacent to a two-story wood-furnished gathering area, undergraduates had come to hear Avery Johnson speak about the "business of basketball," which sounded like a misplaced panel from the Sloan Conference nine days earlier.

Johnson was at Penn to visit his daughter. He had brand credibility, and chatty students seemed excited by the prospect of his arrival. In town to see the Nets play the Sixers, I rerouted my trip to University City and loitered with a friend, a Penn law student and occasional moonlighting sportswriter. We were chatting when Tim Bontemps, the *New York Post*'s Nets beat writer, showed up.

Johnson eventually arrived and exchanged pleasantries and handshakes with Tim and me. I made an awkward crack about how talking to Johnson would trump any story that could come out of that evening's game. He immediately made it clear he wasn't interested in having any sort of revelatory conversation about his time with the Nets, but fully engaged in updates about his life, mostly his ability to be a bigger part of his son's life with more free time. He seemed refreshed, more at ease, relatively at peace. He said he had watched four Nets games since being fired and spoke of an affinity for the coaching staff—Popeye Jones, Mario Elie, Patrick Spurgin, Doug Overton—that he put together.

Shooting the breeze with Avery Johnson in a hallway at the Wharton School of Business was more natural than one of his pregame pressers. In parting, Johnson noted with a laugh that he had to go to work. A man made almost entirely out of an indomitable spirit saying that in academia, the land of gifted adolescents and legacy WASPs, strangely, sounded right.

We each gave Avery a business card in hopes that he would call, but that was a shot in the dark—especially for me. As a beat writer, Tim was at or near the top of the Avery Johnson Recognition Pyramid, no doubt influenced by the Nets' PR staff, who specialized, as much as or more than most teams, in putting the beat reporters on a collective pedestal, at times arranging practice times to meet their needs and giving them talking-head time on *The Association*.

I found myself in the middle tier, between the beat and the faceless masses; he definitely knew me, but he did not speak my name.

Johnson often utilized the analogy of a classroom to explain how he operated as a coach, and such a comparison could easily be applied to the media as well. Part of me didn't blame him. The Nets' PR department told Billy King about my book around the time of training camp but neglected to tell Johnson, leading to me awkwardly telling Johnson myself during a preseason practice. As the season wore on, I would periodically wonder if that gesture said everything about what Johnson's final season would inevitably be.

It seemed like the Nets had already won before they even stepped onto the court. Fans had made the journey down I-95 south, were happy to be repping a winning team, and a "BROOOOOK-LYN!" chant sounded off in the Wells Fargo Center. Blatche picked up where he left off on the court, scoring with ease and occasionally turning the ball over, the incident at the Four Seasons a distant memory.

The Nets were riding a three-game winning streak against a team that had lost twelve of thirteen. Williams was shooting more than 50 percent from behind the arc since the All-Star break. On this night in Philadelphia, the Nets were a band that chose to play a series of incredible solos instead of a full concert. Brook Lopez sank absurdly difficult fadeaways. Degree of Difficulty Joe got in the act. For Deron Williams—reinvigorated, reinvented Deron Williams—it was all about rhythm. His ability to subtly change speeds in transition kept him momentarily in control of the proceedings, his defender unsure and off balance. His spin moves were fluid and the pitter-patter of his feet leading up to a catch-and-shoot release—perfect. He split the defense and banked in an absurd shot with his left hand—his off hand—while falling down. He was calm, almost hypnotically in control.

Williams brought the Nets back during a virtuoso third-quarter performance. Once injured and unsure of himself, he sought out contact, charging full steam ahead into Sixers big man Spencer Hawes. When Williams scooted by his man, he took one step into the foul lane and flipped in a scoop shot—a shot that was delicate like fabric softener and looked like something out of a relaxed game of H.O.R.S.E. Wells Fargo Center was his personal playground, and the Philadelphia police (wherever they were) were treating him like a superstar.

Williams hit 10,000 points for his career in the fourth quarter. His counterpart, Jrue Holiday, went twenty-two minutes without a field goal. Yet the Sixers won going away. Williams was in the zone, but the Nets weren't working together—especially on the defensive end. Gerald Wallace missed three shots and registered a personal foul in the third quarter. He didn't play in the fourth and declined to speak to the media after the game; in the shadow of a franchise player's reemergence, the voice of the team had gone silent. Who to play and when to play them—those were never easy decisions for Carlesimo.

THE BULLPEN

Mirza Teletovic, a Bosnian national and Nets power forward, was unfailingly polite and gracious, a multilingual man with sharp features and appreciative of his life's blessings. He grew up in a very small town in Bosnia and lived a much more low-profile life in the States. He appreciated space and the outdoors. Driving into games in the big city, only to have an undefined role, it wasn't hard to tell that he wasn't always having fun.

There was a philosophical conundrum that haunted the Nets' inaugural Brooklyn season. They could hinder the offense at the expense of greater rebounding proficiency and play Humphries and Evans over Teletovic. Or Teletovic and Blatche could play more, giving up easier looks on defense but making life easier for Johnson, Lopez, and Williams on offense. Evans made his case for playing time by snatching rebounds at a historic rate. Blatche was held at arm's length at times, while Humphries and Teletovic were consistently inconsistent. (Dealing with these two players showcased two different sides of player/reporter inconsistency. In tone and occasionally body language, Humphries was direct when it came to giving interesting answers to people he trusted. In responding to others, not so much. Yet the size of the circle around him only seemed to depend on how well he played, and everyone who was there had use of his quotes. Teletovic was friendly, but rarely sought after by English-speaking reporters. Occasionally, Teletovic and I would riff about Spanish soccer—I saw Teletovic play basketball in Madrid during the lockout—and we'd chat about the two main teams in the Spanish capital.)

There was pressure on Carlesimo from the Nets' management to play Teletovic, but the coach still wasn't able to take full control of the situation. He was the same guy who walked up and down the aisle of the team plane offering players snacks when he was an assistant coach, the same guy who didn't change his habit of strolling through the locker room during media availability when he became the head coach. Apparently it was funny when he was cursing during practice because it was hard to tell if he was serious.

"We got squeezed by Mirza," Carlesimo said in late February. "He played well."

Carlesimo was the consummate substitute teacher in Brooklyn; everything was easy and free until he didn't have time for you.

"The guys off the bench should be very unsettled because of the way we've subbed," he said.

Whereas players such as Teletovic, Humphries, and MarShon Brooks had to adapt to a bullpen psychology, Carlesimo was suddenly yanking Brook Lopez out of the game after three quarters. It happened in three of four games in Lopez's return from All-Star Weekend. It was like Lopez was a starting pitcher and Carlesimo was his manager. Blatche was playing well, but part of it was Carlesimo's inability to truly trust a Lopez-Blatche partnership at the expense of the Evans-Humphries-Teletovic power forward trio.

After a loss to the Rockets, Billy King escorted Lopez out of the locker room to avoid media questioning.

"This situation, I created this situation," Carlesimo said. "And it's not a good situation, so yes. I worry about it that I need to address it and I worry about it that I need to watch what I do going forward."

He added, "But it's—I've gone too far with this. I've abused it, where I shouldn't have done it as much as I have with Brook."

Carlesimo probably couldn't have benched Lopez the next day anyway. Brook was going up against his twin brother, Robin.

Brook got the better of Robin in both encounters. Robin didn't have his brother's offensive skill set. In the second matchup at Barclays Center, Brook sank a ridiculous step-back baseline fadeaway over his brother to start the game and delighted the crowd by crushing a single-handed dunk over his brother. When Brook got his brother with a rip-through move, Robin flailed his arms in disgust and argued against the call. Off the court, Robin, a better defender, exuded similar friendliness while wearing a meaner demeanor. The writer/illustrator brothers always said they didn't talk about basketball.

"I guess it just isn't in our nature," Robin said.

PRELUDE TO A ROAD TRIP

After four days off, the Nets hosted the Hawks on a Sunday night in mid-March. Deron Williams, appreciative of your concern for his health, was wearing shoes the colors of highlighters (for a half), Joe Johnson was reacting to the tendencies of his former teammates, Gerald Wallace couldn't find the range, and the crowd was mostly clad in green for St. Patrick's Day. The Nets were part of a jumbled mess in a mediocre Eastern Conference.

Wallace was getting older, and his inability to convert near the rim had grown more apparent. When he attacked the basket, one might as well have dropped a ball in a roulette wheel.

Wallace wanted to be an FBI agent and watched shows such as *Law & Order* religiously. With *Law & Order*'s Mariska Hargitay and actor Ethan Hawke of *Training Day* fame courtside, Wallace shot 1-for-8, but the crowd still appreciated his hustle. The Hawks came back, and Hawke would later tell *Late Night* host Jimmy Fallon, a Nets fan, about wanting to exchange his new Nets fandom back for the Knicks, but how the Knicks suddenly didn't want to give him tickets.

The Nets lost in dispiriting fashion, blown out in the fourth quarter. In one strange small sample size anomaly, the Nets played the Hawks even with Wallace on the floor. The other four guys, even Reggie Evans, scored in double figures, but finished negative in the plus-minus column. I pressed Wallace on what he needed to do to raise his game.

"I don't know, make a shot, probably; a layup or something, any fuckin' thing," he said. "It's just—fuck. Throw trash in the trash can. Anything."

"They came like they wanted the game," he said. "We came like we were already on the road."

In minutes, they were.

CHAPTER 10

No Sleep 'Til Brooklyn

The Nets hit the road for a franchise-record-tying 8 straight road games: 8 cities, 17 days, 44 bus rides, 10 flights, 4 time zones, and 8,299 miles according to the team's broadcast crew.

There was cold, biting air in Detroit and Cleveland and sunshine everywhere else. There were practices in Pac-12 gyms on the campuses of UCLA and Arizona State; drinks in Dallas; flirty girls in Denver Laundromats and Cleveland hotels. Instead of the Bed-Stuy Grill on the concourse at Barclays Center, there was Mongolian Barbecue in downtown Denver and Jake's Crawfish in downtown Portland. Instead of taking the subway to the game, there were leisurely strolls through Dallas and Salt Lake City. Instead of poor third quarters from the Nets—okay, there were poor third quarters from the Nets.

Apparently most of the NCAA tournament happened during the time away, but it was hard to notice. This is how it played out.

"OLD-SCHOOL MUSIC"

Less than twenty-four hours after losing to the Hawks in front of Ethan Hawke, the Nets faced a struggling Pistons squad. Inside a suburban Michigan arena that calls to mind a cavernous B. J.'s Wholesale, the Nets resembled vultures. An exasperated Pistons fan shouted to Williams as he spoke to a referee, "Deron, you're up thirty-two! Don't think you need to worry about it, buddy!"

Carlesimo called his team "day to day" and it was never entirely clear how much of that was about what the Nets were doing or what the schedule was putting in front of them. The eight-game road schedule included five sub-.500 teams, and five wins would probably yield a successful trip.

Williams, Johnson, and Lopez* scored 25 of the Nets' first 27 points and then the bench took over. With Bogans out, Stackhouse returned. He hadn't played since January 26 and turned in an efficient performance on the court he called home when he led the NBA in scoring. He blocked shots, drained his midrange jumper, and corralled a full-court pass before finishing a circus layup. MarShon Brooks came out connecting as well, hitting his first three shots—including a four-point play in front of the Nets' bench—and made a vicious block on Kyle Singler.

The Nets were up so big that when R&B songstresses En Vogue took the stage for a halftime concert, the concert became the rarest thing about the evening. Stackhouse ran out near the court to take a peek and other Nets were also aware of the group that belted out such early '90s hits as "Don't Let Go" and "Free Your Mind." Joe Johnson called En Vogue "old-school music," which was very VH-1 *Behind the Music* of him.

"Man, I was a young buck!" he said. "My mom and my uncles was jamming to that. I was probably riding in the backseat, just jamming or something."

The game seemed to provide something for every Net. Teletovic airballed three shots in quick succession in the Nets' previous trip to the Palace of Auburn Hills, but he delighted a corner of fans

---

* Then Pistons coach Lawrence Frank used the Kevin Durant rule in arguing against Lopez's "rip through" move, in which Lopez would begin a shot attempt by initiating contact with his defender. According to *The Oklahoman* in December 2011, "Shooting fouls will now be called only if contact occurs after the player has begun his shooting motion and not after he has initiated his leap." Lopez rarely elevated noticeably on faceup post moves and his rip-through move often drew the ire of opposing players and coaches, because of how inorganic the motion seemed.

waving Bosnian flags by contributing. In many arenas, those with Bosnian ties showed up to cheer Teletovic, a hero in his homeland who revealed after the game that in the past he has been greeted by a thousand people in an airport back at home. There was a chasm in perception between Mirza the Jump-Shooting Import Whose Name Fans Couldn't Pronounce (Brooklyn) and Mirza Teletovic Bosnian National Treasure Who Could Do More Than Just Shoot if You Watched Film on Him (Europe).

Blatche scored 15 points and grabbed 8 rebounds in another positive performance. In the visitors' locker room in Auburn Hills, Blatche joked about trading his teammates in the NBA 2K13 video game.

When it was suggested after the game that Blatche might not want to trade his virtual reality renditions of his Nets teammates, he wasn't having it.

"Hell yeah, I still trade," he said half jokingly. "They've got to go."

Yeah?

"Yeah, that's my team. I'm the franchise player."

Late in the first quarter, Blatche tracked down a rebound when Williams, continuing to look healthier and healthier with every passing day, smashed the ball off the back of the rim in his most aggressive—and nearly successful—dunk attempt of the season. Fittingly, the ball returned to Williams's hands and he hit a 3-pointer to end the possession, a small time capsule of exactly how well the road trip began.

Moving to Dallas, the story line shifted to Williams's choosing the Nets over the Mavericks in free agency.

"Usually, I get cheers," he said on his way out the door, of returning to play in his hometown.

"Now I'll probably get booed. I don't know why. I didn't leave."

Williams was good at presenting arguments on technicalities, politicking, ignoring the intent of poorly worded questions.

He paused. "I never said I was going to go there."

HOMELAND

The home locker room at the American Airlines Arena in Dallas features a ceiling window pane design in the shape of a basketball. The room was distractingly plush, and players milled about comfortably. The locker room opened to a fully functional gym with brick columns. It looked like a private Crunch Fitness gym in a trendy New York neighborhood. It's easy to see why so many Nets fans were scared shitless that they would lose Deron Williams to the resplendent amenities and world-class everything of the team he rooted for before turning pro.

Past the locker room, inside this sprawling gym, Mavericks owner Mark Cuban talks to the press before games—while climbing a StairMaster. It's strange enough to interview an outspoken billionaire, but interviewing Cuban while he climbed a StairMaster—literally feet above you—bordered on surreal.

You stand on one side of the machine, its whirring rising up and bleeding into your tape recorder, and thrust your arm as close to Cuban as you can. As the stairs continue to rotate through one continuous loop, as he continues to push himself—because that's one of the seven habits of highly effective billionaires, you lazy, fucking sportswriter—he slowly begins to perspire. His hands are red from gripping the sides of the apparatus, elbows about seven and a half feet high in the air, ready to smash an imaginary Shawn Bradley across the face.

Soon he's sweating more and you realize you're in the line of fire. He's got a towel at the ready, but who's to say if he'll spare you by using it; he's Mark Cuban, he chose filming an episode of *Shark Tank* over showing up to his free-agency meeting with Deron Williams. He missed the Mavericks' game in Brooklyn two weeks earlier to attend the Sloan Conference in Boston. Cuban wasn't interested in speaking directly about Williams—calling what had happened "old, old, old news"—but he wasn't tired of talking about how to build a championship team. He was the zany philosophy professor, tired of a specific question but not of evolving philosophy.

"There's all kinds of limitations . . . it's going to be tough to improve," he said of the NBA world post-2011 lockout. "And that's what's guided our approach."

"If you just have seventy-five million dollars in payroll, you're stuck," Cuban added. "And I didn't want to be stuck."

The Nets' payroll for 2012–13 was well over $75 million.

"Let's just see who's holding the rings and who's not," he said on his StairMaster.

"That's it. Period. End of story."

Still, he conceded, "It's just about the approach of the organization. Every team is different."

With the Nets on the brink of their first playoff appearance in six years but not exactly looking like contenders, Cuban's words carried some weight.

The Nets played the Mavs on the tenth anniversary of the Iraq invasion, also a night when LeBron James returned to Cleveland again, leading the Heat to a ridiculous comeback win, a highlight of their twenty-seven-game winning streak. Like James, Williams would bask in the reality of being back at home, playing in front of friends and family.

Initially, as it often was, Lopez felt at home early. Lopez scored 38 points in Dallas in one of only five games he played in during the 2012 season, and poured in 15 first-quarter points on his way to doing the same thing a second time around.

"Our team played well in both games," he said. "I think that's the correlation."

Lopez's offensive game was at maximum efficiency; he reeled in some very difficult passes as if there were stickum on his hands and rumbled to the rim with confidence and agility. Aided by the reality that no Maverick big man could contain him, he was aggressive, scoring the Nets' first 8 points, all of them off of work inside.

Lopez didn't have much help scoring in the first quarter, and the Mavs built a 10-point lead, but led by Blatche and Bogans, the Nets erased the deficit in a four-minute stretch that set the tone for the trip. Blatche, his wing jumper a parabola that sometimes briefly disappeared from television sets while in flight, scored 14 second-quarter points, continuing to make his case for playing time.

The Nets took an 8-point lead in the fourth quarter. The Mavericks cut it to 4 and then Williams took over, scoring 8 points in a row. Statistically, 2-point jump shots are the least efficient in basketball. Straightaway step-back jumpers and baseline fadeaways—normally low-percentage shots—were easy for an in-rhythm Williams during the spurt. Williams sunk the Mavs in a way that affirmed his place as a top eight-to-ten player when healthy, the kind of talent that could both dictate pace and rhythm and make an opposing coach just shrug about such unguardable exploits. The Nets were +27 after falling behind by 10. Williams dropped in 31, points like flowing water, and Cuban looked like an anvil had fallen on his head. It was a good night for the Brooklyn Nets.

After the game, King really put the general in general manager, carrying Williams's wailing toddler into the locker room as Carlesimo was giving his postgame presser. Carlesimo relayed an on-court conversation with Williams at about the same time.

"I kept telling him, 'I'm going to get you out for a minute or two' in the second half, and he goes, 'Are you watching what's going on out here?' Obviously we didn't take him out until the end."

Even though Williams repeated the gesture and carried Evans's son over to his father in the Nets' locker room after a game a few weeks later, it was never clearer who was in charge. Dallas was home to Deron Williams, but the Nets were his house and he most definitely appreciated your concern for his health.

BROOKLYN BOUNCE

MATCHUP MADNESS

The most talented position on the 2012–13 Brooklyn Nets wasn't point guard and it wasn't center, where Lopez and Blatche put up stellar numbers unmatched around the league. It was broadcaster, where the Nets consistently went three deep at both positions. In an industry sprinkled with blathering buffoons, the Nets' play-by-play talent—veterans Ian Eagle and Chris Carrino and the young Ryan Ruocco—was a comparative marvel, on both television and radio.* The analysts, who included former coaches (Mike "The Czar" Fratello, Tim Capstraw) and former players (Greg Anthony, Jim Spanarkel) more than held their own, whether breaking down hoops or bantering; Carrino and Capstraw discussing a horse named after them (Chris and the Capper) or Eagle guessing what The Czar was doodling on his Telestrator.

On the first fourth-quarter possession against the Clippers three nights later, Joe Johnson missed a runner in the lane. There was a loose rebound. Humphries got there first, surrounded by three Clippers: Chris Paul, Lamar Odom, and Blake Griffin. Giving up about half a foot and sixty pounds, Paul wasn't trying very hard to rip the ball away. Griffin had challenged Johnson's shot, so he entered the fray late. This left Odom, Khloe Kardashian's husband—technically Humphries's brother-in-law at the time—to try to wrestle the ball away. The call was a jump ball. The referee pointed to Griffin.

"The world is spared the Humphries-Odom showdown," Carrino said. "A picture that might have broken the Internet."

In the background, at Staples Center, Busta Rhymes's voice was booming, "Don't this s*** make my people wanna jump, jump?!?! Don't this s*** make my people wanna jump, jump?!?!"

---

* Eagle had a Kodak moment earlier in December. With Jerry Seinfeld sitting courtside, he referenced a famous *Seinfeld* episode and Terri Hatcher's breasts in connection to a Joe Johnson game winner. ("That was real, and it was spectacular!")

The officials conferred, and Odom was selected to jump instead. The crowd roared.

"The most enthusiasm in NBA history ever on a jump ball," Carrino said, the dip in his voice a classy, humorous touch.

Odom won the jump ball, and the Clippers won the game.

The moment was covered on celebrity gossip websites such as Terez Owens and CelebrityBalla.com. Odom's jump-ball victory overshadowed a positive return to the lineup for Humphries after a three-week absence, his second-quarter hustle paying dividends for the Nets.

C.S.I.T.P.B.

In the hallway leading to the visitors' locker room at the US Airways Center in Phoenix, images of classic moments in Phoenix Suns history decorated the walls, threaded with inspirational quotes.

"We are what we consistently commit to doing."—Aristotle

The Nets were committed to playing well on the road and beating bad teams, but generally confounding those following them when it came to assessing how good they could actually be. Johnson, Lopez, and Williams were pretty consistently committed to taking turns playing dangerous basketball, maybe because there was only one ball. Placed in an untenable situation, Carlesimo was committed to sacrificing rotation continuity in an attempt to please everybody.

"Nothing great was ever achieved without enthusiasm." —Emerson.

The Nets did not have the most enthusiastic locker room. Reggie Evans as well as Gerald Wallace, Andray Blatche, and Tyshawn Taylor masked this on occasion.

"You are the only person on earth who can see your ability." —Anon

Those words, to a frequent observer of the Nets, seemed specifically targeted at Deron Williams, who looked better and better by the day.

But in the context of Nets-Suns in late March, a day after his return to the lineup and brother-in-law jump ball with Lamar Odom, the statement was also about Humphries. Humphries had posted a then-season-high in points (17) and grabbed 8 rebounds. The Nets weathered a late comeback when Iranian center Hamed Haddadi missed a put-back at the buzzer; it almost seemed like they wanted to test the theory that they were nearly invincible against bad teams in the home of the worst team in the Western Conference.

Needled by his choice reporter about whether the numbers were career highs, Humphries sounded almost offended. "Check stats in the past, bro," he said. "Come on, bro." For once Humphries's fratty bewilderment was understandable; he was one of eight players to average a double-double in the 2010–11 season.

REG-LANDIA

After a few days off in Phoenix, the Nets jumped out to a 44–17 lead in Portland, and Williams spent most of his energy selflessly running the show and making sure the Trail Blazers' prized rookie Damian Lillard didn't score. The Blazers selected Lillard, the eventual Rookie of the Year, with the draft pick the Nets sent over in the Wallace trade. Perhaps the most telling sequence of a remarkable first quarter occurred when Evans grabbed a rebound in traffic and Williams passed ahead to Wallace. Wallace posted up Lillard, the mismatch of that trade reversed.

Wallace stood about half a foot taller than Lillard, and he found Lopez cutting into the lane, but Lopez missed the off-kilter layup. Evans didn't see Lopez streaking down the court and bumped him, which increased the shot's degree of difficulty. Still, Evans corralled the rebound and was fouled. Evans missed both foul shots. Not only did Evans not see Lopez heading into open space, Evans could barely see, or so he said.

Squinting because of what he described as a virus in his eyes, Evans posted a career-high-tying 22 points and a career high 26 rebounds. Two negatives were multiplied and the result was a positive: arguably the NBA's least-scoring-inclined player tied a career high in points with compromised vision. Evans played as if he had a heightened feel for where the ball would be. His touch with his left hand, a trademark when he did decide to take high-percentage shots, was soft. Twice on the Nets' first offensive sequence, he corralled a rebound among three Trail Blazers.

One game after "Check stats in the past, bro" the Nets on the bench wouldn't leave Evans's record-setting rebounding alone in the present.*

"Typical of my teammates," Evans said. "'Oh, you've got this many' . . . 'You've got this many' . . . 'You've got this many' . . . 'You've got this many.'"

Off the court in Portland, Evans wore massive designer, gold-rimmed shades to protect his eyes.

"It's just the way my head's structured," he said. "This fit the frame of my head, you know what I'm saying? Just trying to keep the light out of my eyes and stuff . . . not for no style." Then Evans went on a spiel about the style of designer sunglasses.

It was marketed as Instagram Night in Portland, and whichever picture you wanted to take of Evans, it was there: Scoring Reggie, Rebounding Reggie, Motivated Reggie, "And Stuff" Reggie, Wearing Giant Sunglasses Because of a Virus in His Eyes Reggie, etc.

Evans was acquired from the Clippers with the trade exception that the Nets received from the Trail Blazers in the Wallace deal. The Blazers had given the Nets the trade exception, the monetary credit, they needed to acquire Evans and so they had, in a way, facilitated Evans's arrival in Brooklyn as a third party. As innocent bystanders on the court, they also helped to facilitate one

---

* Whereas "Check stats in the past, bro" was something one might want to do in the desert at Joshua Tree or Burning Man, Reggie Evans frequently came off as a vision quest tour guide.

of the greatest nights in Evans's career. The Blazers, a team that relied on its bench less than any other in the league, were coming off of their own long road trip. So Evans and his feisty mates, refreshed after a few days spent at a golfing resort outside Phoenix, did what they did best: pounded a weaker team and guaranteed the Nets' first winning season in six years.

ALTITUDE ADJUSTMENT

The 2012–13 Denver Nuggets were a unique, fun, strange team. They played the second-fastest brand of basketball in the NBA without a brand-name superstar. Their progressive power forward, Kenneth Faried, was proud to be raised by two moms. Their backup center, Javale McGee, battled ADHD, boasted an alter ego named Pierre, and was famous on YouTube for running the wrong way, requesting All-Star votes through Twitter, and throwing himself an alley-oop in the middle of a loss. McGee was talented but confused; Williams once riffed about McGee's ability to land frequently on *SportsCenter*'s "Not Top Ten" Countdown.

One of the Nuggets' point guards, Ty Lawson, pushed the ball up the court like he was trying to break the sound barrier. His backup, Andre Miller, threw long passes—and alley-oops—better than anyone else.

The Pepsi Center experience was surreal. The PA announcer referred to visiting players by last name only after scores, and *South Park*'s acid-tongued cartoon character Eric Cartman led Nuggets fans in a pregame "Let's Go Nuggets!" chant. At one point, part of the instrumental from King Missile's "Detachable Penis" played over the loudspeakers. There was a leak in the ceiling during Carlesimo's postgame presser. It was like two former ABA franchises were trying to honor a bizarre past through mostly modernized humor.

Running opponents ragged and thriving off of impressive depth, the Nuggets were also 32-3 at home, riding a seventeen-game home winning streak. On the heels of a dominant performance in Portland, the Nets were looking for another win as the playoffs neared.

"It's a monster game," Carlesimo said. "It's almost set aside from the rest of the trip."

The run-'n'-gun Nuggets got plenty of looks in the half-court early on. Brook Lopez struggled against the more mobile Kosta Koufos. Koufos worked well away from the ball and was rewarded with 10 of the Nuggets' first 20 points. The Nuggets finished with five dunks and five layups in the quarter, good for 20 of 26 total points.

In one of the more bizarre sequences of the season, C. J. Watson picked up three fouls in fifty-one seconds early in the second quarter. He grabbed Nuggets rookie Evan Fournier around the waist in an attempt to stop a drive to the basket. When the Nets didn't crash the glass as a unit, Watson pushed off while boxing out the much taller Danilo Gallinari. Then Fournier pushed ahead and Watson fouled him on another drive. Freshly called up from the Developmental League's Springfield Armor, Tyshawn Taylor checked in for the Nets. A 7-point Nuggets lead quickly doubled, and the Nets never threatened again. It was a weird moment for Taylor. He and Shengelia traveled across the country from Springfield, Massachusetts (the birthplace of basketball), and joined the Nets in Denver. Taylor's former teammates at Kansas were playing in the Final Four. Suddenly he was in the spotlight. Taylor had a few nervous moments, and the Nets as a whole were discombobulated.

Turnovers led to transition opportunities. The Nuggets finished with 26 fast-break points to just 2 for the Nets. The Nets missed 18 of their 36 free throws. Right when you thought they might shock everybody and turn a corner, the 2012–13 Brooklyn Nets were there to remind you that, to paraphrase Denny Green, they were who you thought they were: a roster that rarely rose above its superiors or expectations.

BROOKLYN BOUNCE

For the first time all trip, it looked like the Nets played like they were ready to head back East.

"I'm ready to go home," Evans said at the team's shootaround. "From day one I've been missing my kids; ready to go home, but I'm not going to disrespect my opponents—know what I'm sayin'?"

HOMECOMING II

After seven flights in thirteen days—including six in the morning—and living the highs and lows of caffeine and the Brooklyn Nets, it was nice to sit courtside at Energy Solutions Arena and observe a little slice of NBA pregame life.

Humphries worked on midrange shots with assistant coach Popeye Jones. Blatche and Brooks did ball-handling tricks with Carlesimo's young kids, Kyle and Casey. Carlesimo's wife, Carolyn, a retired sports psychologist, sat a few seats down. It was especially nerve-racking to be sitting next to the coach's wife when the coach had shaken your hand but not formally introduced himself.

Blatche saw me taking notes.

"What's that, your diary?" he asked.

That night, Jazz fans greeted Deron Williams warmly before the game. As he ran through the tunnel, a sea of screaming kids clamored for his autograph. An elderly lady working usher shook his hand. The Jazz mascot even gave him a hug. At other points, the crowd seemed confused, unsure whether to clap for him or boo. Williams spoke of his former team and its fan base before the game. How could he resist Jazz fans who held signs that read "D-Will U Stud"?

The teams started the game a combined 20-for-25 from the floor, hot shooting indicative of two tired defenses on the second night of a back-to-back. Williams had some nice moments en route to 21 points and 11 assists, but Newark native Randy Foye did the Nets in from behind the arc. Foye needed only eleven field-goal attempts to score 26 points, and his eight 3-pointers tied a Jazz record. Foye's five 3s turned the tide in another unfortunate third quarter.

Foye, wearing a Jazz uniform and Williams's number, shot the lights out as Jerry Sloan, Williams's former coach with the Jazz, watched the game from the stands.

"It feels like your body is numb," Foye said of the performance.

A night after being whistled for three fouls in fifty-one seconds, C. J. Watson (22 points, 8 assists) led a strong effort from the Nets' bench, but it didn't matter; Foye was feeling it.

The Nets went home to rest for a few days before hitting the road again to complete the journey.

MISTAKE-FREE BY THE LAKE

MarShon Brooks had scored 27 points and dished out 7 assists, both career highs. The youngster with the contract that moved from Jersey to Brooklyn dominated. He made nifty passes. He made the right plays. The game slowed down for him. He sank his first ten shots.

"I was going to make sure I missed," he joked.

The Nets obliterated a demoralized Cavaliers team, shooting 73 percent in the first half with a season-high 31 assists. And yet it still felt like Brooks was pledging. With Brooks wearing an orange and blue ensemble highlighted by a Mets hat in the visitors' locker room at Quicken Loans Arena, his teammates criticized him for looking "like a Knickerbocker." Maybe he didn't care, maybe he could take it, but sometimes it just felt like Brooks couldn't win.

Even Blatche, a player who needed a franchise to have his back, openly discussed trading Brooks in a video game during the beginning of the road trip in Detroit. Moreover, he had discussed trading Brooks for Nick Young, Blatche's former teammate with the Wizards, a man known as Swaggy P. (Through his tenure with the Wizards and Sixers, Swaggy P was the definition of the player at Sloan that Stan Van Gundy described as "jacking up horseshit shots." It wasn't a compliment in the continuity-on-offense sense. Somehow he landed with the Lakers, one of Kobe Bryant's back-ups.)

Brooks's defense usually did him no favors, but even Carlesimo, a coach in a substitute teacher's situation, had no problem knocking MarShon while avoiding more pointed critiques of other players. The mind wandered, wondering what Brooks could do in a healthier situation. Would his shortcomings doom him or would he blossom?

Williams had his first dunk of the season in Cleveland. Most importantly, the victory locked in the Nets' first winning road record since entering the NBA in 1976. Beating the bad teams while racking up wins against the Thunder, Knicks, Celtics (twice), Pacers (twice), Bucks, Hawks, Mavs, and Blazers pointed to a veteran team performing as such. And for all the questions about its inaugural Brooklyn season, the team's consistent success away from Brooklyn was indisputable.

CHAPTER 11

Coming Attractions

From Cleveland it was quickly on to Brooklyn for a playoff preview against the Chicago Bulls. The news of the day was the death of legendary *Chicago Sun-Times* film critic Roger Ebert. I vividly remember scrolling through tributes as the subway rumbled aboveground toward Brooklyn, the East River in the distance. Ebert wasn't into basketball like his late partner Gene Siskel, a noted Bulls fan, but he loved *Hoop Dreams* so much that the documentary's criterion collection DVD came with a bonus feature of Siskel and Ebert tracking its acclaim.

Ebert touted *Hoop Dreams* as "one of the best films about American life I've ever seen." He ranked it as the best film of the nineties and the best film of 1994—beating out *Forrest Gump* and *Pulp Fiction*. In discussing *Hoop Dreams'* worthy three-hour running time, Siskel praised the film's reach and discussed why it was snubbed by the Academy.

Hoop Dreams highlighted Chicago's dominant basketball culture. It popped up in the fall of 1994 with Michael Jordan on hiatus. That year a seven-game Rockets-Knicks Finals was upstaged by O. J. Simpson's arrest.

Hoop Dreams begins with a scene from the 1988 All-Star Game at the old Chicago Stadium. Michael Jordan steals the ball from Karl Malone, and the scene immediately shifts to Chicago's Cabrini Green housing projects, home to William Gates, one of the film's protagonists. Later, Arthur Agee, the other protagonist, meets his favorite player, Isiah Thomas. Agee and Thomas, two point guards, share a bonding moment in slow motion on-screen, and Agee beams. Agee was being evaluated by St. Joseph's High School head coach Gene Pingatore when he met Thomas. "I could see the playground in him," Pingatore said, a moment that underscored an ugly racial undertone partly explaining why Agee couldn't keep his scholarship.

In that regard, the film showcases Chicago as heaven and hell divided—a city haunted by old prejudices and high crime rates. In a bizarre irony, the Michael Jordan fan (Gates) has to follow in Thomas's footsteps while the Thomas fan (Agee) has to learn about life by getting booted from his hero's world. The twists and turns are staggering. About a decade later, Gates was involved briefly with the Wizards when Jordan played for the franchise.

The 2012–13 Bulls were the epitome of a team. They hunkered down on defense and were third in points allowed. The Bulls shared the ball, too, assisting on 64.5 percent of their made field goals, second in the NBA. The roster was filled with unselfish players. The center, Joakim Noah, was a defensive savant born in New York to tennis great Yannick Noah and Cecilia Rodhe, a former Miss Sweden. Taj Gibson, a Brooklynite, was born to a father who played basketball for the US Army National Team during the Vietnam War. He listed his favorite players as Jamaal Tinsley and Lamar Odom, legends of the New York City streets with solid NBA careers.

Five of the players on the Bulls had won a combined seven NCAA championships. They could play over their heads—breaking the Knicks' thirteen-game winning streak and the Heat's twenty-seven-game run—but they were the first team in NBA history to finish an entire season without a four-game winning streak or a four-game losing streak. With a healthy Derrick Rose, they went eighty-six games between February 2011 and April 2012 without losing two in a row. Even though he didn't play in 2012–13, Rose was Chicago's hoop dreams actualized, a product of Simeon High School in downtown Chicago.

BROOKLYN BOUNCE

The first game back from the circus trip followed trends from earlier in the season. The Bulls were shorthanded. The Nets were happy to be home early on. Lopez hit his first six shots, and the Nets built an 18–4 lead. But Lopez struggled down the stretch, throwing the ball away before getting blocked in the paint by Nazr Mohammed on the ensuing possession. Nate Robinson connected on a floater over Lopez before Lopez's baseline jumper to tie the game spun out. The ball bounced around the rim—and the roll, well, it just wasn't friendly.

Speaking about the final play, Lopez said, "I guess I can be thankful it happened in the regular season. It wasn't the postseason."

For the third time the Nets had lost to the Bulls. Joe Johnson didn't make a 3-pointer until well into the third quarter, but Williams carried the Nets in the second half, weaving into traffic for tough scores and playing with a spring in his step. One of his dunk attempts left press row slack-jawed, as he exploded off the ground with gale force. Williams was fouled but he made his point.

Carlos Boozer scored 29 points and grabbed 18 rebounds for the Bulls. The loss put the Nets five games behind the Pacers. Instead of a sequel to the Battle of the Boroughs, the Nets and the Bulls would match up again soon.

CHANGE CLOTHES

Other musicians had been involved with NBA franchises: Nelly with the Charlotte Bobcats; Usher with the Cleveland Cavaliers; and Justin Timberlake with the Memphis Grizzlies. But no minority owner rubber-stamped the style and culture of a team quite like Jay-Z did with the Nets. That might explain why he bounced from his position to become a sports agent.

"My job as an owner is over but as a fan it has just begun," he said in a statement released on April 18. "I'm a Brooklyn Net forever."

His Roc Nation Sports agency merged with Creative Artists Agency, home to Carmelo Anthony and Mike Woodson of the Knicks. Jay-Z immediately struck a deal with Yankees second baseman Robinson Cano and would soon sign Thunder star Kevin Durant, who was ejected for the first time in his career against the Nets in early January and led the Thunder to an entertaining victory in Brooklyn on Jay-Z's birthday.

Interestingly, Jay-Z left the Nets to align himself with an agency that represented no members of the inaugural Brooklyn Nets. Instead the Nets had a number of Excel Sports Management clients (Williams, Taylor, Teletovic, Stackhouse, and Watson, who switched over to Excel at the end of the season). Excel was led by Jeff Schwartz, who also represented Devin Harris and Jason Kidd, the two point guards preceding Williams, as well as Paul Pierce. Arn Tellem's Wasserman Sports Management represented two of the Nets' soft-spoken main scorers in Johnson and Lopez. Andy Miller Sports Management represented a few members of the Nets' frontcourt. If a good time was being had in the locker room, there was a decent chance it was, in a way, Miller Time; he represented Evans and Blatche, and his most high-profile client was Kevin Garnett.

Wallace was alone on the Nets with Rob Pelinka, who represented Kobe Bryant. Pelinka was a benchwarmer on the Michigan Fab Five NCAA tournament teams that changed the style of basketball with baggy shorts and black socks. Kris Humphries acted as an agent of change, switching agents frequently while playing for four teams in eight seasons and appearing on countless supermarket tabloid magazine covers.

FOUR ROOKIES, RECHARGED BATTERIES

The Nets rested all five starters along with Stackhouse and Bogans for a matchup against the Wizards in the second-to-last night of the regular season, as they had locked up the fourth seed regardless of opponent. The Wizards jumped out to a big lead, but the

Nets fought back and a funny thing happened on the way to the playoffs: the crowd woke up. With underdogs to root for, Brooklyn stood up.

A ridiculous comeback was highlighted by the exploits of the four rookies: Taylor, Shengelia, Teletovic, and Kris Joseph. Being a rookie, especially a second-round pick (Taylor, Shengelia) or D-League call-up (Joseph) wasn't always easy, whether learning a foreign language or periodically fetching Deron Williams his *New York Daily News*. Finding one's place in a locker room dominated by men with guaranteed contracts and money to burn never seemed easy.

The NBA locker room can be an odd place. Teammates can't seem to find enough lotion, but everyone is rocking the latest Louis Vuitton handbag. In this world, second-round picks float around like missing pieces to a puzzle. Against the Wizards, those proverbial missing pieces led a stirring comeback, and an infectious innocence was in the air.

Teletovic tied a career high with 14 points and got a friendly roll on key 3-pointer. Shengelia scored 11 points and grabbed 11 rebounds, his raw, high-energy style of play at its best. Joseph, a Montreal native, made sure everything moved fluidly. Taylor's speed was once again on display and he sank the decisive 3. The Nets won by 5, but their four rookies together were a plus-55. Blatche held it together, logging thirty-seven minutes to get in shape for the playoffs.

THE BROOKLYN BACKFLIP

When he served as the Nets' head coach, Lawrence Frank combined the diminutive stature and emphatic gesticulations of a young Avery Johnson with some of P. J. Carlesimo's biting sarcasm. After serving as student manager at Indiana University for four seasons, Frank spent time at the University of Tennessee, Marquette, and the Vancouver Grizzlies before joining the Nets in 2000 as an assistant coach. When Frank was promoted to head coach, the Nets won thirteen in a row, a record for a new coach. Frank was the only NBA coach at the time to have never played pro, college, or even high school basketball. He was the youngest coach in the league at the time.

Ultimately Frank could not overcome the franchise's cheap ways and overmatched roster. He went through the guillotine by losing the first sixteen games of the 2009–10 season.

The record-setting seventeenth-straight loss to start a season came against the Mavericks and Kidd. It was one of those nights when a coach would look at a box score and simply shrug. Kidd exemplified the Mavericks' efficiency, scoring 16 points while taking only 6 shots. The IZOD Center was overrun with excitable media types as history was made, leading to a bizarre and somewhat macabre feel in the air. Frank landed in Boston as an assistant under Doc Rivers, and the Celtics made it to a seventh game against the Lakers in a rivalry battle royale. Frank took over as the Pistons' head coach the next season. The Nets' media interviewed him before the regular-season finale.

Frank sidestepped a question about whether the Pistons' preseason playoff expectations were realistic. He spoke about the difference in camaraderie between good teams and bad ones—the idea that players on bad teams aren't unified and operate in cliques. Frank took questions about the playoff-bound Nets too. I asked Frank if he would share notes with Carlesimo heading into a potential playoff matchup. Frank explained how dicey it was in the coaching fraternity to choose sides.

"P.J.'s a good friend. Potentially, they could play Chicago. Tom [Thibodeau] is a very, very good friend of mine. Potentially, they could play Atlanta. Larry Drew worked with me in New Jersey . . . so sometimes you just stay out of it."

"They might not ask me," he said, oozing cynicism. "Have you seen our record?"

The New York City native and graduate of Teaneck High School—where the Nets began in 1967, as the New Jersey Americans—would be returning to the Nets about two months later after getting fired by the Pistons, reunited with his New Jersey–based family and reunited with old friends at work, reportedly the highest-paid assistant coach in the NBA. From a maturity-starved roster and all of the responsibility on his shoulders to an essential, guiding role on a veteran team was quite the role reversal.*

A VERY REGGIE PLAYOFF PREVIEW

The Nets were set to take on the Bulls, and East Rutherford was buzzing. Carlesimo was talking about the prospect of Derrick Rose making a dramatic return.

Reggie Evans was in game mode: "Got to hoop," he said. "It's do or die right now. I got all summer to relax. You know what I'm sayin'? It be May, June; I can last 'til June, I'll be aight."

You expect it to be a physical series?

"Hell, yeah . . . I'd rather have that than a track meet. I ain't wantin' to be playin' no D'Antonio Phoenix Suns.

"This our first [postseason] practice," he said. "Look how many media. I'm seeing faces I haven't even seen all season. So everything is different. Everything is tense. Even y'all can feel, like, the intensity . . . Brooklyn first year. You know what I'm sayin'? Excitement . . . so everything is at an all-time high. I mean, at an all-time high. That goes for the referees, the ballboys, the fans, janitors, you know what I'm sayin'?"

* Haha.

CHAPTER 12

Respiration

> Prokhorov watches the game nervously, fidgeting, cracking his knuckles, and, when Chicago takes the ball up-court, roaring, "Those S.O.B.s will now score!"
>
> —*Forbes* magazine watches the Nets play the Bulls on February 1, 2013, with Nets principal owner Mikhail Prokhorov as part of a Prokhorov cover story

Nothing felt quite as self-serving as the idea that Michael Jordan was born in Brooklyn and should be represented as a Brooklynite. For a long time, it was a strange duality; arguably the greatest player ever was born in a basketball mecca without a professional team, where shifty point guards made names for themselves and dreams lived and died with a ball and a hustle.

Jay-Z and others trumpeted Jordan's Brooklyn birth as if the borough were a heavenly manger. It was strange until it wasn't. "Birthplace of Michael Jordan!" made sense when the birth of the Brooklyn Nets was defined in Chicago and the Nets were branded in Jordan's former place of business, an arena built between two three-peats. But the series began in Brooklyn.

REINTRODUCTIONS REVISITED

There was a loud BROOOOO-KLYN chant right before Jerry Stackhouse sang the game 1 national anthem. After an early hitch, Stackhouse nailed the anthem by singing with unmistakable soul and passion. His introduction was cause for raucous applause, and his eighteen-year career was distinguished both on and off the court. Everywhere you looked, it seemed like Stackhouse was kicking ass. He stood up with LeBron James during All-Star Weekend and fought for the firing of Billy Hunter, the leader of the Players Association who was accused of nepotism. James, the best player in the league, and Stackhouse, the player who earned preeminent bad boy status for a number of altercations, formed quite the tandem. James could dunk on anyone; Stackhouse had the capacity to fight a player only for his adversary to come back and apologize, as was the case with Kirk Snyder.

The Nets took a 60–35 lead into halftime and led by as many as 28. Williams got whatever he wanted. Lopez was dominant. Contributions came from everywhere except Stackhouse, who fired up multiple airballs after contributing an excellent anthem. The crowd chanted for Wallace and Evans. Williams punctuated a 17-point win by stealing the ball from Luol Deng and converting a reverse dunk. The atmosphere was electric. It was a party.

"Hopefully, we can do the same thing the next night, when it's not our first playoff game," Williams said.

TYPICAL. NETS. BASKETBALL.

In an interview with Bloomberg News in Moscow, Prokhorov said something that had been on the minds of many before the season began: the Nets were one really good player away from being a championship-caliber team. The timing of the statement could not have been worse. Even if the odds of beating the Miami Heat were slim, teams need to believe in the postseason. Prokhorov's comment killed the momentum.

Carlesimo, ever the diplomat, called Prokhorov's assertion "an astute statement" while claiming that he "loved" the Nets' current roster.

"So Mikhail's right and I love all of our players," he said.

The Nets lost game 2 to the Bulls in disappointing fashion, unable to climb out of a hole created by an 11-point third quarter. Joakim Noah, the face of the Bulls in Derrick Rose's absence, sounded like a relaxed warrior during his postgame press conference. He talked about being a New Yorker who repped Chicago. He answered questions about his pain threshold in French and looked like a long-haired hipster. Despite his Bulls jersey, he would have fit right in at a gastro pub in Brooklyn's Williamsburg.

"Our team played passionate basketball tonight," he said.

Among Noah, Boozer, Gibson, and Nate Robinson, the Bulls were loud and expressive on the court. It became apparent that screaming motherfuckers was something the Bulls, especially without Derrick Rose, had in spades against the comparatively silent Nets. Then again, even Rose was whooping it up on the bench.

The coaches exhibited their different approaches. Carlesimo played eleven Nets—including five reserves at the same time during the second quarter—while Thibodeau put nine Bulls on the court, and all of whom made significant contributions.

Gerald Wallace coined an expression midway through the season to define the Nets' up-and-down play. "Typical. Nets. Basketball."

The three words became a negative slogan that followed the team in its first year. Whenever the Nets seemed ready to take the next step, Typical. Nets. Basketball. was right around the corner. As Wallace was speaking to the media after game 2, somewhere in the vicinity of the Watson-Bogans locker area, the rapper Kendrick Lamar's "Bitch, Don't Kill My Vibe" crept into the background. Bogans, playing for his seventh team in nine seasons, wouldn't play again for the Nets, and the ball would end up in Watson's hands with game 3 on the line.

THE EX-BULLS

Replacing Derrick Rose proved no easy task for Watson in the 2012 playoffs against the 76ers. Watson shot 24 percent in the series and, with the Bulls up by a single point in a win-or-go-home game 6 in Philadelphia, he controversially passed up a chance to run out the clock or ice the game at the free-throw line. An 81 percent free-throw shooter, Watson instead passed to Omer Asik. Asik missed both, and Andre Iguodala won the game for the 76ers with two free throws of his own. Watson's desperate heave missed at the buzzer and he received death threats on Twitter.

Even though Watson's salary was meager by NBA standards, Brooklyn was a safe landing spot for the Las Vegas native. His relationship with Williams dated back to an international competition in Thessaloniki, Greece, after their freshman year of college. Watson backed Williams up for Team USA then, too, and the pair roomed together abroad. After going undrafted, Watson followed a stint playing in Italy with a brief return to Thessaloniki, suiting up for the Greek League team PAOK. He used the NBA Developmental League to pave his path to the NBA, catching on with the Warriors before the Bulls.

Watson was the valedictorian of his high school and was direct and focused in his infrequent interviews. Sort of like a supporting Shakespearean character whose actions and words defined a larger work, Watson had a propensity to pop up and play a major role during key moments in the season, such as the opening-night win over the Raptors and important sequences against the Bulls. When Watson struggled with Williams out in a mid-February game in Indianapolis, Tyshawn Taylor took the reins and played the best game of his rookie season. Watson rebounded immediately from what was dubbed as the Tyshawn Taylor Game by shooting the lights out for the rest of the regular season as he accepted his creative limitations with the ball and focused on spotting up and converting from distance at a supreme clip.

The other ex-Bull, Bogans, always seemed to be around; the guy to snicker and look down at the floor if you had something funny to say. In the Nets' locker room, Watson's stall was two over from Williams's, with Bogans between them. The Watson-Bogans duo seemed to compose a quiet cocoon of sorts around the franchise player; Watson in his natural state and Bogans's penchant for joking around taken down a notch, at least publicly.

THE WINDY CITY FREEZE

Prior to tip-off at the United Center before game 3, the Bulls' reserves danced along the baseline. Rows of banners hung from the rafters, the Bulls' on one side, Blackhawks' above the other baseline. Scottie Pippen, arguably the best defender of his generation, sat courtside.

The action started out tough. Williams took a shot from a pick-setting Carlos Boozer, and Joakim Noah bled from his elbow. Despite an airballed finger-roll and a bumbling turnover from Wallace, the Nets jumped out to a 15–5 lead before everything fell apart. From the 6:25 mark in the first quarter to the 3:38 mark of the second, the Bulls' defense held the Nets to just a single field goal in twenty-six tries. It was astonishing.

Noah missed a layup, the Nets rebounded, and Williams was off and running. He attacked the basket hard from the right wing and missed a layup, but the Nets retained possession. Williams drew a foul on Kirk Hinrich quickly on the inbounds play — earning two free throws. He made both to put the Nets up 17–5.

After another six misses, Lopez committed his second foul and was subbed out. He was the Nets' best counter against Chicago's pack-the-paint defense. The Nets had consistently counted on him early in games. He sat out for eight minutes while the Nets struggled to penetrate.

Fresh off his divorce from Kim Kardashian, Humphries went for a layup that failed to touch the rim. The Bulls pushed the other way and Taj Gibson dunked on Humphries so forcefully, it felt like he was trying to cram a tabloid romance into a trash compactor. The Bulls extended a 7-point halftime lead to 16 at various points in the third quarter, and took a 13-point lead into the final frame. The Nets had scored 52 points through three quarters, and Carlesimo finally decided to mix things up. In the fourth quarter he subbed in a squad of his five best scorers, despite the mismatches on defense. The move kept the Nets from getting completely blown out. Brooks, ever the black sheep, was a part of the all-offense lineup.

"Honestly, I was just on the bench just waiting for my name to be called," Brooks said. "Kind of figured it was going to get called because we couldn't score."

"It seems like I'm the last resort, honestly," he said the next day. "If things aren't going well for the team, throw MarShon out there. That's been the rhythm all year. I kind of know when my name is going to be called, in a sense."

On offense Brooks was the fourth option. "I just wanted to get in where I fit in," he stated earnestly. Buoyed by a late 12–0 spurt, the Nets were in position to tie the game with 14.4 seconds left. Lopez, who also blocked 7 shots, dominated down the stretch, and 77–62 had become 77–74. Brooks inbounded the ball with the game on the line.

His pass to Johnson was off target. Brooks's man went to double Johnson, and Johnson threw the ball back to Brooks.

"I actually looked at the rim," Brooks said. "I was about to shoot it. Seen two seconds left . . . and [Watson] was just wide open. That's just the right play to make."

Watson said the play wasn't designed to go to him as a first option.

"Did I think it was good? No. It felt good. Got a good look."

BROOKLYN BOUNCE

The Nets were in a 2–1 hole.

"I just keep repeating myself," Lopez said, sitting at his locker after game 3. "I think a lot of it's on our end. A lot of it's just the simple fact that a lot of the normal shots we make aren't going down."

FIVE-STAR THERAPY

The press enters the United Center in Chicago at gate 3½. Instead of meeting with the press on the days between game 3 and game 4 at the arena, the Nets handled their media obligations in the open area adjacent to a ballroom at their swank hotel. Sleepy reserves ambled into an adjoining room with a breakfast buffet while the team's starters took turns in a hot seat in front of the media horde.

"I couldn't tell you my role now," Gerald Wallace said glumly. "I don't have a clue what my role is."

Carlesimo was constantly tinkering with his lineup. Maybe against the Bulls, as illustrated during desperation time in game 3, the special sauce would be a floor-spacing unit with four or five scorers on the floor at all times. Could a player whose primary skill is relentless rebounding (Reggie Evans, Kris Humphries) succeed with Gerald Wallace? Should the Nets fight defense with defense if the opposing team's defense is much better?

"At times it's refreshing, the fact that there's not always a correlation between what we're going to do tomorrow and what we did yesterday," Carlesimo said, opting to stand instead of sitting in a chair.

"If you want, you can call that refreshing. But we can come in tomorrow, play the hell out of it, get the series back to two to two, and go back to Brooklyn. We have not . . . we have not built a lot of bridges to prior games, so that's good or bad depending on how you want to look at it."

GAME 4

The Nets and the Bulls fought seven hard games, and the core of their epic slugfest began in the middle, right before game 4. The scene was familiar: a Brooklyn gang, in matching colors, taking advantage of a helpless, smaller victim. Brook Lopez, the leader, stared his target down and approached like a boxer. Andray Blatche, the guy with something to prove, grabbed the victim from behind, opening his body up to Lopez. Tyshawn Taylor, the energetic youngster, leaped at him, and the whole group crashed to the floor. Keith Bogans, the veteran, stopped by for a casual kick from behind. The victim was outnumbered and he never stood a chance. It looked like a class on better borough brutality: how to get jumped by a few guys with Brooklyn scrawled across their chests.

Except it wasn't. The scene wasn't real.

Before what would be the pivotal game of their season, a few Nets interrupted their warm-ups to stage a fake beat-down of their opponents' mascot, Benny the Bull. While not exactly commonplace, faux mascot beatings weren't a new thing in the NBA. And Benny the Bull got his revenge by pantsing Lopez shortly after the attack. Still, it was jarring because New Brooklyn was pretending to be Old Brooklyn; the violent bluster was palpable. Brooklyn native and newly minted Nets fan Mike Tyson even threatened to kick Charles Barkley's ass during one of the live commentary cutaways.

The Nets were edging closer to elimination, down two games to one. The winner would earn the opportunity to pop the defending champion Miami Heat in the mouth in the second round of the playoffs. For the Nets that prospect was dwindling.

The prospect of losing stung Lopez the most. Lopez was the Nets' most consistent player. When his teammates went through their respective funks or injuries, Lopez kept up his end of the bargain. Drafted tenth in 2008 on the night Michael Jackson died, the main on-court link to the Nets' New Jersey past, Lopez was the one you counted on.

He was purportedly the comic book writer and he came up with a great plot point, hitting the first 3-pointer of his career, breaking into a huge smile, on a Sunday afternoon in Chicago that defined the Nets' first season in Brooklyn.

Whereas the Nets' in-arena playlist felt like an ode to Jay-Z, the Bulls intro song "Sirius" by the Alan Parsons Project was the stuff of NBA legend. On the big screen, Bulls run through the streets of Chicago and smash through the opposing team's bus. The introductions combine a proud tradition and a city's reputation. Music was all around before game 4. There were different eight-piece bands on the concourse. In front of one of them, signage read: The Chicago Bulls Present "Knock Out the Nets" featuring Together. A curvaceous older woman belted out the notes to Etta James's "At Last."

It started with a pair of misses from Nate Robinson and then C. J. Watson. Boozer scored over Lopez at the rim. Lopez limped up the court. Watson dribbled around and backed into Robinson. Robinson took offense, in the way that a dog might take offense at a mailman simply for having the audacity to deliver the mail. As referee Ronnie Garretson tried to separate the two men, Robinson drove Watson into the scorer's table.

"He pushed me and I was holding him so I wouldn't fall on the table," Watson said. "So it's nothin'."

Noah, Williams, Thibodeau, Blatche, and Mario Elie all entered the picture. A double technical was called on both players, which made little sense at the time, and Watson's was later rescinded.

"It's unfortunate, but it is what it is," Watson said.

In a game that lasted seven periods, three hours and fifty-seven minutes, the Nets had 1 point unjustly taken away. Carlesimo was looking to call a time-out when Robinson leaped at Watson. Robinson basically grabbed Watson in a wrestling hold and shoved him into the scorer's table, a move Watson thought was bush league.

"I mean, that's in his character, so it didn't surprise me," Watson said.

Robinson ran into Watson in game 1 as well—again with Robinson as the aggressor, and it took nine more seconds for Watson to goad Robinson into a foul.

THE ART OF A COMEBACK

With the Nets up 14 with 3:22 remaining, Watson and Evans double-teamed Robinson, and a loose ball bounced to Williams. Williams passed ahead to a wide-open Watson. Watson went up for a two-handed dunk.

C. J. Watson, though a spry professional basketball player, is generously listed only at six-two. Watson was not one to attempt dunks frequently, let alone in a playoff game. The dunk squirted out.

A few possessions later, Robinson spun away from Watson using a screen and hit a straightaway 3-pointer over Lopez; 14 became 11. A wide-open jumper from Lopez bounced off the rim twice and out. Robinson drove the lane, splitting Williams and Lopez, and threw up a difficult floater over Lopez's outstretched arm that bounced in; 11 became 9. The Bulls fouled Wallace on purpose. Wallace missed both. Robinson curled around a screen and hit a midrange jumper, with Williams doing everything possible not to foul him; 9 became 7. Gerald Wallace and Carlos Boozer received double technicals for pushing each other.

As Johnson was shooting a 3-pointer from the wing, Wallace was called for an offensive foul for grabbing Luol Deng's arm. Robinson received a screen from Noah and fired up a 3-pointer from the wing. It looked like Williams had barely touched him, but he grazed Robinson's arm, and a foul was called. Robinson hit three free throws; 7 became 4. Williams missed a floater in the lane. Robinson scooted around Watson and sank another shot over an indecisive Lopez; 4 became 2. Robinson preened and flexed.

Wallace was called for a 5-second violation on an inbounds

pass, as Robinson denied Watson access to the ball. Then Robinson drew the defense and fed Boozer, who hit a reverse layup; 2 became 0. Nets reporters had gone from contemplating airfare back to Chicago for game 6 to staring at the prospect of overtime.

Lopez backed Noah into the paint and drew a foul, hitting both free throws. Deng missed a 3-pointer, but Noah followed up his own miss, tying the game again, at 111.

Biggie Smalls's "Hypnotize" blared over the loudspeakers, followed by the *Godzilla* theme. It was a protagonist time. Williams dribbled out the clock and took a tough contested fadeaway that didn't quite go down.

"I mean, I couldn't shoot it better," Williams said. "I thought that was in. Looked good. Felt good. Just rimmed out."

THREE OVERTIMES

The Nets carried the lead for much of the first overtime until Robinson hit yet another jumper over Lopez. Boozer then put the Bulls up 119–117 with a layup inside, the Bulls' first lead since 68–66.

Joe Johnson responded with a floater over multiple Bulls; he took on three defenders. Then Robinson responded with a running twenty-foot floater off the backboard that was so absurd, I did not believe that it was an actual shot in basketball. Really, Robinson had seemed to invent a new way for moving one's feet, like he was a dancer playing basketball. It was easy to imagine Dave Chappelle, acting as a loose-lipped broadcaster, noting that Robinson was "on some twinkle-toes shit." The Nets' season was on the line. "Sirius" rang out through the arena.

Johnson silenced the crowd again with another floater.

"I had no clue I would even go back in the game," Johnson said later.

For all of his ability to fade from the forefront at times, he was still so unbelievable, so clutch.

The two teams split 12 points in double overtime. With the

Nets down 4, Johnson did it again, sinking another floater in the paint while getting fouled. Robinson fouled out seconds later.

Lopez split a pair of free throws and Noah missed a layup and it was on to triple overtime, tied at 127. Gerald Wallace, a day after not knowing his role, fouled out, having played forty-nine minutes of hard-fought basketball.

The Bulls hit four of their first five shots in the third overtime. Evans fouled out and Blatche checked in. Despite not missing a shot in the first three quarters, he sat for most of the overtime sessions, and Nazr Mohammed scored 4 crucial points as the Bulls pulled away.

POSTGAME

Evans: "Tomorrow, I'm going to kick it with my kids, sit my butt down, be in the house all day. Eat me some food. Hopefully my mama and them cook. And watch some basketball games. I know my kid will keep me up all day, so there's a good chance I may get no rest tomorrow, but it is what it is. . . . You ain't gonna forget about this game. Heck naw. Naw. Not at all. If you're a true basketball player, you won't forget about this. This hurt. This hurt. Definitely."

Williams: "It seems so long ago what all went on, but we had the missed dunk, the missed free throws, I fouled Nate on the three . . ."

For his part, Robinson compared himself to a character that catches fire in the NBA Jam video game.

BROOKLYN BOUNCEBACK

The Bulls hadn't won four in a row all year. They lost game 5 at the Barclays Center. The series shifted back to Chicago. Winning was simple sometimes.

The game took a backseat to a *Sports Illustrated* cover revealed that Monday, on which former Net Jason Collins became the first male athlete in a professional team sport to come out. On the Nets'

2002 and 2003 Eastern Conference Championship teams, Collins was the consummate teammate, a player whose primary skills were post defense and screen setting. He made the game better for others, and fans paid money mostly to see others do things that Collins had a hand in making happen. In a thoughtful magazine essay, he started the process of changing the complexion of professional sports.

The Nets won game 6 in Chicago—finally winning in the United Center on their fifth try. Williams tapped the ball to Johnson. Johnson dribbled the ball as time expired. Humphries tapped a despondent Bulls fan on the chest. Watson jumped up and down on assistant coach Doug Overton. Carlesimo waved to people.

"That's it!" Brooks yelled to the fan whom Humphries tapped.

Williams was interviewed by TNT's Rachel Nichols. He looked weary but victorious, the prizefighter who had just won one of the biggest fights of his life.

The first do-or-die game on the road in Brooklyn Nets' history boiled down to Andray Blatche—"The Zero Hero," as he was known—at the free-throw line. Blatche had struggled in the fourth quarter, but he hit both free throws. He had to wait until January to have his contract guaranteed for the whole season, but the ball was in his hands with the season on the line.

"No pressure," he said. "Just focus. I ain't gonna lie to you; it was loud." From playing in the shadow of the Four Seasons incident to the season's two biggest free throws, Blatche showcased impressive fortitude in tuning out background noise.

The Bulls were battling unparalleled injury and sickness. Rose, Robinson, Deng, Hinrich, Noah, Gibson were out. Deng had a spinal tap. Trying to get concrete info on the lineup from Thibodeau was impossible. Carlesimo compared the Bulls to a medevac unit. Maybe Thibodeau was really testing out the "beat them with one hand tied behind your back" theory. The only Bulls' rotation regular was Jimmy Butler.

Joe Johnson was on his game early, scoring 8 points in the first eight minutes. Watson checked in amid boos. Marquis Teague, little brother to the Hawks' Jeff Teague, and veteran Richard Hamilton joined Nazr Mohammed, Taj Gibson, and Marco Bellinelli to form the ultimate ragtag lineup.

A Bulls fan yelled at Bellinelli, who scored a team-high 22 points.

"Bellinelli, you're going to be making pizzas tomorrow!"

Robinson scored 18 points, his pyrotechnics from game 4 a faded memory.

"Nate a good player," Evans said. "If you asked me, 'What's our focus against Derrick Rose?,' that's something different. You know, you talking about an MVP player. You talking about Nate Robinson—he had a good game. No disrespect to him because he's a good player, but . . . you know, come on."

Evans listed All-Stars and former All-Stars who should be a bigger focus.

"It's beyond my imagination how it's gonna be," Johnson said of game 7. "It'll definitely be a frenzy in there. That sixth man will definitely come into play. I know Brooklyn will be ready."

I met Bruce Ratner in the United Center media room at game 6. Told by a Nets employee that I was writing a book on the first season of the Nets, he suggested I write a book about Nassau Veterans Memorial Coliseum or the Islanders—I don't completely recall. He was in the process of competing against Madison Square Garden for the rights to transform Nassau Coliseum. An article in Long Island's *Newsday* the next day outlined different proposals. *Newsday*'s parent company owned the Knicks. The Nets had taken over the Islanders' business operations and were moving them to Brooklyn in 2015. It was the business side of a still-developing rivalry, and Ratner's team won the bid.

Jay-Z stood by Ratner, there to lend support and push the idea that major music acts would be attracted to a venue developed by Ratner. Brett Yormark was doing Brett Yormark things, utilizing the phrase "Brand Nassau." Renovating Nassau Coliseum was the next development—a much smaller project than Atlantic Yards, but still a project, and that's what mattered. There was a game 7 less than forty-eight hours away, and Ratner was already immersed in the possibility of the next deal. He was never a basketball fan, so it made sense that with the inaugural season of the Brooklyn Nets on the line, he didn't seem to care. Caring about results and funneling money into the franchise was Prokhorov's role.

Together, they seemed to comprise one new-age George Steinbrenner. From his father supplying cement and gravel to an uncle who started Forest City Ratner, a national real estate company, Ratner's money was rooted in Cleveland, like Steinbrenner. With the Atlantic Yards project losing steam, Ratner's family grilled him in Cleveland. About a year later he made a deal with Prokhorov. Prokhorov was willing to try to win at any cost and had a history in basketball, a lack of which was Ratner's Achilles' heel. Playing basketball on YES (Yankees Entertainment and Sports), a network representing a brand built by Steinbrenner, it was Prokhorov's job to right the ship that Ratner—dubbed "the absent-minded professor"—delivered at his Russian doorstep.

Business development must make linear sense to Ratner. He was born on January 23, 1945. On important documents, he must write 1/23/45 next to his name. He went into business with Jay-Z, the artist with the song "On to the Next One."

It's no secret that the Atlantic Yards project was a land grab for Ratner. He bought the Nets, stripped them down, sold them to Prokhorov, and received some land to develop. Prokhorov did the same with nickel and mining companies on the other side of the globe. The state government gave Ratner twenty-five years to build up the properties surrounding the arena, essentially license to dawdle on a plan that promised "hoops, jobs, and housing."

Building up Atlantic Yards immediately meant glossing up Brooklyn even more and further distancing the Nets from the past of the borough they were settling into, unquestionably a tricky issue. Cultural assimilation required more than the remnants of a culture. How can you plant the official Ebbets Field flagpole into the ground outside Barclays Center one day, and push toward a galactic high-rise future the next?

The Reverend Clinton Miller of Brown Memorial Baptist Church, a few blocks from Barclays Center, was caught in an interesting predicament. He was a community leader with hoops history, recruited to play at Southern University, where Avery Johnson finished his college career. Like Golden State Warriors coach Mark Jackson, Miller played high school basketball at Bishop Loughlin in the eighties. He watched the Nets, but hadn't attended a game and wasn't fond of the way Ratner and Prokhorov did business. On the night the Nets drafted Derrick Favors, Miller led a protest outside Madison Square Garden, asking that the NBA fully vet Prokhorov's business dealings.

If there wasn't much Miller could do about new expensive Brooklyn, a reality that forced residents to leave the area, he could still educate members of his congregation, many of whom attended Nets games and wore the gear.

"I would like for them to get the big picture about how government works, how money works, how when we don't organize ourselves, actually whole communities can be taken away and changed away from us," he said.

Miller referenced Andy Warhol's fifteen minutes of fame quote and compared Jay-Z to Magic Johnson in the way he helped sell a business to the black community. There was a picture of Magic Johnson on the wall in Miller's office. Miller spoke of Johnson's role as a figurehead with the hedge fund Canyon Johnson, which purchased Williamsburg Savings Bank in 2005 and transformed Brooklyn's then-tallest building, installing luxury condo units. Back when he was a prodigal Coney Island point guard, Sebastian Telfair (whose journeyman career has included stints with the Trail Blazers, Celtics, Timberwolves, Cavaliers, Clippers, Suns, and Raptors, thus far) would link up with his AAU teammates by the Williamsburg Savings Bank clock tower.

Miller was asked to protest the Canyon Johnson purchase.

According to Miller, he called the hedge fund and asked if it would be interested in seeing other spots in Brooklyn to do affordable housing and building a balance, but nothing came of it despite Magic Johnson saying he was open to it.

Quite a bizarre situation for a basketball-loving reverend to be in: attempting to get arguably the greatest point guard of all time—now a successful businessman—to see business his way, or the way of his politics. The everyman hustle of Brooklyn had evolved into a publicly funded bourgeois endeavor, a new reality that probably allowed the Nets and Barclays Center to exist. Yet that reality made no real promise of a devoted marriage between team and borough like Brooklyn had with the Dodgers, purchased by a Magic Johnson–led ownership group and outspending everybody but the Yankees.

Miller and I finished our lengthy conversation, and Deron Williams went out and lit the Wizards up for 42 points and an NBA-record nine 3-pointers in a half.

The nostalgic cynic says the Dodgers were religion in Brooklyn and the big-business Nets will never tug at the borough's heartstrings that way. The optimist says there have always been players, owners, and affiliated businesses in professional sports. The realist wonders if the Nets can thrive somewhere in the middle.

"So, how did we get here?" Ratner asked at the Barclays Center ribbon cutting. "We first needed to buy a basketball team, and against all odds we did it."

It was the job of the basketball team to not give a fuck about what was going on with the real estate part of the deal and respect a more wide-reaching fan base while building on Brooklyn culture with a ball, two hoops, and ninety-four feet of prime real estate surrounded by sleek black seats and real fans.

There were newspaper covers throughout the United Center media room, honoring the days in June when the Bulls and the Blackhawks became champions. Some of the headlines from days when the Bulls won championships:

1991: Anti semitic out break stuns Leningrad Election
1992: Perot camp tries to keep up unbridled momentum
1993: Somali Warlord like Elvis: Everywhere and nowhere
1996: Russians lift Yeltsin into Runoff
1997: McVeigh Sentenced to Die
1998: GOP Wooing Main Street, Not Wall Street*

Six simple reminders that the world is a crazy place that continues to evolve as time flies. It was back to Brooklyn for the greatest two words in sports: game 7.

GAME 7

You spend a season around a team, at games, practices, thinking about the team and everything pertaining to it. Time passes by in environments both new and old. Lines are straddled, jokes made, laughs shared, grievances filed through words, and tweets dissected. You have conversations with players, meals with writers on the road. The team and the beat become your extended family. Seemingly every day someone asks, "How's the book?" You never know what to say, so you offer an answer and move along, sometimes into more words, sometimes into your own inertia.

You take the D train to the arena for game 7 seated next to a guy with a "Kings County" tattoo in the style of *New York Times* newsprint. A Bulls fan takes a picture in front of the arena, middle finger raised. You arrive inside for game 7 and find yourself seated in the upper deck between two Knicks fan sportswriters who live in Brooklyn.

Then, even though you don't realize it at the time, you're like Max Zaslofsky, coach and general manager of the New Jersey Americans who played for the Chicago Stags and New York Knicks, trying

* "GOP Wooing Main Street, Not Wall Street" is a curious headline to run the day after Jordan's final championship when considering his famous "Republicans buy sneakers too" line.

to understand this franchise, now the Brooklyn Nets, while surrounded by a Chicago team and Knicks fans. It's one final paradox, rammed down your throat without mercy, a 6-point loss that feels like 60, a team booed off the floor at halftime down by 17.

Tired of the guttural noises being made by the game-changing sportswriter to your left, you go to your favorite spot in the arena and stand among a group of fans. A guest services staff member named David keeps watch. Joe Johnson is struggling mightily to score. Fans are both angry and drunk. But the Nets come back, Wallace playing out of his mind; he's suddenly, in the biggest of spots, playing up to his contract, leaving it all on the floor, stepping on Nate Robinson's head (though Robinson would get up and hit a floater).

It's refreshing to see people hanging on every call, every bounce of the ball, roundball religion in full force. The Nets grab 10 offensive rebounds and outscore the Bulls by 10 in the third quarter. You go back to your seat for the fourth quarter because your computer is up there and, sigh, you've gotta write.

The French New Yorker who attended high schools in New York and New Jersey, the hipster-looking dude with the Miss Sweden mom, the tennis pro father, and the grandfather who played soccer for the Cameroonian national team; that guy needs to decide the first game 7 in Barclays Center history after Kim Kardashian's ex-husband makes things a little bit easier on the Bulls by missing three out of four free throws.

On the season's biggest possession, the Nets play hot potato and Johnson misses a 3-pointer from the corner. The nomads have not fully settled into their new surroundings.

"If this wasn't the playoffs, he wouldn't have even been playing, getting cortisone shots and injections in his foot just to be able to play in the game," Stackhouse said.

"Regardless of what was going on in my foot, I played," Johnson said.

"Before this series, I didn't know if I was going to be able to play," Noah said. "I could barely walk."

The juxtaposition of Joe Johnson and Joakim Noah, both battling plantar fasciitis, was touted by sportswriters as Plantar Fasciitis Joe vs. Plantar Fasciitis Jo. Jo thanked his osteopath Sharon and his physical trainer ("David I don't even know what his name is") and the Bulls' training staff. Joe sternly disagreed with the notion that he would have sat out games 1 and 2 against the Heat had the Nets advanced.

An exit sign leading to the staircase out never looked so red. A drunk fan was talking about how it felt so familiar. Maybe the point was how crowded the staircase was.

The next day, on Cinco de Mayo, the Nets held exit interviews. Williams wore a Running Sucks shirt with sky blue lettering with a matching light blue Nike logo on his hat. The Nets were both positioned to maintain a Running Sucks philosophy on the court while making a run at the championship, as strange as that would have sounded at the time.

EPILOGUE

New Point Guards

For all of their fluctuations and for all the cynics who judged them by the money they spent, the Brooklyn Nets had a mostly successful launch campaign. The first-round knockout enabled the Nets to get back up before the playoffs ended. Exhaled air from the Brooklyn launch still lingered when the second party began, a fiesta that called to mind Prokhorov's "good . . . basketball . . . strategy" statement from before the regular-season home opener.

On the cover of the first issue of *SLAM* magazine, the publication that brought hip-hop and basketball together, a story about Kidd, then a college prodigy for the California Golden Bears, boasted "Jason Kidd's Krazy Mad Moves." The tagline lingered as an inside joke. Kidd's arrival as the Nets' coach was surreal, like the Kraziest of the Krazy Mad Moves.

"Hello, Coach! J-Kidd back where he belongs," the team's message read on various screens. The Nets had named Kidd the eighteenth coach in franchise history despite a blank coaching résumé. Kidd had retired from the NBA nine days earlier. In October 2012, when the Knicks played the Nets at Nassau Coliseum in the preseason, Jason Kidd—in his final season, and in his one and only season in blue and orange—looked like he was meditating on the bench. He played one game in Barclays Center and he won it—controversially.

On the court, Kidd threw passes that dictated extended

sequences of action and brought fans out of their seats. As a coach, he would look to lead a roster that shared the ball and followed that lead.

Billy King made an obvious comparison: hiring Kidd was akin to Donnie Walsh hiring Larry Bird to coach the Pacers in 1997. Both were once nearby heroes with rich NBA legacies. Bird had led the Pacers to the Finals in 2000, losing a hard-fought series to the Lakers that paved the way for the Shaq-Kobe era. The Nets were hoping against hope for a little bit more.

On the sideline, Kidd brought many reinforcements: Lawrence Frank, Roy Rogers, Eric Hughes, John Welch, Joe Prunty, and Charles Klask. King and the Nets' ownership selected Kidd over Brian Shaw, the well-regarded associate head coach of the Pacers. Shaw had the better coaching résumé, but Kidd was the best player in the Nets' NBA history, the point guard who served as a coach on the court.

In scale and panache, Kidd's well-attended press conference brought to mind the 2012 media day, when Gerald Wallace talked about being afraid of the city, and Deron Williams from the *Deron Williams News* asked Avery Johnson which New York team was best.

Williams, back from vacation and trim in a shiny suit, attended the new coach's presser, too. Kidd was Williams's favorite player growing up, and they'd since become friends and golfing buddies. They shared an agent, Jeff Schwartz of Excel Sports. Realistically, Kidd was an unknown quantity on the sidelines, but help was soon on the way.

Jay-Z told Irina Pavlova that the Nets needed to make the B their own when Pavlova said that a plain "B" logo reminded her of Boston. That's exactly what the Nets did when Barclays Center hosted its first NBA draft. The Nets acquired Kevin Garnett, Paul Pierce, Jason Terry, and D. J. White for Wallace, Humphries, Brooks, Bogans, and three draft picks.

Bogans received $5 million just to be traded. The team jokester, the swingman with the personal trainer's look and deep voice, Bogans experienced an interesting end to the Nets' first Brooklyn season, transitioning from floor-spacing, 3-point-shooting wingman to playoff afterthought.

It wasn't surprising to see Humphries go; he looked like a trucker, rocking a mustache on exit interview day. Many wondered if Humphries and Rondo could coexist in Boston after their November scuffle. Whatever the case, on a rebuilding team, Humphries would have the chance to fill up the box score again because, really, the only thing he could do that could possibly yield more press than a seventy-two-day marriage to a starlet whose father served as O. J. Simpson's defense attorney would be to chuck cases of Snapple into Boston Harbor with his two trade amigos.

Brooks had been hyped up as a possible Sixth Man of the Year candidate in the preseason, but with the way the season played out, he never got much of a chance.*

That the Nets were able to unload Wallace was the huge shock. Wallace's contract was an albatross—at least that was the popular perception—but he often played like a futuristic gladiator and embodied the sound and symbol of the Nets' first season in Brooklyn.

C. J. Watson signed with the Indiana Pacers, and the Nets replaced him with veteran point guard Shaun Livingston. The Nets were Livingston's ninth NBA team. Despite being a highly touted preps-to-pros high school sensation, Livingston had his career derail when he suffered one of the most gruesome injuries in NBA history. While playing for the Clippers, he dislocated his left kneecap in a game against the Bobcats.

Very much Livingston's opposite in look and style, Nate Robinson signed with the Denver Nuggets, putting Watson and Robinson on franchises that began in the ABA. After a year of good development, Blatche re-signed with the Nets, a portion of his

---

* Brooks bounced from the Nets to the Celtics to the Warriors to the Lakers to a top team in Milan, Italy, in the span of a year.

salary still paid by the Wizards. The Nets drafted Duke's Mason Plumlee with the twenty-second pick of the first round. Mason became the second of three Plumlee brothers to enter the NBA.

Prior to the trade, Pierce was a lifetime Celtic. He speaks with a rasp and boasts a slow-moving but psychologically brilliant game. He lulls defenders into false comfort zones and then beats them by changing speeds. He understands defense schematically.

Pierce has a track record for nailing big shots. His game embodies the creative process relative to spatial dynamics, the idea that every move is interconnected. When Pierce, with his lingering gait, pulls up for a three-pointer in transition, it feels like time slows down as the ball floats through the air. Like Joe Johnson, he often lives the on-court motto "keep your teammates close and your defenders closer."

The first player since Moses Malone to make the leap from high school to the pros, Garnett keyed the Celtics' recent success. A lethal midrange jump shot and his ability to turn team defense into an art form were two of his calling cards. Projecting a proud warrior's attitude, he banged his head on the basket stanchion before the game and rode his teammates hard. He radiated alpha intensity without needing to be an alpha scorer.

Garnett, Pierce, and Terry were roughly 108 years old combined on opening night. Concerns about the Nets' depth were partially allayed on July 11 when the Nets signed Andrei Kirilenko, a.k.a. AK-47, a Russian forward and defensive stalwart with a pterodactyl's wingspan, for well under market value.

The Nets also turned the NBA's financial system upside down, owing roughly $82 in luxury tax and $101 million in salary. From the in-arena signage to the salary structure, the Nets weren't afraid to spend big. That the Nets staked their claim as a contender by signing Kirilenko for under market value while also acquiring Garnett, a player whose six-year, $126 million contract in 1997 shocked the NBA world and helped bring about the 1999 lockout, philosophically hoisted the NBA financial system on its own petard.

BROOKLYN BOUNCE

YEAR TWO—BK, HOME AND AWAY

The Nets doled out record money for salaries but found value in a cost-effective bench. They provided the avenue for a landmark moment in history, but didn't make a huge deal about it. In the middle of an early-season mess, they spilled things on purpose but did a decent job of cleaning up their season. The paradoxes continued in year two, perhaps none more striking than the reality that, on the court, the Nets—winners of a season-high fifteen straight games at home at one point—continued to find definition on the road.

Everything changed in Philadelphia in December when they lost Brook Lopez for the season to a broken right foot. The Nets immediately faced a long winter of discontent, a financial colossus and preseason contender crumbling before the eyes of expectant pundits who predicted championship-caliber play after the summer roster remodel.

They hit rock bottom in San Antonio, blown out for the second straight New Year's Eve, and found a turning point in Oklahoma City, notching their biggest win of the regular season at Chesapeake Energy Arena on January 2 for the second straight season. The P. J. Carlesimo whirlwind alumni tour was still the P. J. Carlesimo whirlwind alumni tour, even without P. J. Carlesimo.

They made fans cry, out of respect, in Boston and Los Angeles, and turned Toronto upside down—twice, almost three times—before facing their fate in Miami.

They were the Brooklyn Nets, a thriving and fashionable global brand still seeking greater meaning in a major media capital.

OKLAHOMA CITY

On the night the season turned, the Thunder were without star point guard Russell Westbrook, and Williams, exactly a year after telling everyone in Oklahoma City that it was a new year, carried the offensive load for much of the night. In arguably his season's best performance, Williams scored 29 points and spearheaded a remarkable comeback, hitting a thirty-seven-foot 3-pointer at the end of the third quarter to bring the Nets within 11 heading into the fourth.

With the game tied and six seconds left on the clock, Degree of Difficulty Joe returned to the fold, hitting an almost impossible top-of-the-key fadeaway over the 6'10" Serge Ibaka to win the game. Just like against Luc Mbah a Moute in year one, Johnson attacked a talented, muscle-bound defender who was draped all over him with a slow-motion dribble, and, almost literally, held his opponent's hand after releasing the game-winner.

Four days later, Garnett noted that the Nets called Johnson, "Joe Jesus," because "he might not be there when you call on him, but he's there when you need him."

In Oklahoma City, the Nets stopped trying to replace Lopez with similar size, instead inserting Shaun Livingston into the starting lineup. Almost overnight, the Nets became a team predicated on length and interchangeability on defense. Mismatches lost meaning when attacking the Nets. A squad that was profoundly bad at defense early on found its identity, got a little bit healthier, and dug in.

The Nets quickly went from slow and plodding in year one to funky and fun—out of necessity—for most of year two, forcing turnovers and shooting the 3-pointer with impunity. After going 10-21 in 2013, they finished the 2014 portion of the regular season 34-17. At times, the ball moved too much, players passing up good shots in order to keep the good vibes flowing. A large image of Johnson, Pierce, Garnett, Lopez, and Williams decorated a huge section of the Barclays Center's main entrance, but the season was largely defined by lesser-known Nets stepping into the breach.

Playing next to Williams and often bringing the ball up the court, Livingston was the beneficiary of many open seams through which to maximize his rare—and very fun to watch—

midrange game. Livingston's length, skill, and decision-making down low against smaller guards, in tandem with the attention-drawing, perimeter-oriented talent surrounding him, enabled him to lead the NBA in points scored per postup. In glossy year two of the Brooklyn Nets, the player with arguably the most gruesome injury in league history on his résumé revitalized his career and went from a journeyman on the brink to a hot commodity commanding big dollars on the open market.

Liberated from coaches who didn't (or wouldn't) see his value, Mirza Teletovic more than doubled his minutes and scoring. Teletovic's long-range shooting (39 percent, on nearly five attempts a game) was an enviable weapon at Kidd's disposal once Teletovic shook off a dreadful start to the season. A 34-point explosion against the Mavericks (including 24 in the second quarter) and an unimpressed smirk during a dust-up with LeBron James were two signature sequences at Barclays Center, courtesy of the King of Bosnia, as Mirza was known to Nets fans. Watching Teletovic when he was feeling it—catching on-point passes and bouncing back up in the air with just the right rise and rhythm—was an underrated aesthetic pleasure tied to the Nets' resurgence.

Aside from a four-game stretch when Kidd left him at home—ostensibly to improve his conditioning—Blatche continued to provide big minutes off the bench and straddle the line between brilliance and brain fart. Despite helping lead a massive comeback in game 5 of the Nets' first-round series against the Raptors, it looked like Blatche may have tossed away the Nets' season, literally, when he threw a pass over Williams's head and into the backcourt with precious seconds ticking away.

The moment didn't prove decisive because the Nets won the next two games, so Blatche could forget about it and enjoy the offseason focusing on becoming a naturalized Filipino citizen in order to play for their national team. Asked if he knew Blatche was half-Filipino, Johnson cracked, "No, but he's full of shit." At one point, Blatche noted that he wanted to be known as "Young Seymour," because fans wanted to "see more" of him.

After signing Andrei Kirilenko for well under market value, Kirilenko played to the approximate value of his contract, appearing in only forty-five regular-season games, with a noticeable decline in individual stats. However, the Nets were unquestionably a better team with Kirilenko. With the gangly Russian in uniform and wreaking havoc, the Nets lost only one home game (by one point) before mid-April. It came as no shock to anybody paying attention that the Nets' New Year's resurgence coincided with Kirilenko's return to everyday action.

Mason Plumlee filled in admirably with Kevin Garnett out for two months in the middle of the season, starting at center as the team continued to win. The team defense wasn't as strong with Plumlee on the court, but his athleticism and activity, blocking shots and converting quirky reverse-style finishes in the paint, were hallmarks of a season that netted him All-Rookie First Team honors.

Alan Anderson went from barely making the team to earning important playoff minutes and converting a few clutch four-point plays. Anderson's better moments highlighted the reality that the Nets would have been lost in year two if not for their depth.

That depth was bolstered when the Nets sent Reggie Evans, who had no defined role on a team with improved offensive firepower, and Jason Terry to the Kings in February for Marcus Thornton, an isolation scorer from Baton Rouge known as the Bayou Bomber. The Nets were in Utah when the trade went down.

"Just dap everybody up," Evans recalled. " 'I'm out.' That was it. 'I'm out.' "

Evans returned with the Kings in March and met with the reporters who already missed him. He seemed accepting of his fate, a little somber but not bitter. The hardest part was having four kids still in school in the area, although he missed the "brotherhood" of the team, shouting out Lopez, Blatche, and Williams.

"I just left all my brothers and stuff like that," Evans said.

LONDON

The Nets had paid the price for a time-consuming London visit earlier in the season with an unforgiving schedule—no three-game homestand until December 23—and a team and coach with little chemistry and fluctuating health paid the price.

The 17-point victory over the Hawks on January 16 at the 02 Arena fell right in the middle of the early 2014 resurrection. The Nets had a five-game winning streak snapped in Toronto before they crossed the Atlantic, and the victory over the Hawks started another five-game streak.

Johnson starred in the win, scoring 29 points on 11 of 15 shooting, including 6 of 8 from beyond the arc. That Johnson was the Nets' best export in the London game was fitting. There wasn't really much time for Decoy Joe in 2014. Johnson was an All-Star in 2014 and the Nets' most consistent player, unquestionably the team's MVP. With Lopez hurt, Williams bothered by nagging ankle injuries, and Pierce taking his time early in the season getting into the flow, Johnson played like a franchise player, using a quality season to elevate the perception of his game among many of the naysayers.

The Nets returned from London and promptly crushed the Knicks at Madison Square Garden in the biggest meeting between the two teams all season. Johnson led the Nets with 25 points. The Nets' official rock bottom in year two was a blowout loss to the Knicks on December 5, two days after Kidd controversially reassigned Lawrence Frank. Frank purportedly stayed involved with the organization, writing reports, but the demotion left few believing that Frank, the highest paid assistant coach in league history, would do much of anything. Less than two months later, that victory over the Knicks, a second consecutive Martin Luther King Jr. Day matinee win over their crosstown rivals, signaled a changing of the guard in New York's pro basketball hierarchy for a season at least.

BOSTON

Paul Pierce was talking to somebody as he entered the Celtics' locker room. It was the wrong locker room, but it was also, in the most obvious sense, the right locker room, a pathway bracketed by an iconic image of Red Auerbach exhaling cigar smoke and a leprechaun logo gleaming green.

"We in the back, we in the back," Pierce said. "We gotta talk, dog."

It didn't really matter who he was talking to, who was the recipient of his broad smile, because he could have been talking to anybody in the familiar hallway at the TD Banknorth Garden. Everything about the return of Pierce and Garnett to Boston felt right, from video presentations that spared no iconic detail—Garnett doing knuckle pushups, Jack Nicholson bellowing, "You can't handle the truth!"—to music selections (Aerosmith's "Sweet Emotion" as the game was about to tip), to Garnett's game-sealing steal with seventeen seconds remaining.

The on-court play was dreadful. The teams combined for 69 first-half points, the lowest in any game during the 2013–14 season up to that point. In a way, that simply placed more attention on the event itself. Pierce said it was the toughest game he'd ever had to play in; Garnett called it his hardest day to focus. Even afterward, Garnett was playing big brother to Pierce, urging him to cry in front of a packed media horde.

"I think we'll always bleed green as long as we're playing basketball and as long as we're living," Garnett said. "Even when they bury us six feet, this is what it's gonna be."

The return of two future Hall-of-Famers to Boston was a condensed master class on player/media relations, a simple illustration of why the Pierce/Garnett locker room was generally more enjoyable, or at least exciting in big moments, than the plainer collective that debuted the black-and-white threads.

Pierce was happy to talk about buying mojo at Cotsco or being clutch since he was eight months old. Garnett was easy to listen to in a way that athletes aren't supposed to be. Early in the season, the Nets had Garnett address the media in pregame press conferences before Kidd spoke, until the team got off to a terrible start and it became obvious that anybody, let alone the soft-spoken and coy Kidd, would struggle to follow Garnett at the dais. Not that Garnett minded. There was no point in being a figurehead for a woefully underperforming team. And when the Nets turned it around in January, he was perfectly at ease in the locker room, comparing his jump shot to a booty call.

"I want it to be there when I dial it up, I want her to pick the phone up," Garnett said after a win over Golden State in January. "Tonight, I dialed and she was right there, answering like she's supposed to."

The Nets clung to the idea of Garnett and Pierce improving their culture, of handing them readymade respect, as if basketball culture were like a Christmas gift: there to provide a lengthy adrenaline rush, entertain you, and improve your quality of life. It was a nice sentiment, but definitely not that simple.

LOS ANGELES

The Brooklyn Nets had taken over the interview room in another opposing arena. Just as it was in Boston, where it was about two men and their relationship to a city, this wasn't really about the Nets. It was about Jason Collins becoming the first openly gay man to play a game in one of the four major American sports, about his relationship to himself and his relationship to his teammates and his relationship to the NBA. Shortly after dealing Evans and Terry, the Nets signed Collins to a ten-day contract. The timing allowed Collins, who had been working out in Los Angeles, to debut in front of family and friends.

The Lakers were accommodating hosts. The media room was swollen to capacity. Collins walked a fine line between professionalism and earnestness. He was organic and bashful in telling moments, seemingly interested in expounding at times, but not keen on overloading a feeding frenzy when there were games to be played.

Collins had already spent six seasons with the Nets, including the back-to-back NBA Finals appearances in 2002 and 2003. He played with Garnett and Pierce in Boston, Johnson in Atlanta, and Kidd with the Nets in New Jersey. His twin brother, Jarron, had played with Williams and Kirilenko in Utah. The Nets were the right fit.

Collins set hard screens, aided spacing on defense, and used his fouls frequently and wisely. The nuances that defined his play both guaranteed that the issue itself would take center stage and that the complexity of the issue could be better appreciated through a basketball prism. Jason Collins wasn't going to dunk over two guys, put them on a poster, and then watch as T-shirts honoring the poster became a fashion statement all across America. He was going to cover for a teammate by knocking an opponent to the ground during a play that would otherwise be just another overlooked moment. In a really nice way, his teamwork-oriented game was something of a metaphor for the give-and-take germane to positive public discourse and societal growth.

Collins checked in to a surprisingly soft reception. Pockets of fans were vocally appreciative, but the moment passed many others by. It took Collins two minutes and two seconds of action to commit a foul.

"My favorite part of the evening was when, I think it was Jordan Farmar was complaining to the refs that I was setting an illegal pick," Collins said.

It wasn't all that obvious that Collins had made history upon entering the postgame locker room. Led by Pierce and Blatche, many Nets couldn't stop mocking Dennis Rodman's recent bizarre appearance on CNN where Rodman defended his decision to lead a touring group of former players to North Korea.

"You don't know!" Pierce said in imitation. "These guys! They're here! See, they're all here!"

So on the night of Collins's debut, the loud political story in the locker room wasn't gay rights. It was, indirectly, North Korean dictator and basketball fan Kim Jung Un.

The world was the same, but it also wasn't.

Not much of narrative substance transpired in the two months between Collins's debut and the playoffs. The Nets followed up the win over the Lakers by flipping the script from the team's previous West Coast trip, suffering the third-worst loss in franchise history in Portland against a team missing almost all of its frontcourt, only to bounce back and defeat a much weaker Denver Nuggets team. Collins was re-signed to a second ten-day contract and eventually for the remainder of the season.

As the victories piled up, Kidd started to win back credit from critics. The seamless integration of Jorge Gutiérrez, a point guard from the D-League, only seemed to highlight the reality that Kidd was getting a feel for coaching and the team's unselfish play was reflective of Kidd's own playing style.

At first, Kidd's success was half-jokingly attributed to his wardrobe. He stopped wearing a tie when 2014 began and the team won ten of eleven. Kidd letting his neck breathe became an actual thing that people talked about, including Kidd. Actual NetsDaily headline: "Haberdashers be afraid! Kidd says no tie!"

Yet by the end of the season, the Nets, by virtue of maintaining the best record in the Eastern Conference for much of 2014, could slow down—or tank, as the conspiracy went—for the sixth seed in order to play the Raptors. And the coach looked more like a budding behind-the-scenes leader than a lucky, automated fashion statement who released clichés into the ether almost as if he worked for a manufacturer of failed fortune cookie sayings.

Kidd's turnaround was certainly a positive development for the Nets. Barring some unforeseen disaster, Kidd will be the face of the franchise, a power broker with permanence.* When the Knicks hired Derek Fisher just days after the seventeen-year veteran retired, Kidd even became a trendsetter of sorts.

TORONTO

Paul Pierce provided the memorable bookends to the first playoff series win in Brooklyn Nets history. After making four clutch fourth-quarter shots against a plucky Raptors defense in Game 1, Pierce, cross-referencing his own clutch history while storming back up the court, spoke the words now famous to all Nets fans: "That's why they got me here! That's why I'm here!"

It was a 180-degree turn for Pierce. Nine months earlier, Pierce had struggled to hide his discomfort after being shipped out of Boston. When they arrived in Brooklyn, Garnett was the megatrade's emotional center, playing to a huge media crowd and sweating in a suit like it was the fourth quarter.

Now, with Raptors general manager Masai Ujiri having drummed up interest in the series earlier in the day by yelling, "Fuck Brooklyn!" to a crowd of fans assembled outside the Air Canada Centre, Garnett was the supportive aging veteran playing restricted minutes and a mic'd up Pierce was the charismatic hired gun who could lead the Nets to victory in the "Fuck Brooklyn" knife fight.

Pierce drained a pull-up 3 over an outstretched hand; made a layup with the aid of a sneaky ball fake and some slow-motion old-man steps; sank a fadeaway with a seven-footer running at him; and hit a midrange fadeaway with his man tracking his every move. All of the scores were vintage Pierce, but the final basket was especially in character, Pierce taking a half-spin back into Patrick Patterson, as if to illustrate that he was shooting the shot he wanted to take all along and he wouldn't be stopped.

* Stay tuned for more on this sentence, originally filed a few days before the shit hit the fan.

Game 1 had a throwback feel. The shot clock stopped working because of a power outage. A stopwatch—an actual stopwatch—took center stage. The Raptors' PA announcer counted down at 24, 10, 5, 4, 3, 2, 1, before yelling, "Horn." That Pierce made all of these shots, his rhythm backed by a stopwatch, only enhanced the idea that fans were watching Old Man River in full flow.

The Raptors took control down the stretch in game 2, and then the pattern repeated itself in Brooklyn, the Nets taking the series lead followed by a loss that featured a dominant fourth quarter from the Raptors. In game 4, the Nets scored 12 points in the fourth quarter, were outscored by 8 in the period, and lost the game by 8. Both games in Brooklyn were noteworthy for late-arriving crowds, which compared poorly to the atmosphere in Toronto.

Garnett, the living embodiment of expended energy and noise as related to basketball, made the point simply. "They could do better," he said after game 3. "I was expecting Brooklyn to be real hostile, New York–style. I know what it's like to come here as the opposition, so our crowd could do better, but they were there when we needed them, and we fed off of them."

Game 5 in Toronto featured more Toronto crowd theatrics (loudly mocking the BROOOOOK-LYN chant), but more important, it may go down as the most epic performance of the Nets' season. A comeback from 26 down fell just short when Blatche over-threw Williams. The game was most notable for how unstoppable Johnson was in the second half (26 points) and the fact that Kidd stuck with the same five-man lineup (Williams, Johnson, Anderson, Blatche, Teletovic) for almost the entire fourth quarter. Pierce and Garnett sitting in what could have been the stretch of play that defined the Nets' season highlighted both Kidd's command over decision-making and the interchangeability of a squad that featured no 20-point scorer after Lopez was lost for the season.

The Nets won easily in game 6 and pushed the series to seven, where Johnson's heroics (13 of his 26 points came in the fourth quarter) set the stage for Pierce's second Toronto bookend, when he blocked Kyle Lowry in the paint. Pierce barely elevated on the block after Lowry had taken on three Nets en route to the rim.

Up next? The defending champs whom the Nets had swept 4-0 in the regular season.

MIAMI

It's tempting to say that the year-two Brooklyn Nets met their fate at Barclays Center in game 4 of the Eastern Conference Semifinals when LeBron James poured in 49 points and Chris Bosh nailed a corner 3-pointer in the season's biggest defensive possession, because the season ended two nights later in Miami. The Nets coughed up a 9-point fourth-quarter lead in game 5 with under six minutes remaining, despite a thrilling 34-point performance from Johnson that seemed to restore the amount of hope in the season akin to the amount of space Johnson needed to score on a slow-motion maneuver. Still, the Nets weren't going to beat the Heat in four out of five games after dropping the first two, unless the series was directed by the folks from *Friday Night Lights* and shot as impossible-is-nothing Adidas performance art.

The Nets flew to south Florida immediately after outlasting the Raptors and looked the worse for wear in game 1, falling by 21. An immediate 1-0 hole put all of the pressure on game 2. The Nets equipped themselves well until an 8–0 run in the middle of the fourth quarter was quickly followed by a sixty-nine-second possession, during which the Heat corralled three different misses. Basketball is often seen as a game of *put ball in hoop*. Watching a season's hope fade away during three different mini games of *no, sorry, you cannot retrieve ball* is the type of sequence that strives to redefine anguish. Game 3 was a party in Brooklyn and the Nets won with relative ease, but it ended up as little more than a nice memory to pocket from a season that ended in disappointment.

BROOKLYN

Befitting an organization that takes in-arena sponsorships and cross-promotional synergy too far, the Nets' most talked about year-two Brooklyn moment inadvertently involved product placement. Late in an early-season matchup against the Kobe Bryant–less Lakers, Kidd was out of time-outs and needed time to draw up a play. Caught on camera while holding a cup of ice and soda, Kidd said, "Hit me!" to Tyshawn Taylor. Taylor obliged and the desired spillage caused the desired delay in the action. Kidd was fined $50,000 by the league and the story blew up.

The idea of a drink sold on the concourse sticking to the playing surface evoked the common criticism that too many folks went to Nets games to eat dinner with a basketball game in the background.

"Our goal is making this arena all about Brooklyn—even the food and drink—and one thing that became clear to me is Brooklyn's a Coke town," Brett Yormark said in 2011, after the Nets made Coca-Cola an official team sponsor.

The Nets sold sponsorship time at Barclays Center as if game night was an hourglass and each grain of sand needed to be accounted for. They were a local car dealership's town in the third quarter and a frozen yogurt company's town in the fourth quarter. When they were playing historically poor defense, they were sponsored by a security company. When they improved their defense, they were still sponsored by a security company. The team's dancers had different sponsors for their hair, their makeup, and, implicitly, their physiques. Maybe consistent in-arena corporate sponsorship was no big deal in pro sports, but for a franchise making a first—and then a second—impression, all the while knowing that its value was soaring, the advertising felt over the top.

Understandably, confusion persisted as the Nets continued their push into Brooklyn. The word "Brooklyn" was thrown around with much greater emphasis than the word "Nets." Were fans supposed to be supporting Brooklyn (the odds of making it out of a housing project) or Brooklyn (the $11 fois gras doughnut only a few blocks from that very project)? Were they supporting the rough-and-tumble Coney Island of winter, once a basketball hotbed, or the Coney Island of the Nets official team store, open only when the weather warmed and tourists started hitting the beach? Did rocking the gear in impressive numbers count as fandom or merely fashion?

In New Jersey, the Nets were a cynic's safe haven. In Brooklyn, they fast became a cynic's lament. Then again, if you understand what goes into packaging an NBA game, maybe a little bit of errant high fructose corn syrup on the floor at the coach's behest is just par for the course.

EVEN . . . MORE . . . POINT GUARDS

Jason Kidd preached process. Especially when things seemed dire early in his first season, Kidd preached process. Kidd preached process when we knew what he was talking about and he preached process when he needed to say something because it was a Tuesday in January and there were sixty eyeballs and eight cameras on him.

Even if you were ready to declare that after one season Kidd looked like a "power broker with permanence" (in a revision for a paperback update of a book about the Brooklyn Nets), you probably had to believe that Kidd believed in process, in improving situations, because that's what he did as a player.

But for Kidd, circumstance trumps protocol and it probably always has. Kidd joined the Milwaukee Bucks in a bizarre turn of events in late June. The Nets had to allow the Bucks time to interview Kidd and they received compensation (two second-round draft picks) for allowing Kidd to leave. For all of the improvement that Kidd showed in his first year as coach, he was essentially traded for the fourth time in his storied career, the soda barely dried from the floor.

Kidd has now left the Suns, Knicks, Mavericks (twice), and Nets (twice—once as a player, once as a coach), usually moving from a situation with less promise to one with more. Like a skilled Wall Street broker, he gets out before he sees the stock about to fall. That he has usually looked prescient after extricating himself from a job (in part due to removing his own capacity to help a team win) may frighten Nets fans. In fact, each of the four times he changed teams as a player, his new team won at least thirteen more games in his first full season than the team he left. Of course, Kidd the coach has shown little compared to Kidd the player; Kidd's Nets won five fewer regular season games in 2014 than in 2013.

Kidd's move to Milwaukee from Brooklyn featured two interesting primary components: Kidd leaving to join Marc Lasry, a member of the Bucks' new ownership group who was once Kidd's financial adviser, and Kidd wanting more power than Billy King (or King gone altogether). Remarkably, Kidd attempted to usurp King even though the Nets' slow start had management thinking about firing Kidd early in the season.

In a way, each ended up with what might have been predictable all along: King still has his job and has now outlasted three Nets coaches—perhaps reelected somewhere in a back conference room—while Kidd is on to a greener situation that he can leave a positive mark on. Before Kidd was tasked with turning around the worst team in the NBA, the *New York Times* wrote that Lasry and Wesley Edens, the new Bucks' owners, specialized in "distressed assets" in the hedge fund game. For what it's worth, a distressed asset is exactly what the Nets were when Kidd landed in New Jersey in 2001.*

---

* Following Kidd out the door, the BrooklyKnight was laid to rest in the summer of 2014. A graduate of the School of Hard Knocks, according to his NBA .com bio, the late "walking nightmare" never quite grasped his position as Nets Guardian. However, despite his comic look, he still performed acts of generosity, such as opening locked doors to help stuck reporters arrive at their media seats in time for a game to start.

• • •

Ten minutes into his introductory press conference as the Brooklyn Nets' fourth coach in less than two years, Lionel Hollins said something that struck a chord: "I've been out of the league before. I've gone and done other things."

Indeed he had. It wasn't my idea to wake up before the crack of dawn on my final day at a U.S. Army base in Mannheim, Germany, in the spring of 2008. Hollins, somewhere in the middle of a long conversation while seated in the back of a bus, suggested I ride down to the Frankfurt airport with the team I was covering, even though I would have to double back to the army base. It was sound advice, especially as it related to process: it made me think and assess and make a sacrifice and do my job better.

In Mannheim, Hollins led a high school all-star team assembled by a travel coach and then-Adidas employee named Darren Matsubara to compete in the biannual Albert Schweitzer Tournament. (Matsubara's other main gig was coaching a regional travel team in Fresno, California, and he was a few months away from watching two of his prized pupils—Brook and Robin Lopez—get drafted. Matsubara is now Brook Lopez's agent.)

Hollins's understanding of various processes—shifting his focus from baseball to basketball, learning about his own value during contract time, bringing hard-learned, hardworking values to a new team—is thoroughly chronicled in David Halberstam's seminal book *The Breaks of the Game*, about the Portland Trail Blazers of the late seventies. Hollins was the point guard of the Blazers' 1977 championship team and he enjoyed a ten-year career, which segued into coaching at various levels.*

• • •

---

* Team USA's leading scorer at the 2008 Albert Schweitzer Tournament was Erving Walker, a diminutive point guard from Brooklyn who played four years at the University of Florida before beginning a career overseas. Well before I learned in person that Nate Robinson could be a decisive player in a playoff series, I nicknamed Walker "Straight Robinson," because his game was reminiscent of Nate Robinson's sans some of the ridiculous flash and zany antics.

Four years after watching him coach high schoolers in Germany, I spotted Hollins at a gym in Las Vegas and we caught up, getting lunch with a member of the Grizzlies' PR staff. The Barclays Center was still two months from opening; the Brooklyn Nets still a logo and an evolving idea.

We left lunch and Hollins drove me back to my hotel. We reached the hotel's parking lot and, as I remember it, I jokingly told him I'd have Prokhorov call him, which made little sense; Hollins's stock was on the rise after a second consecutive trip to the playoffs and he lived in the Memphis area. (The other less likely possibility is that he jokingly told me to have Prokhorov call him.) Intertwined tidbit from a bizarre literary journey or just a random moment in time, the fuzzy memory popped back into my mind when the Nets hired Hollins two years later.

"I did speak to Mr. Prokhorov and we had a nice conversation," Hollins said. "And [Prokhorov] said, 'I approve of this contract and I approve of you.'"

Hollins had come to the Nets after parting ways with the Grizzlies despite helping the Grizzlies to 56 wins and the franchise's first-ever conference finals berth in 2013. A rift between Hollins and the Grizzlies' statistically inclined front office was defined when the team traded small forward Rudy Gay to the Raptors against Hollins's wishes.

"When you have champagne tastes, you can't be on a beer budget," Hollins said of the trade on national TV.

The Grizzlies won a lot without Gay, negotiations for a new contract that summer didn't yield anything, and Hollins spent a year away from coaching. Molded in an era when players and reporters were more open with one another, Hollins arrived in Brooklyn understanding that his straight-shooter wings might need to be clipped in a world that often sought to keep reporters at Durant-arm's length.

"I think I have to be careful because I'm a joker," Hollins said with a group of media clustered around him after his introductory press conference. "And sometimes—" He briefly paused.

"And *you* know," he continued, looking at me. "That the first thing out of my mouth is not what I really feel, but everybody has it down and it's written. I have to be careful with that."

He was right. I did know that. And he knew that I could relate, because yakking without cause, especially in a big city like New York, is how bored sportswriters often pass the time. In Brooklyn, Hollins spoke resonantly about the idea of showing different personality traits at different times—basically, of people *being people*.

I had seen him speak honestly and in a fatherly manner to younger players—Hollins grew up with his coaches as his father figures—and I had seen him lightly kick a chair in frustration during an international game dominated by a young Enes Kanter, a player later drafted by the Utah Jazz with a pick acquired from the Nets in the Deron Williams deal. Like Reggie Evans, I had seen Hollins keep his starters in, maybe a bit too long, while his Grizzlies blew out the first rendition of the Brooklyn Nets. I watched as his squabbles with the Memphis front office hurt his reputation, especially on the internet. He wasn't perfect, but as a person and a leader Lionel Hollins had range and he thoroughly understood process, especially as it related to paying dues and putting time in.

I had no idea how his new team would perform. Pierce was suddenly a Wizard and Livingston a Warrior. The Nets' unwillingness to give Pierce a second year on a free agent deal, with ownership finally wary of luxury tax payments, dampened the championship expectations that seemed so bright only a year ago. For better or worse, the Nets retooled. Prized European prospect Bojan Bogdanovic was on his way over. Point guard Jarrett Jack was acquired in a deal that also helped the Cavaliers clear cap space in order to sign LeBron James.

Yet Lionel Hollins's Brooklyn Nets were still very much at their core a fast-forwarded version of Avery Johnson's Brooklyn Nets, with Johnson, Lopez, and Williams in the middle of everything. The plans for a new practice facility in Sunset Park were unveiled in June, signaling a future with players new and old call-ing Brooklyn home. Kidd was at the unveiling, speaking about the team.

And then, like a magic trick, he was gone, "as quick as a tick in a New York minute," as the rapper Fabolous spits in "Breathe."

Following in the footsteps of Michael K. Williams—the actor who introduced the Nets before games 3 and 4 of the first round at Barclays Center—Fabolous was rehearsing to a mostly empty arena hours before a do-or-die game 6. Deron Williams, seemingly oblivious with red earphones in his ears, was rotating around the 3-point arc, receiving passes from an assistant coach and firing up shots. Fabolous, who, like Michael K. Williams, was part of the Nets' first-season NBA TV promotional package, read the start-ing lineup.

It went swimmingly until the end.

"A six-three guard from Illinois, Duh-ron Williams."

Eighteen months after Jay-Z opened the arena with a concert that featured a lyrical shout-out to Duh-ron Williams, a Brooklyn rapper of lesser stature made the same mistake in a nearly empty arena. In a series that featured the rapper Drake, a Raptors fan, caught using a lint roller on his pants during game 1 (promotional lint rollers were given out before game 5 in Toronto), the Fab-olous faux pas called back to a time when Jay-Z, for better and worse, was the first front man of the Brooklyn Nets. Someone walked up to Fabolous and told him of the mispronunciation, Williams still alone in his own zone down at the other end of the court. Fabolous pronounced the point guard's name correctly the second time around and again during player introductions.

Williams was one game removed from getting badly outplayed by Lowry, set to the backdrop of twenty thousand promotional Drake-inspired lint rollers. Surrounded by Johnson's stellar sea-son, Livingston's emergence, and the larger-than-life presence of the ex-Celtics, Williams had faded from the limelight somewhat in year two. He suffered through a subpar, injury-plagued season, yet still managed to lead the Nets in plus/minus, both when they were bad in 2013 and good in 2014, highlighting the idea that, for all his struggles, the Nets were still at their best with Deron Williams on the floor.

Even so, Nets fans were losing patience with their franchise point guard's inconsistencies. Williams's game 5 performance inspired one creative observer to pin a poster of the point guard's face on a pole across the street from Atlantic Terminal, across the street from Barclays Center. "MISSING," the flier read in all red caps letters, followed by "Have you seen this person?" According to the flier, Williams was "LAST SEEN: getting a legendary coach fired in Salt Lake City," and the reward was $63,128,400 (Williams's remaining salary). The message went viral quickly.

Early in the game, Williams went crashing into a basket stanchion and twisted his ankle. As he suffered, a small pocket of fans chanted his name in support—and pronounced it correctly. Williams turned out to be okay on the night, scoring 23 points to lead the Nets to their most lopsided win of the series, but he would still need the same surgeries after the season to clean up his wobbly ankles—removing bone spurs in the left and a bone chip in the right—that the Nets deemed unnecessary in 2012. Platelet-rich plasma therapy and cortisone shots were temporary solutions. Still, small steps were small steps and the Brooklyn Nets, in reality and in metaphor, continued to move forward—hesitantly, gingerly, some of them on surgically repaired feet and ankles—led by a new guiding hand into an unknown future.

Acknowledgments

"It's done?"

"Yeah."

Thanks to anyone who supported me in bringing this book to life. Special thanks to Brant Rumble, John Glynn, Kyle Radler, Katie Rizzo, Jud Laghi, Davy Rothbart, Peter Cunningham, Howard Beck, Ryan Jones, Lang Whitaker, and Ben Couch.